EXPORT POTENTIAL OF INDIAN TEA

G.D. BANERJEE
SRIJEET BANERJI

ABHIJEET PUBLICATIONS
DELHI 110094

ABHIJEET PUBLICATIONS
2/46 Tukhmeerpur Extension
Delhi 110094
Phones: 011-22960492, 65698474
e-mail: abhijeetpublication@gmail.com
abhijeet_singh1@indiatimes.com

EXPORT POTENTIAL OF INDIAN TEA

First Published 2008

ISBN 978-81-89886-48-6

PRINTED IN INDIA

Published by J.K. Singh fo Abhijeet Publications, Delhi 110094, Lasertypeset by Gaurav Graphics, Delhi and Printed as Himanshu Printers, Delhi.

Dedicated to

Guru Maharaj Revered Swami Bhutesananda,

the 12th World President, Ramakrishna Math and Ramakrishna Mission of Ramakrishna Order, Belur Moth, Hoogly, West Bengal. His continuous inspiration, encouragement etc. have piloted the authors to make this journey possible. Let Guru Maharaj's blessings shower on us.

Dedicated to

Our Beloved Father/Grandfather

Late Dr. Indra Narayan Banerjee

Foreword

The book on "Export Potential of Indian Tea" refers to export markets of Indian tea in the world. Indian tea has been aggressively marketed in countries like United Kingdom, Poland, United States of America , Canada and South America. India has also identified suitable strategies to strengthen her base in Arab Republic of Egypt, Arab Republic of Syria, Arab Republic of Libya, Jordan and Iran. Her aggressive marketing ventures are directed towards Singapore, Nigeria, Middle East, Mauritius, Taiwan, Japan, and South Africa. Importance of Britain in World Tea and the areas of concern like production, propagation, funding development projects, financing, generic advertising, communication, tea and health, the world tea market, the UK tea trade have been studied in depth. Indian tea constitutes major share (70 per cent) in total tea imports for consumption in Poland. She exports both bulk teas and value added teas mainly packet tea. A small quantity of tea bags and instant tea is exported. In the United States of America more than half of the population is now drinking tea. "Tea is becoming more and more the beverage of choice because of its refreshing taste, and its 'perfect fit' with desire for healthier life styles. Served hot tea is soothing. It is a relaxing cold weather beverage choice perfect any time." Changing consumer needs, the growth areas, liquid consumption trends, features of US market, chalking out well coordinated campaign, medicinal and health properties of tea are some of the areas, which draw attention. Canada ranks fifth position among the tea importing countries. India accounts for major share in total tea imports for consumption in Canada and could increase her exports from 8 million kgs in 1951 to 15 million kgs in 2006. Packet tea exports enhanced from 6 thousand kgs in 1980-81 to 90 thousand kgs in 2006-07. This calls for introspection and identification of specific strategies to capture tea bags and instant tea markets. Tea Board has already taken various promotional measures to arrest slow growth of these value added teas.

Indian tea has export potential in South American countries like Chile, Mexico, Guyana, Venezuela, Trinidad, Peru, Colombia etc.. The quantity of tea entering into such countries is of Argentina or Brazil origin, which could be hardly quality tea. Thus, there is scope for quality tea of Indian origin, which can cater to the needs of the sections of higher income brackets. The entry of such quality tea could be in the forms of packet tea and tea bags. Indian tea has attained fame by way of quality in Arab Republic of Egypt, Arab Republic of Syria, and Arab Republic of Libya. India has to further equip with new innovations in export strategies to attract markets of Iran and Jordan, Singapore and Nigeria. The Tea Board, Government of India, Tea Associations, Tea Research Associations, Calcutta Tea Traders Association, and others involved in this trade must also adopt suitable mechanism in this regard. The United Planter's Association of South India (UPASI) sent delegation to some middle east countries such as South Africa, Egypt, Syria to study the markets and design appropriate strategies to explore the possibility of exporting Indian Tea in these markets. Major findings of the studies have been documented in this book. Tea is grown in Mauritius, Taiwan, Indonesia etc.. However standard of tea appears to be far from satisfactory. Now it is the opportune time for India to penetrate into the markets. Further tea cultivation took its roots in Mozambique, Tanzania, Rwanda, Uganda, Nyasaland. As the quality of tea in these countries is not up to the mark, India's possibility to grab the market is of paramount importance. India must identify the strategies to be adopted for exporting tea in Rhodesia, Turkey, Malawi, Cameroon, Australia, New Zealand, Vietnam, Peru, Brazil, Argentina, Equador, Bolivia, Colombia, Bangladesh etc.

The Indian Tea industry got momentum with the discovery of wild tea in Assam, formation of a Tea Committee, tea cultivation in North and South India, research and development activities undertaken by Tea Research Association, Tocklai, United Planters' Association of South India etc. Issues relating to import of tea for re-exports, standard of quality, renovation of old tea bushes having more than 60 years, product diversification, exports of value added teas have been documented with probable solutions. Long term marketing strategies of value added items of tea focussing on production and productivity, cost of production, skewness towards black tea (CTC variety accounting for 90 per cent of total production) have been worked out. Interestingly, the treatise on "Export Potential of Indian Tea" identifies major areas affecting India's export performance, and suggests well coordinated efforts with brand building of Indian Tea, new outlets, preference of emerging markets, strengthening of market share in matured markets, India's competitive position in the world tea trade.

Tea was first planted in Kenya in 1903, although tea production in Malawi had started on a commercial scale since 1891. The Kenya Tea Growers Association (KTGA), set up in 1931, was the driving force behind the recognition of Kenya teas in the world tea market. The Kenya Tea Development Authority, formed in 1964, promoted small tea growers of Kenya. At present, the small growers own nearly 80 per cent of the planted tea area and large estate owners 20 per cent. The KTGA alone directly employs nearly 60 thousand people, which accounts for about 50 per cent of total production. The average size of holdings in the small holder is only 0.38 hectare. Production, export and sale; disposal of tea to various countries, origin of Mombassa Auction, market behaviour and promotional efforts are some of the aspects that have been incorporated in the treaty. The Tea Board of Kenya exercises licensing control over tea planting and manufacturing facilities and is financing Kenyan Tea Research Foundation. The Board of Kenya now undertakes the task of tea promotion in the world.

Sri Lanka has unique agro-climatic zones, each is producing a different type of tea. Officially, there were 24 grades of black tea. A committee of marketing experts was constituted to oversee 24 grades and see whether there is need to reduce some. They did a lot of work and came up with interesting answer, increasing the numbers to 30. It may sound odd, but actually what they are doing is that they are catering to each market. The more segmentation is done, the more is the value addition. Colombo the Hub is one of the biggest strengths and the largest auction of its kind in the world. It is also probably the largest packing operations of its kind in the world. Colombo town has the largest number of tea bagging machines in the world. Sri Lanka is third largest tea bagging supplier in the Asia-Pacific Region. The transfer of state owned plantations to private sector, nationalization of foreign companies and setting up of 22 independent 'Regional Management Enterprises', each with 15 to 25 states are some of the issues that got due weightage.

The Pu'er Tea in China has many health giving properties. People largely have three attitudes towards goods: commodities should provide novelty, beauty and health. Of these requirements, health is major one. This is also the basic factor for any commodity to excel on the market. Books such as *Diannan Record,* and *Supplements to the Compendium of Materia Medica* recorded the pharmacological and health giving properties of Pu'er tea. The China's medical profession provided the clinical evidences that Pu'er Tea has shown significant effect reducing cholesterol level, preventing and curing dysentery and enteritis together with weight reducing and anti steroid actions. Clinical trials conducted by the National Research Institute for Health and Medicine (NRIHM) in France demonstrated that Pu'er Tea (Tuo Cha) can lower the blood fat level. The book *Pu'er Tea—The Tea with Miraculous Function* written by Nu Setsuao and Soyama Ichiro created a Pu'er Tea fad in Japan. The Kunming Medical College undertook the clinical trials. Some of the researchers in China doing in vitro experiments with sections of rats have found that the Pu'er tea possesses functions such as helping digestion, appetising, relieving over stuffiness and weight reduction. Pu'er tea has strong flavour, better reusability, moderate nature, health giving properties and affordability.

Japanese green tea has lemon yellow or greenish yellow liquor without any thing of brown. The manufacture of green tea, typical non-fermented tea, developed by Japan has been discussed. Further, a comparison on the method of production of green tea between Japan & China has been made. The hand processing of green tea *Temomi,* which covers nine different operations and takes about four hours. Japan has opted *Aracha,* that means crude tea mechanically produced. Besides, processing freshly plucked leaf, manufactures of refined tea, health aspects of green tea, and prospects of liquid tea market, retail ready black teas etc. are the areas that find special attention. Prospects of Indian tea in Japan, herbal tea, green tea, black tea, Oolong tea, barley tea have been documented. Area, production, yield, exports, value of exports of tea from Japan during the last decade has been analyzed. In addition, share of Japan to world production and export of tea; exports of tea from Japan by destination and Import pattern of tea in Japan has been covered.

Dr. Banerjee is scholar in his field and gained experience both as an academician and a practitioner. He served as a lecturer both in college and university levels; worked in UNDP, Global Project; Agro-Economic Research Centre, Visva Bharti, Santiniketan; Rice Research Institute, Chunchura, Hooghly, Government of West Bengal, Sundarban Development Board, Development and Planning Department, Govt. of West Bengal, Tea Board, Kolkata; Uttar Pradesh Development System Corporation under State Planning Board, Lucknow; National Council of Applied Economic Research, New Delhi etc. At present he is serving as Deputy General Manager (Officer-in-Charge), NABARD, Nagaland, Regional Office, Dimapur. He was awarded Ph.D. degree in Economics from the Jadavpur University, Kolkata; and graduated in Law. He has published four books namely, *Tea Plantation Industry in India Between 1850 and 1922—Structural Changes,* 1966; *Challenges before Small Scale Industries,* 1997; *The Tea Industry Survey,* 2005; and *Darjeeling Tea—The Golden Brew,* 2007. The books on *Agricultural and Rural Development Policy Agendas in the New Millennium,* and *Sustainable Tea Plantation Management in India* are under printing and will be published in first quarter of 2008. He also contributed more than 160 papers in reputed journals/

national dailies like *Yojana, Kurukshetra, Indian Journal of Agricultural Economics, Indian Journal of Agricultural Marketing, Man and Development, Afro-Asian Journal, Financing Agriculture, Indian Association of Social Science Institutes (IASSI) journal, Agriculture Today, Waste Land Development News, National Bank News Review (NABARD), NAB Law (NABARD), Technical Digest (NABARD), Suvikalpa, NABCON, NABARD, Tea Association of India (TAI) News Letter, The Assam Review* and *Tea News, Chai ki Bat, Financial Express, Economic Times, Eastern Mirror, Nagaland Post, North-East Times, India Today* etc. I am sure, the present publication will be useful to not only the academicians and researchers but also to the students, tea companies, tea associations and those involved in tea trade etc. in various capacities. Shri Srijeet Banerji, a post-graduate student of computer science of Mumbai University, is involved in compilation, tabulation and analysis of data presented in the form of tables. He is also associated in many ways for giving the final shape of the book.

With these few words, over to the readers, for the rest, let the book speak (or whisper into their ears) for itself.

Shri Khulu, IAS
Principal Secretary and Finance Commissioner
Government of Nagaland,
Ministry of Finance, Kohima

Preface

The book *Export Potential of Indian Tea* explores the possibility of further strengthening export markets of tea world. Indian tea has gained reputation for its quality in the United Kingdom, Poland, United States of America, Canada and South America. The value added teas also captured these markets. India has also identified suitable strategies to prevail upon more markets like Arab Republic of Egypt, Arab Republic of Syria, Arab Republic of Libya, Jordan and Iran. Her aggressive marketing ventures in popularising teas in the markets namely Singapore, Nigeria, Middle East, Mauritius, Taiwan, Japan, and South Africa are well acknowledged. The book outlines the importance of Britain in World Tea. The issues relating to production, propagation, funding development projects, financing, generic advertising, communication, tea and health, the world tea market, the UK tea trade have been addressed in the first UK Tea Convention (21-24 May, 1990). Indian tea constitutes major share (70 per cent) in total tea imports for consumption in Poland. She not only exports bulk teas but also value added teas mainly packet tea. A small quantity of tea bags and instant tea is exported. The popularity of Indian tea in the United States of America is "Skyrocketing" as reported by Sir Joshep Simrany, the then President of Tea council, USA. More than half of the population is now drinking tea. A little over 48 million cups/glasses of tea is consumed. Tea is becoming more and more the beverage of choice because of its refreshing taste, and its "perfect fit" with desire for healthier life styles. "Served hot tea, is soothing and relaxing cold weather beverage choice perfect any time." Changing consumer needs, connoisseurship to appreciate tea, the growth areas, liquid consumption trends, features of US market, chalking out well coordinated campaign, medicinal and health properties of tea are some of the areas, which draw attention. Canada occupies fifth position among the tea importing countries. India accounts for major share in total tea imports for consumption in Canada since 1950. She could increase her exports from 8 million kgs in 1951 to 15 million kgs in 2006. Packet tea exports enhanced by 15 times. It was 6 thousand kgs in 1980-81 to 90 thousand kgs in 2006-07. Exports of tea bag and instant tea declined over the same period. Tea bags and instant tea fell from 206 million kgs to 10 million kgs and 55 million kgs to 11 million kgs respectively. This calls for introspection and identification of specific strategies to capture tea bags and instant tea markets. Tea Board has already taken various promotional measures to arrest slow growth of these value added teas.

Indian tea has export potential in South American countries like Chile, Mexico, Guyana, Venezuela, Trinidad, Peru, Colombia etc.. Analysis of production, exports and tea consumption of those countries reveal the fact that the quantity of tea entering into South American Countries is obviously of Argentina or Brazil origin, which could be hardly quality tea. Apparently there is scope for quality tea of Indian origin, which can cater to the needs of the sections of higher income brackets. The entry of quality tea could be in the forms of packet tea and tea bags. Indian tea has attained highest esteem by way of quality in Arab Republic of Egypt, Arab Republic of Syria, and Arab Republic of Libya. India has to further strengthen her export strategies in the markets of Iran and Jordan. Singapore and Nigeria are the major markets for Indian tea. All-out efforts are to be ensured to have enough quantity of Indian tea in these markets. The Tea Board, Government of India, Tea Associations, Tea Research Associations, Calcutta Tea Traders Association, and others involved in this trade must also adopt suitable mechanism in this regard. The United Planters' Association of South India (UPASI) sent delegation to some middle east countries such as South Africa, Egypt, Syria to study the markets and design appropriate strategies to explore the possibility of making Indian Tea available in these markets. The major objectives of the study were to promote export of South Indian Tea both bulk and value added teas; assess the current tea import situation and policies of the middle east; know the product profile (tea) in each country; match Indian resources and positioning the same and appraise the importers of middle east about changing ground realities. Major findings of the studies have been inked in this book. Tea is grown in Mauritius, Taiwan, Indonesia etc.. However standard of tea appears to be far from satisfactory. Now it is the opportune time for India to penetrate in to the markets. Further tea cultivation took its root in Mozambique, Tanzania, Rwanda, Uganda, Nyasaland. As the quality of tea in these countries is not up to the mark, India's possibility to grab the market is of paramount importance. India must identify the strategies to be adopted for exporting tea in Rhodesia, Turkey, Malawi, Cameroon, Australia, New Zealand, Vietnam, Peru, Brazil, Argentina, Equador, Bolivia, Colombia etc. All endeavours have been made to facilitate presence of Indian Tea in these countries. Tea in Bangladesh highlights area, production, yields, exports, destination wise exports of tea, quality and average price realisation at different auctions in India and World. To strengthen the tea economy of Bangladesh emphasis may be made on quality of products. All efforts must be made to maintain consistency in standard of products throughout.

India's popular slogan since independence has been "World's largest producer, exporters and consumers". India's share in world production and world exports in 2007 have been registered at 25 per cent and 12.50 per cent respectively as against 50 per cent and 45 per cent in 1950. The factors responsible for sluggish growth in export are on account of fall in production, inability to make a headway in exploring potentials for emerging markets, inadequate efforts in marketing and brand equity in overseas markets, and over dependence in Commonwealth of Independence States (CIS). Besides Indian tea is beset with problems of entering in emerging higher markets by competing with Sri Lanka, Kenya, China etc.. All these call for elaborate study outlining "Export Potential of Indian Tea" in other countries. The major break through of Indian tea started with the discovery of wild tea in Assam, formation of a Tea Committee, tea cultivation in North and South India, research and development activities undertaken by Tea Research Association, Tocklai, United Planters' Association of South India etc., and exports of Indian tea in other countries. Issues relating to import of tea for re-exports, standard of quality, renovation of old tea bushes having more than 60 years, product diversification, switching over from primary to processed goods, exports of value added teas have been documented with probable solutions. India has been facing various problems of value added teas. These are dearth of indigenous know-how, lack of investment for establishment of firms, brand name, imposition of various tariff and non-tariff barriers created by developed countries against the entry of Indian tea in consumer packets. Long term marketing strategies of value added items focussing on production and productivity, cost of production, skewness towards black tea (CTC variety accounting for 90 per cent of total production). Interestingly, the book identifies major areas affecting India's export performance, and suggests well coordinated efforts with brand building of Indian Tea, new outlets, preference of emerging markets, strengthening of market share in matured markets. India's competitive position in the world tea trade with remedial measures, quality of production and export of tea in relation to world, sale and imports of tea for re-exports are some of the issues that got due importance. Incentives provided to such tea have been discussed.

Kenya, being one of the African countries, entered into the world of tea at relatively a later date. Tea was first planted in Kenya in 1903, although tea production in Malawi had started on a commercial scale since 1891. The Kenyan Tea Growers Association (KTGA), set up in 1931, was the driving force behind the recognition of Kenyan teas in the world tea market. The Kenyan Tea Development Authority was formed in 1964 to promote small tea growers of Kenya. At present, the small growers own nearly 80 per cent of the planted tea area and large estate owners 20 per cent. The KTGA alone directly employs nearly 60 thousand people, which accounts for about 50 per cent of total production. The average age of tea bushes under small growers is lower than that of the large estate sector. The average size of holdings in the small holder is only 0.38 hectare. The share of area under tea cultivation and crop produced by small tea growers to total area and production are the focal points. Data relating to area, production and yield over a period of 56 years, quantity of exports, value of exports and unit value of exports have also been studied. Production, export and sale; disposal of tea of various countries, origin of Mombasa Auction, market behaviour and promotional efforts are some of the factors that deserve special attention. Further types of manufacture, taxes and duties, tea prices are the aspects, are given due consideration. The Tea Board of Kenya now exercises licensing control over tea planting and manufacturing facilities and is financing Kenyan Tea Research Foundation. The Board of Kenya now undertakes the task of tea promotion in the world. At present Kenya is the topmost tea producer in Africa and ranks fourth in the field of world tea exporters after India, Sri Lanka and China. Tea is Kenya's second most important foreign exchange earner after coffee. Kenya occupies the second position accounting for nearly 19 per cent of the global production. About 99 per cent of the total tea production of Kenya is of CTC type. Kenya produces negligible quantity of Orthodox teas.

Sri Lanka is relatively a small country, but it has unique agro climatic zones, each is producing a different type of tea. The industry decided a long time ago—let's promote teas. Further the country has unique products. Some of which are familiar with everybody—various grades. It is not catering to the mass markets; it is catering to the individual customer—giving the consumer a range of whatever teas he or she wants. Officially, there were 24 grades of black tea. This is the part from green tea, instant tea and the concentrates. So a committee of marketing experts was constituted. The Committee was to oversee 24 grades and see whether there is need to reduce some and may give up some, they did a lot of work and came up with interesting answer, increasing the numbers to 30. It may sound odd, but actually what they are doing is they are catering to each market. The more segmentation is done, the more is the value addition. The CTTA made hub in Colombo. Its Rules ensured that all the packing houses are in Colombo (in the north of Colombo exact). All the warehouses come in the same area, which is called Colombo the Hub, one of the biggest strengths and the largest auction of its kind in the world. By doing so, the industry has been able to increase the demand. It is also probably the largest packing operations of its kind in the world. All the packers are doing their jobs with 3.5 million and odd tea bagging machines. Colombo town has the largest number of tea bagging machines in the world. Sri Lanka is third largest tea bagging supplier in the Asian-Pacific region.

Efforts have been made to document the legendary perseverance at perfecting the art of tea manufacture since 1857 by John Tailor, the Father of Sri Lanka Tea. The transfer of state owned plantations to private sector, nationalization of foreign companies and setting up of 22 independent 'Regional Management Enterprises', each with 15 to 25 states are some of the issues that got due weightage. Major recommendations of South Indian Tea Convention held in 1990s emphasizing the cooperation between India and Sri Lanka on marketing, value added exports and follow up measures have been incorporated. The conventions cautioned the industry in this regard. Sri Lanka's share, mis-matched between price realization and cost of production along with strategies have been spelt out. Various suggestions by planters associations of Sri Lanka for development of the tea industry were documented. A comprehensive note on the 'Reformist Zeal' indicating distribution of tea area by district/elevation/ holding was made. Further, exercises have made to include export of value added products. In the process, attempts are endeavoured to cover strength and future of Sri Lanka Tea industry. The strength includes formation of Tea Association, Tea Propagation Board, Sri Lanka Tea Board, enactment of Tea Control Export Act, implementation of new levels of marketing, exports of value added products, introduction of Colombo Hub, existence of tea bagging machine and tea bag supply, etc. The future of the industry suggests further ensuring quality and customer focus, more transparency in auction system and propagation of tea as tourist industry.

The Pue'r Tea in China has many health giving properties. In modern times, people largely have three attitudes towards goods: namely, commodities should provide novelty, beauty and health. Of these requirements, health is the major one that is also the basic factor for any commodity to excel on the market. "High mountains shrouded with clouds and mist yield famous tea" is an old saying. This together with the unique processing technology permits full oxidation of the polyphonies and caffeine, substances beneficial to the human body, and yield a product of unique flavour and quality. In ancient times many books such as "Diannan Record" and "Supplements to the Compendium of Materia Medica" recorded the pharmacological and health giving properties of Pu'er Tea. The China's medical profession provided the clinical evidences that Pu'er Tea has shown significant effect in reducing cholesterol level. It can be taken for long periods of time without any side effects, and also has bacteria static effects, being able to prevent and cure dysentery and enteritis. Since 1978, Dr. Emile Karoubi, Head of the Clinical Instruction Department of the Saint Antoine Medical College, Paris, has subjected the Pu'er Tea (Tuo Cha) of Yunnan to tests, focusing on the weight reducing and anti steroid actions of Pu'er Tea in human beings. Clinical trials conducted by the national Research Institute for Health and Medicine (NRIHM) in France since the eighties have demonstrated that Pu'er Tea (Tuo Cha) can lower the blood fat level. The patients' with very high blood fat level, 20 per cent showed a reduction of 22 per cent within two months. Professor Lu Tong of the Laboratory of Nutrition, Orson, also performed similar tests and concluded, "This kind of tea apparently contains one or more constituents which can influence the metabolism of lipoids". The book "Pu'er Tea—the Tea with Miraculous Function" written by Nu Setsuo and Soyama Ichiro created a Pu'er Tea fad in Japan. The Kunming Medical College under took the clinical trials. Some of our researchers in China doing in vitro experiments with sections of excised rat intestine, have found that the Pu'er Tea possesses functions such as helping digestion, appetizing, relieving over stuffiness and weight reducing functions. They think that the Green Tea is cold in nature, Black Tea hot in nature, whereas Pu'er Tea is neither cold nor hot, easy to afford and worth one's money, and so is a popular drink given the name "Baoli Tea". Pu'er Tea is moderate and mild in nature, can strengthen the body's defense mechanisms, and is suited to the digestive system of the people in Hong Kong. This may be the main reason why the Hong Kong people prefer to drink Pu'er Tea. Pu'er tea is strong flavour, better reusability, moderate nature, health giving properties and affordability.

Japanese green tea gives a lemon yellow or greenish yellow liquor without anything of brown. The manufacture of green tea, a typical non-fermented tea, developed by Japan has been discussed. Further, a comparison on the method of production of green tea between Japan and China has been made. The hand processing of green tea known as 'Temomi', which covers nine different operations and takes about four hours. Japan has opted 'Aracha' that means crude tea mechanically produced. Besides, processing freshly plucked leaf, manufactures of refined tea, health aspects of green tea, and prospects of liquid tea market, retail ready black teas etc are the areas that make special attention. Prospects of Indian tea in Japan, herbal tea, green tea, black tea, oolong tea, and barley tea have been documented. Area, production, yield, exports, value of exports of tea from Japan during the last one decade has been analyzed. In addition, share of Japan to world production and export of tea; exports of tea from Japan by destination and Import pattern of tea in Japan have been covered.

The Authors are indebted to their father\grandfather Dr. Indra Narayan Banerjee, and mother\grandmother Srimati Chaya Rani Banerjee for their moral support in this venture. Unfortunately they left for heavenly abode few months back. Let their blessings shower on the Authors. We must place on records our heart felt thanks and love to Shri N.S. Dawood and Shri S.K. Dey who took trouble day in and day out to make this manuscript error free. Thanks are due to Shrimati Shikha Banerjee, wife/mother and Sarada Banerjee, daughter/ sister respectively for helping in many ways in publication of the treaty. We are obliged to M/s. Abhijeet Publications, Delhi and their staff-members for taking trouble in publishing the book. We are sure that the present publication will be useful to the academicians, researchers, students, planners, policy makers, tea companies, tea estates and those involving in tea manufacturing and trading etc.

Authors

Contents

List of Tables

1

Export of Indian Tea—Strategic Alliances of Major Markets

Introduction

The students of Indian Tea are aware of Sri Maniram Dewan, a patriot and a pioneer of tea gave clue to Major Bruce to discover wild tea growing in Assam hills. Therefore, the credit to discover tea should go to Maniram Dewan, contrary to the Britishers' view in favour of Major Bruce. The tea committee appointed by Lord William Bentinck in 1834 played a major role in starting tea in India, although the members on this committee were doubtful of tea cultivation here in our country. The historical shipment was sent to London in 1839 and commercial success was seen which later eluded until about 1869. The commission appointed by the Government in 1868 to study the viability, however, found basic soundness of the industry. In 1840, tea holdings of the government were given to the Assam Company, which was started in 1839. The credit of being world's first successful tea company goes to this organization. India contributes about twenty-eight percent to world tea production. In fact, modern tea industry's extension started in India. Whatever India produces, seventy-five percent of it comes from NE India. Biggest tea area is in Assam followed by West Bengal. In south, maximum tea areas are in Tamil Nadu and Kerala. An area over 2128 hectares of tea is there in Karnataka. Tripura has a tea area of about 6700 hectares. Tea is there in areas other than what mentioned here also and they comprise over 10000 hectares. Entire Indian tea is spread in about 512450 hectares. Tea areas in Assam, West Bengal, Tamil Nadu and Karnataka increased in each decade from 1960 onwards, highest increase being in Assam followed by West Bengal and Tamil Nadu. Marginal increase has been there in Karnataka. Tea is there in Dehradun, Kangra, Ranchi, Manipur, Sikkim, Arunachal Pradesh, Nagaland, Orissa, Meghalaya, Mizoram, etc.

Tea in North and South India

The first tea state came up in Cacher of North Eat Indian (NEI) in 1856 and discovery of tea was made in Sylhet and Khasi and Jaintia hills. Plantation in Tukvar in Darjeeling was also done until this time together with some gardens on Kurseong and Darjeeling slopes. Darjeeling produces the queen of world tea with fantastic flavour. In 1862, tea estate started in Terai and in Doars in 1874. N.E. Indain soil has alluvial deposits by rivers, tributaries and the bulk is alluvial in origin. Sand and silt proportions are high and the excess of iron and aluminium are low. Compared to Assam, potash amount is normally higher in the soils of North Bengal. Twenty percent oxides are there in those parts of Dooars where older red bank soil is there. Cacher and North Bengal soils have higher nitrogen and organic matter contents in general compared to Brahmaputra valley. Nitrogen and organic matter are quite rich in Cacher bheel soil. Tea is grown in Almora and Garhwal Kumaon districts, Dehradun, Kangra valley and Ranchi etc in North India. Main tea area of Kangra valley is near Palampur. Almora and Garhwal Kumaon and Dehradun areas suffer due to the lack of soil acidity. Ranchi area faces the problem of young leaf wilting and dieing back during spring flush. Plants take longer time in coming into bearing. Although the period of gestation is longer, tea has already been cultivated in non-traditional areas of Manipur, Arunachal Pradesh, Orissa, Meghalaya and Uttaranchl.

Maximum of *South Indian tea was planted after 1893*. Coffee, Cardamom etc. are also there in tea estates in South India. Benefit of virgin forest was there to plant out nearly all South Indian tea after clearings. Forest humus enriched soils are there. Except the bheel, organic matter, potash and nitrogen are in soils there compared to N.E. Indian soils. South Indian tea does not have winter dormancy. About forty percent of the bushes in India are old. Further, land is practically not available for extension to the extent. By the year, 2025 India Government sets the target of 1200 million kgs of tea. In 2005, production suffered because of unfavorable weather. A record of 900 million kgs was achieved in 2003. The Government is taking keen interest in tea. In India, maximum production is of CTC teas followed by Orthodox and green tea. Some instant tea is also produced. Our research scientists also manufactured green tea by CTC method. It may contribute to some increase in green tea production depending upon market situations and the policies of the tea companies here.

Tea Auction Centres: There are many tea auction centers in India. The Kolkata auction center has been there since 1861 and apart from it, auction centers operate at Guwahati, Siliguri, Coonoor, Coimbatore, Cochin and Amritsar. For many years, the export of Indian tea has been static at about 2000 million kgs and has been meeting the domestic consumption. In India, the per capita consumption of tea is 550 gm, on an average.

Tocklai Experiment Station and Tea Board

Tocklai: The world renowned Tocklai Experimental Station of Tea Research Association is situated at Jorhat, Assam, This provides very useful services. It is world's oldest research station for tea. UPASI (United Planters Association of Southern India) located in South India also contributes to the growth of Indian tea. It has its tea research station at Cinchona. Both TRA and UPASI are engaged in R & D and they keep on updating the information and knowledge of the planters. Very useful videocassettes on plucking, pruning and soil management also been brought out by TRA. In 1912, Tocklai Station was established. A chemical laboratory was set up at Heeleakah not far from Tocklai. This chemical laboratory at Heeleakah was started after an entomological laboratory was set up in Cachar at Kannykoorie in 1904. The first laboratory was established in Kolkata in 1900 in the Indian Museum there.

Tea Board: The Board in India has award scheme for quality and production. Its development schemes are there for setting up tea nursery and demonstration plots, training small tea growers and crop diversification also. For creating irrigation and drainage facilities, it has interest subsidy scheme on bank loan. For tea extension, also interest subsidy on bank loan is there. For non-traditional areas, Tea Board has New Tea Unit Financing Scheme. Tea machinery- irrigation equipment- hire scheme and tea plantation finance scheme comprise its loan schemes. Loan scheme is available for setting up cooperative tea factories. Tea Board's capital subsidy schemes include subsidy schemes for replanting and replacement and consolidation and rejuvenation of tea areas.

Area, Production, Yield and Exports of Tea during 1918 to 2005

The details of growth variables are shown in Table 1 below:

Table 1.1: Area, Production, Yield and Exports of Tea in India during 1918 to 2005

Year	*Area (Thousand ha)*	*Production (Million kgs)*	*Yield (Kgs per ha)*	*Exports (Million kgs)*	*Year*	*Area (Thou-sand ha)*	*Production (Million kgs)*	*Yield (Kgs per ha)*	*Exports (Million kgs)*
1918	275	173	625	–	1995	427	756	1770	167
1928	314	183	584	–	1996	431	780	1809	160
1938	337	205	607	–	1997	434	810	1865	201
1948	311	262	843	202	1998	474	874	1844	208
1958	325	325	997	230	1999	490	825	1685	190
1968	351	402	1146	208	2000	540	847	1679	205
1978	369	563	1527	176	2001	510	854	1675	179
1988	414	700	1689	201	2002	513	860	1674	185
1990	416	720	1730	219	2003	518	870	1679	195
1993	418	760	1819	174	2004	523	881	452	200
1994	426	752	1768	149	2005	528	897	1700	205

Source: Various Issues of Tea Statistics, Tea Board, Kolkata, India.

It is evident from the table that area under tea increased almost by 1.92 times during the period from 1918 to 2005, while production enhanced by 5.19 times. The increase in production was mainly due to improvement of productivity (2.71 times) and partial extension of area. Exports hovered around 200 million kgs. It was minimum at 149 million kgs in 1994 and maximum at 205 million kgs in 2005. India's share in world production stood at 27 percent and its share in world exports was 14.50 percent.

Country-wise Export of Indian Tea during 1947 to 2004

Indian tea's popular slogan since Independence has been "world's largest producer, consumer and exporter of Tea". In 2004, however, Sri Lanka forged ahead and exported 238 million kgs against Indian exports of 184 million kgs. Again, in 1991 and 2003 Sri Lanka exported more than India. Sri Lankan exports for these years were 212 million kgs. and 235 million kgs respectively, against Indian exports of 201 million kgs and 202 million kgs. Another feature of Indian exports has been the sea change in its profile between 1947 and 2004. In 1947 U.K's share of Indian exports was 66 per cent and in 2004 it has declined to 12 per cent. On the otherhand, the former Soviet Union, which bought no Indian teas till the 60's became the major importer of Indian tea, it accounted for 44.9 per cent of Indian tea exports in 2004.

Table 1.2: Countrywise Exports of Indian Tea from India during 1947 to 2004

(In million kgs)

Country/year	*1947*	*1957*	*1967*	*1977*	*1987*	*1991*	*1997*	*1999*	*2004*
United Kingdom	127.20	135.40	117.20	74.30	22.40	22.50	25.40	25.00	25.10
Per cent of export	66.30	68.00	53.80	32.40	11.09	11.09	12.70	12.10	12.11
Ireland	9.00	8.30	6.20	6.40	2.10	2.50	2.60	2.50	2.50
Per cent of export	4.70	4.20	2.80	2.80	1.04	1.23	1.28	1.20	1.19
Netherlands	1.50	0.90	3.70	3.40	1.60	1.90	2.70	2.60	2.60
Per cent of export	0.80	0.50	1.70	1.50	0.79	0.90	1.33	1.27	1.26
West Germany	–	1.90	2.20	5.80	4.70	4.70	6.90	6.60	6.65
Per cent of export	–	0.90	1.00	2.50	2.33	2.30	3.40	3.20	3.21
Rest of West Europe	0.60	0.10	0.50	0.90	0.50	0.60	0.80	0.80	0.80
Per cent of export	0.30	0.05	0.20	0.40	0.20	0.30	0.40	0.40	0.40
Poland	–	–	1.80	5.30	10.70	11.90	14.00	14.70	14.75
Per cent of export	–	–	0.80	2.80	5.30	5.90	6.90	7.10	7.11
Yugoslavia	–	–	0.50	4.70	1.40	0.20	0.30	0.40	0.40
Per cent of export	–	–	0.20	2.00	0.70	0.10	0.15	0.17	0.16
Rest of East Europe	–	0.10	1.70	1.40	3.30	1.00	1.60	1.40	1.40
Per cent of export	–	0.05	0.80	0.60	1.60	0.50	0.80	0.70	0.70
USSR	4.00	7.30	20.70	47.70	96.60	104.50	90.70	92.80	94.10
Per cent of export	2.10	3.60	9.50	20.80	47.80	51.50	44.70	44.90	44.95
Afghanistan	–	–	5.70	8.60	3.60	1.60	0.80	1.20	1.20
Per cent of export	–	–	2.60	3.70	1.80	0.80	0.40	0.60	0.60
Iran	3.90	5.60	1.80	6.60	18.90	14.80	11.70	12.80	12.80

Per cent of export	2.00	2.80	1.10	2.90	9.40	7.30	5.80	6.20	6.15
Iraq	1.40	0.02	2.50	4.60	8.80	–	0.10	0.04	0.40
Per cent of export	0.70	0.00	1.10	2.00	4.30	–	0.01	0.02	0.02
Persian Gulf Ports	4.40	2.60	3.00	6.20	7.00	5.20	6.80	7.02	7.02
Per cent of export	2.30	1.30	1.40	2.70	3.50	2.60	3.35	3.40	3.40
Jordan	–	–	1.40	0.60	–	0.50	0.10	0.60	0.60
Per cent of export	–	–	0.60	0.30	0.05	0.20	0.20	0.30	0.36
Rest of Middle East	0.60	0.30	0.05	0.07	0.30	–	0.20	0.20	0.20
Per cent of export	0.30	0.10	0.02	0.03	0.10	–	0.10	0.10	0.10
Pakistan	–	–	–	4.60	0.60	0.30	0.40	0.4	0.40
Per cent of export	–	–	–	2.00	0.30	0.15	0.20	0.20	0.26
Japan	–	–	0.30	0.80	1.40	2.00	1.90	2.30	2.30
Per cent of export	–	–	0.10	0.30	0.30	1.00	0.90	1.10	1.10
Arab Rep. of Egypt	1.80	7.30	16.60	14.10	7.80	7.90	7.20	7.60	7.60
Per cent of export	0.90	3.70	7.60	6.10	3.90	3.90	3.50	3.70	3.76
Sudan	0.70	2.00	10.00	13.60	0.10	–	0.10	0.10	0.10
Per cent of export	0.40	1.00	4.60	5.70	0.05	–	0.05	0.06	0.06
Tunisia	–	–	3.80	1.20	1.00	1.70	1.50	1.90	1.90
Per cent of export	–	–	1.70	0.50	0.50	0.80	0.70	0.90	0.90
Rest of Africa	–	–	–	0.40	3.70	7.00	9.80	9.50	9.50
Per cent of export	–	–	–	0.20	1.80	3.40	4.80	4.60	4.60
Canada	8.20	7.70	3.90	2.50	0.80	0.60	0.10	0.15	0.15
Per cent of export	4.30	3.90	1.80	1.10	0.40	0.30	0.05	0.07	0.07
USA	17.30	10.60	8.40	10.00	1.80	2.50	2.90	3.30	3.30
Per cent of export	9.00	5.30	3.90	4.40	0.90	1.20	1.40	1.60	1.60
Australia	7.00	3.40	5.40	4.60	0.70	0.80	0.50	0.60	0.60
Per cent of export	3.70	1.70	2.50	2.00	0.30	0.40	0.25	0.30	0.30
New Zealand	0.50	0.70	0.40	1.30	–	–	–	–	–
Per cent of export	0.30	0.40	0.20	0.60	–	–	–	–	–
All other countries	3.60	5.00	0.10	0.50	4.30	8.10	13.40	11.95	11.95
Per cent of export	1.90	2.50	0.05	0.20	2.10	4.00	6.63	5.81	5.81
Total	191.70	199.20	217.80	229.60	201.90	201.72	200.71	189.02	183.64

Source: Same as Table 1.1.

Countries like Poland, Yugoslavia, Afghnistan, Japan, Tunisia and even Germany bought no teas from India in 1947 but today they are strong supporters of the Indian produce. Iraq, Iran, Gulf, ARE have been buying more teas but Canada, USA, Australia, New Zealand and the UK, reduced their purchase from India substantially. In the 57 years period since 1947, African Countries, particularly Kenya, have been giving stiff competition to Indian CTC teas and gained popularity in the red currency areas. Sri Lanka, on the other hand, a major producer of orthodox tea, has been stepping into the Indian orthodox exports. She took credit for catering to the entire expansion and demand in the orthodox segment. The only exception has been the former USSR who has supported Indian orthodox varieties strongly. Sri Lanka has been catering to the growing markets of ARE, Iran, USA, and Pakistan.

India and World—Tea Exports during 1947 to 2004

India exported 191.07 million kgs in 1947. It increased to 199.20 million kgs in 1957, 217 million kgs in 1967 and 229 million kgs in 1977. The quantum of tea exported, however, hovered around 200 million kgs. India's share in world exports reduced from 53.30 per cent to 18.25 per cent during 1947 to 2004. Details are given in Table 1.3 below:

Table 1.3: India's Share in World Exports during 1947-2004

(In million kgs)

Country/Year	*1947*	*1957*	*1967*	*1977*	*1987*	*1991*	*1997*	*1999*	*2004*
India	191.70	199.20	217.80	229.60	201.90	201.72	200.71	189.02	183.64
Per cent	53.30	39.90	35.60	28.20	20.70	17.90	13.20	18.50	18.25
Sri Lanka	130.30	166.80	216.50	185.50	201.20	212.40	234.85	238.05	291.01
Per cent	36.30	33.40	35.40	22.70	20.60	18.80	21.24	21.52	21.60
Indonesia	3.90	38.80	26.60	51.30	90.40	109.60	103.90	102.50	86.42
Per cent	1.10	7.80	4.30	6.30	9.20	9.70	9.40	9.60	9.70
Bangladesh	N.A	4.50	Negl	26.00	21.60	25.30	24.30	25.40	12.45
Per cent	Negl	0.90	Negl	3.20	2.20	2.20	2.40	2.30	2.32
Kenya	4.40	8.20	19.70	70.20	135.00	191.60	245.50	251.10	326.20
Per cent	1.20	1.60	3.20	8.60	13.80	16.90	22.20	22.70	22.73
Uganda	1.10	2.80	9.60	14.70	2.10	4.70	15.20	15.10	16.10
Per cent	0.30	0.60	1.60	1.80	0.20	0.40	1.40	1.40	1.42
Tanzania	0.50	2.40	6.20	12.00	11.40	15.00	18.80	19.90	24.95
Per cent	0.10	0.50	1.00	1.50	1.20	1.30	1.70	1.80	1.82
Malawi	5.90	8.80	16.80	29.90	33.40	41.20	36.50	35.40	47.20
Per cent	1.70	1.80	2.70	3.70	3.40	3.60	3.30	3.20	3.21
Mozambique	1.50	5.90	14.40	15.60	2.10	1.00	0.42	0.95	0.97
Per cent	0.40	1.20	2.40	1.90	0.20	0.09	0.04	0.05	0.08
Others	20.20	61.70	84.40	180.60	277.50	338.40	223.23	213.60	216.15
Per cent	5.60	12.30	13.80	22.10	28.40	29.90	25.12	18.93	19.25
Total	359.50	499.10	612.00	815.40	976.60	1132.10	1105.70	1106.20	1501.00

Source: Same as Table 1.1.

In the domestic front also, the scene has changed. In 1947, Indian consumption was only 39 per cent of production and in 1999 this figure reached 76 per cent. In the past, the equation was "Indian consumption equals production minus exports". In the eighties, this equation was reversed and on several occasions, the government restricted export to conserve tea for the domestic market. The details of Indian consumption of tea in given below:

Table 1.4: Growth of Consumption of Tea in Indian during 1947-2004

(In million kgs.)

Particulars/Year	*1947*	*1957*	*1967*	*1977*	*1987*	*1991*	*1997*	*1999*	*2004*
Consumption	98.5	112.9	180.7	302.0	446.0	520.0	635	670	740
Growth (percentage)	—	14.6	60.1	67.1	47.6	16.6	22.1	5.5	10.5
Average annual rate of growth (percentage)	—	1.46	6.01	6.7	4.76	4.1	3.6	2.3	2.1

Source: Same as Table 1.1.

Table 1.5

Indian Tea Consumption, Production and Share of Consumption to Production during 1947-2000

Particulars/Year	*1947*	*1957*	*1967*	*1977*	*1987*	*1991*	*1997*	*1999*	*2004*
Consumption in million kgs	98.5	112.9	180.7	302.0	446.0	520.0	635.0	670.0	740.00
Production in million kgs	254.8	310.8	384.8	556.3	674.3	741.7	810.6	880.2	820.00
Per cent of production	38.7	36.3	47.0	54.3	66.0	70.1	78.3	76.1	90.12

Source : same as Table 1.1.

The break-up of the Soviet Union has therefore had a strong impact on the Indian tea market. However, it gained momentum over the years. Russia and other CIS members did not cross 45 million kgs. Total Indian exports thus touched 205 million kgs. Indian domestic market continues to grow at around 2 per cent per annum. In the 1999 domestic consumption was about 670 million kgs. By 2004 this figure was 725 million kgs. If export of 205 million kgs is added, production in 2007 would be about 940 million kgs. The CTC element of Indian consumption is over 94 per cent. It is estimated that in 2010 the Indian requirement for CTC teas has been estimated at 1034 million kgs, which would go up to 1050 million kgs in 2012. State-wise split of estimated consumption of tea is furnished below:

Table 1.6: A state-wise Split of Estimated Consumption in India during 1991-2004

(Million kgs)

Particulars/Year	*1991*	*1995*	*1999*	*2004*
Uttar Pradesh	44	50	57	67
Bihar	18	23	25	25
Mahharastra	67	76	86	99
West Bengal	38	43	48	52
Andra pradesh	25	30	32	33
Madhya Pradesh	32	38	40	43
Tamil Nadu	21	23	26	28
Rajasthan	45	48	52	56
Gujarat	45	50	57	67
Orissa	10	12	18	20
Kerala	33	37	40	44
Assam	18	20	23	25
Punjab	40	45	50	55
Haryana	18	20	22	24
Jammu & Kashmir	10	15	20	22
Karnataka	26	30	34	36
Others	30	35	40	44
Total	520	595	670	740

Source : same as Table 1.1.

New strategies will to be evolved for the Russian Federation, CIS and Pakistan. Above all, exports will to be given a clear priority over domestic need. While future supply and demand, on the overall, appears *'hand to-mouth'* the future of specialty varieties, such as Darjeelings and Assam orthodox, would depend upon aggressive marketing.

Freely Import of Tea for Re-exports

Proposal of Ministry of Commerce, Government of India, modified the export-import policy (2002-07) with a view to facilitating the EOU/EPZ to freely import teas for bulk-re-exports generated unfathomable dissatisfaction among many Barons of the India's tea industry. Tea imports were allowed with the rider that they should be used only for re-export with a 20 per cent value addition. But the imports were insignificant because the facility was limited to re-export of packaged teas, tea bags and instant tea. The Commerce Ministry sought the industry's view on allowing bulk re-export of tea blended with the imported product. Barons of the Indian tea association asserted: *(i)* tea having an exportable surplus, India does not need to import teas; *(ii)* if the imported low grade teas are blended with better stuff to export as tea bags, packets, instant tea, its image would be damaged at the international market and exports suffer in the long run; *(iii)* under the Exim policy (2002-2007) for tea, exporters were not allowed to sell any portion of the manufactured items in the domestic market.

But the leaders of the Indian tea industry feared that once bulk teas are allowed to import, there would also be an option for unloading these teas in the domestic market. And a few larger business houses, facing stiff competition in the domestic market, would practically use the cheap imported product to reduce their prices in a bid to earn and maintain substantial profit and hold the domestic sectare; (iv) import of teas by India would raise international prices of teas while depressing domestic markets, a situation, which would adversely effect the growth of tea industry that may eventually lead to recession. The aforesaid premises, as a corollary, led many barons of the industry to raise strong objection against the government's intention of further liberalizing the Exim policy, which may open the floodgates for import of teas. They felt that the policy, if implemented, would not, in anyway, help the growth of the country's tea industry. But, however, one should not be touchy and emotional while considering the policy of import. Rather, it was imperative to visualize the necessity of imports in the perspective of reality. And no denying the fact, that only such a study can help comment judiciously either in favour or against the proposed policy.

There are countries like U.K, U.S.A., importing huge quantity of teas, of course, high grade, to re-export them in the value added form. It should not go unnoticed that international buyers are fast leaning towards packet tea, instant tea and tea bags. So, it is high time to catch them young. Indian tea barons should realize this fact. They should further appreciate that endeavour to re-export value added teas will help to find new markets and to contribute more foreign exchange in the national exchequer through nontraditional way. This is likely to attract new investment also. This besides, two other significant matter should not go un-escaped from our view. First, India's overwhelming dependence on traditional buyers was Russia and CIS, who were the principal buyers of Indian tea? Although, at the moment, India enjoys comfortable position the possibility of creating discomfort by the infiltrated sellers in these markets should not be overlooked. The *'seller's market'* at that time was turned to *'buyer's market'*. Second, China is preparing vigorously to exert its pressure in the international market. Tea is listed as one of the key export commodities. Due to over-whelming importance of red currency earnings it was very likely that the China government provided all sorts of incentive to the tea industry. It is worth noting that between 1950 and 2004 total tea area in the country increased by more than 7 times, 155,000 hectares to 1,115,300 hectares. Output increased by more than 3 times over the same period from 255 million kgs million kgs. Export-increase accounted for 10 times from 18 million kgs in 1950 to 182 million kgs in 2004. Nevertheless, China has the greatest range of tea in different grades and varieties. China intends to be at the top of the list of tea traders in the world market. And no denying the fact, China may, at the earliest opportunity, penetrate in the Russian and CIS market. Keeping in view this possibility, the industry should right now find new market, which may easily be possible with selling value-added teas.

Standard of Quality

Of course, the standard of quality matters much at any export trade. It may be recollected that only a few years back the quality of tea sold to Russia was so bad that million kgs of tea were destroyed. Serious complaints were lodged to the Tea Board. Russian television cautioned the domestic consumers with the words: *"Don't sip Indian tea"*. No doubt, industry's goodwill has been severely damaged by this act of the exporters. The questions are obviously, who has *to be blamed for this event; what measures been taken so far to prevent recurrences*. The Tea Board, being the appropriate authority, should devise full-proof measures to ensure quality. Tea Board should: *(i)* scrutinize every export order received; *(ii)* ensure the credit worthiness of the exporter; *(iii)* arrange intensive checking at the time of shipment; *(iv)* arrange random checking after un-loading; *(v)* introduce mandatory use of the Tea Board's logo, subject to the fulfilment of stipulated conditions, for ever

Doemstic Consumer Strangulated with Demand and Inflation

Whilst it was unlikely that the government would impose any restriction on exports in the foreseeable future, the pressure from the domestic market would limit the quantum of Indian tea exports in the years to come. As stated earlier that with the country's population touched more than 120 crore, ever if an Indian was to drink one extra cup a year, the additional requirement of tea would be 2.55 million kgs; again, if ten cups extra were to be taken everyday by every Indian, the additional requirement would be 931 million kgs per annum. But *how much the industry with its present capacity can produce at the maximum*? Thus the tea industry immediately requires more additional plantation area to meet the target of 1,000 million kgs by the end of the twenty first century. Otherwise, tea production will grow at a small rate of around 3 per cent per annum.

Nevertheless, it is necessary to renovate tea areas, which are more than sixty years of age. A replanting programme of 2 per cent per annum will ensure a rotation over 50 years. Obviously, the argument in favour of '*exportable surplus*' needs be reconsidered. It is a plain truth that if not today, tomorrow India will have to import sizeable quantity of tea either, or to curtail its export for the sake of domestic consumer. Otherwise, where is *the guarantee that, in the near future, domestic consumers will not be strangulated with severe pressure of demand-pull inflation? Where is the guarantee that the industry will be able to maintain exportable surplus, as expected*? These matters are, indeed, related with the industry's social obligation *to two segments*. First obligations relates to *domestic consumers in terms of right price for the right product at the right time*. *Second obligation refers to the nation in terms of helping earn foreign exchange.*

Contextually, the observation of Mr Jimmy Hilditch may be referred to. In course of summing up the convention papers presented at the U.K. Tea convention held in May 1993, it was observed during this period India's "production has increased remarkably together with her population and per capita consumption. With these statistics it is difficult to assess how India can feed internal demand and increase exports without increasing production". The following table shows the future of India's exportable surplus of tea.

Product Diversification of Indian Tea

Even 50 years ago, tea drinkers abroad used to buy *'pure' tea* from the producing country of his choice. Trading companies located in the importing countries were selling the teas of different origins under well-advertised brand names. These companies got their merchendise from a number of tea producing countries. In other words, there was a so-called international division of labour under which tea was grown by poor developing countries especially for the purpose of exports in bulk as raw materials to various developed countries. The imported tea was then sold by the developed countries through a network of large sized companies with substantial capital investment who were marketing the tea in attractive consumer packs under different brand names built up by intensive campaigns. This division of labour was not based on any natural advantage as understood in the theory of international trade. It was dependent on historical factors and on advantages artificially created for different companies by virtue of dominant position of their countries over the erstwhile colonies. The companies not only controlled over 40 or 50 per cent of the markets of developed countries but also controlled trade channels for marketing and distribution of tea. Moreover, some bigger companies owned plantations and controlled a large part of retail marketing of packaged tea. Thus, it is of vital importance that an attitudinal change must precede our attempts towards boosting of tea exports by the developing countries. This would work as catalyst to mark a departure from the traditional position of tea producing countries being content with export of tea as a primary product to value added items. This change covers the diversification

Table 1.7: Exports, Production, Population, and Per Capita Consumption of Tea in India 1950 to 2004

Particulars/Year	*1950*	*1960*	*1970*	*1980*	*1992*	*1995*	*1997*	*1998*	*1999*	*2004*
Exports (million. kgs)	181	193	200	224	190	167	203	205	206	183.64
Production (million kgs)	278	321	419	570	704	756	810	870	880	820.22
Population (million)	354	429	539	675	869	915	935	937	952	1105
Per Capita Consumption of Tea (kg)	0.21	0.29	0.39	0.57	0.61	0.68	0.74	0.79	0.87	0.95

Source: Same as Table 2.1.

into blending of tea and its packaging would enable the tea producing countries to free themselves from the vagaries of the wholesale market of tea and enter the consumer markets directly where prices are more stable compared to wholesale markets. Packet tea can help the producing countries to earn benefit because of blending and packaging and thereby earn more foreign exchange. Similar is the case of instant tea and tea bags.

Structural Changes in Tea—Concept and Forms of Value Addition

By introducing structural changes in tea, India entered value added markets. Before making any attempt to define *'value added'* concept it would be worthwhile to mention that despite over a century of India's entry in world tea export market Indian tea has been hardly known by name or origin except in the country like UK and Germany. In these countries, there was good demand for fine Darjeeling Tea while Chinese and Srilankan Tea are well known in export markets abroad. Even the small amount of value that may be added because of the consumer preference for a particular origin of tea has not reached us. The *first value added exercise started with Indian tea known for superior quality* and flavour to create among consumers a purchasing preferecne for Indian tea. The next stage was to create awareness among the consumers about the regional varieties such as Darjeeling tea, the Nilgiris tea, the Assam tea, Kangra tea etc..

There are three methods by which values are added to tea. These are: *(i)* Breaking bulk and blending involving no technology but require skills that we possess. *(ii)* Consumer packing in attractive packets, cans or bags using modern packing materials, if sold in other brand names (to devote attention towards marketing and promotional skills) and cost, if sold under own brand name. *(iii)* Product processing and qualitative improvement extracting tea solubles i.e., solids and flavour. The country must recourse to value addition in order to reach the consumer directly. The value added items of tea which are sold in the retail market, are in the forms of tea in consumer package and tea bags.

Primary to Processed Goods of Indian Tea

Thus, all the developing countries should bring in certain structural changes in the product they export. This will help them in improving their share in world trade and in earning more foreign exchange. Besides, this would enable the developing countries to be known not only as exporters of *'primary'* products but also as exporters of *'convenient'* products or manufactured goods which can directly find place in the display counters of the consumer stores in the developed countries. In other words, a switch over from *'primary' to 'processed' goods* might open up new vistas of economic growth for the developing countries through increased exports. India, which is one of the developing countries, has progressively ushered in diversification in many of its agricultural commodities in recent years. India started by exporting groundnut seeds and then moved to export of oilseeds and thereafter to products like meal. In case of leather products, India has moved from raw hides to tanned, semi-processed to processed and finished leather, and for over a decade, India has been developing markets for shoe uppers, shoes and leather as well as leather garments and goods. The same could happen in the case of tea. The question is what type of structural changes in tea exports i.e. product diversification has been achieved in India so far.

India is the largest producer and exporter of tea in the world and is expected to produce 1100 million kgs in 2010 assuming an average annual growth rate in tea production to the extent of a little over 3 per cent, other things remaining constant. On an average, India produced about 820 million kgs annually during the last five years. India produced 826 million kgs tea in 2002 and her share in world production was 27 per cent. The volume of her tea exports was 201 million kgs in 2002 that accounted for 14 per cent of world exports and these are mostly in bulk form. India has been trying to maximize exports particularly in the form of processed tea such as packets, tea bags, and instant tea.

Exports of Indian Packet Tea

In India, tea packets containing loose tea are still the normal form of packaging. India for the first time started the export of packet tea (in consumer pack upto a size of 1 kg) in 1965. Six years later, she ventured into export of tea bags, instant tea, etc. Since then India has been making steady and consistent progress in the export of packet tea. In 1965, with only two firms in the field, she had exported 2 million kgsof *packet tea* and at the end of five years, with entry of few more firms, her tea exports doubled to 4 million kgs 1971-72 and in another 4 years, exports reached the level of about 11 million kgs (1975-76). The progress, since then, was noteworthy with the entry of more than 200 firms in the field.

The year-wise growth of exports of packet tea in India for the last two and a half decades since 1973-74, is given below:

Table 1.8: Export of Packet Tea from India during 1973-74 to 2004-2005

Year	*Quantity (thousand kg)*	*Value (thousand Rs.)*	*Unit value (Rs/kg)*
1973-74	4744	50216.00	10.58
1974-75	6095	83051.00	13.56
1975-76	10787	172457.00	15.99
1976-77	12612	193635.00	15.37
1977-78	25187	519834.00	20.64
1978-79	38599	787384.00	20.40
1979-80	30024	580703.00	19.34
1980-81	32322	699834.00	21.65
1981-82	20493	468216.00	22.85
1982-83	10101	263232.00	26.06
1983-84	17368	521288.00	30.01
1984-85	21841	930552.00	42.61
1985-86	25690	994063.00	38.69
1986-87	16847	595727.00	35.36
1987-88	21142	785994.00	37.18
1988-89	25541	879841.00	34.45
1989-90	75817	3548148.00	46.80
1990-91	71514	3908642.00	54.64
1991-92	78321	4520917.00	57.72
1992-93	65245	4040263.00	61.92
1993-94	64917	4685722.00	72.18

1994-95	52042	3577669.00	68.75
1995-96	83965	6162394.00	73.39
1996-97	81016	5714458.00	70.53
1997-98	78115	7490434.00	97.89
1998-99	82013	8904328.00	108.57
1999-00	63518	6743290.00	106.16
2000-01	69315	7195601.00	103.81
2001-02	42719	5211372.00	121.99
2002-03	33610	4084300.00	121.54
2003-04	34010	4058000.00	119.31
2004-05	25890	2957000.00	114.23

Source: Various issues of Tea Statistics, Tea Board, Kolkata.

India's export of packet tea increased from 5 million kgs in 1973-74 to 26 million kgs in 2004-05. Year wise data further revealed that on many occasions India could not retain the volume of her preceding year's exports. Export of packet tea showed a record increase of 84 million kgs in 1995-96 followed by 82 million kgs in 1998-99 and 81 million kgs in 1996-97. On an average, India exported about 68 million kgs fetching Rs. 712 crore with average unit price of Rs 105 per Kg. India acquired an important position as the world's largest direct exporter of packet tea surpassing the UK. She is the leading exporter of packet tea and accounts for 60 per cent of world trade in packet tea. It is interesting to note that packet tea imports constituted nearly 20 per cent of total world imports and India constitutes for nearly half of it by way of direct export of this item during the year.

Direction—Region-wise Packet Tea Export

During the last 4 decades, major changes had already taken place in the tea market in the world. Countries like USA, UK, Canada etc. preferred for packet tea, tea bags, and instant tea in recent years. The countries in the region of West Asia and North Africa place their order mostly for these items. The exports of packet tea in the countries of West Europe (United Kingdom, Ireland, Netherlands, Germany, Austria, Finland etc.) are also gradually falling. On an average, about 4 million kgs are exported to West Europe, 21 million kgs to East Europe, 1.5 million kgs to America {North & Latin

America) and 4 million kgs to North Africa during the year 2004-05.

Export of Tea Bags in India

In order to cope with changing consumer preferences, India started production and export of tea bags from 1971 onwards with three firms. Progress made since then has been considerable and at present, there are many firms manufacturing tea bags. The progress relating to export of tea bags in India is set out below:

Table 1.9: Export of Tea Bags in India during 1973-74 to 2004-05

Year	*Quantity (thousand kg)*	*Value (thousand Rs.)*	*Unit value (Rs/kg)*
1973-74	144	3571	24.80
1974-75	108	2752	25.48
1975-76	157	5914	37.67
1976-77	285	10560	37.05
1977-78	390	18522	47.49
1978-79	238	10570	44.41
1979-80	493	20275	41.13
1980-81	754	32591	43.22
1981-82	777	33531	43.15
1982-83	618	23172	37.50
1983-84	514	24259	47.20
1984-85	631	36551	57.93
1985-86	590	37839	64.13
1986-87	467	31845	68.19
1987-88	498	32424	65.11
1988-89	626	44409	70.94
1989-90	546	46875	85.85
1990-91	496	43715	89.20
1991-92	483	71408	147.84
1992-93	520	72536	139.49
1993-94	1007	101456	100.75
1994-95	1008	144180	143.04
1995-96	861	125811	146.15
1996-97	1716	252479	147.16
1997-98	2169	449957	207.45

1998-99	2415	498180	206.29
1999-00	2305	557207	241.74
2000-01	1917	385232	200.96
2001-02	2542	597103	234.89
2002-03	3180	668558	210.37
2003-04	4190	943146	192.46
2004-05	4970	1363649	195.53

Exports of tea bag in 1973-74 were 144 thousand kgs that went up to 4970 thousand kgs in 2004-05 showing an increase of 34.52 times. There was an appreciable increase of this item from 1994-95 on wards. Except 1995-96, exports of packet tea boosted up from 1716 thousand kgs in 1996-97 to 2169 thousand kgs in 1997-98. It further improved from 2415 thousand kgs in 1998-99 to 2542 thousand kgs in 2001-02. The export started improving appreciably from 2002-03 to 2004-05. Average export of packet tea during last five years was to the level of 3360 thousand kgs fetching Rs 206 per kg.

Tea bags are exported to mainly countries like United Kingdom, Irish Republic, Germany, France, Belgium, and Luxemberg of West Europe. A substantial quantity is also exported to east Europe i.e CIS countries (Russian Federation, Ukraine, Latvia, Kazakhasthan, etc.) and Poland. Meagre quantities are exported to USA, Canada and Brazil of America as well as Iran, UAE, Kwait, Bahrain, Muscat, Yemen of West Asia and North Africa. Further, less quantity in the level of 20 thousand kgs is exported to Asia other than West (Japan), Africa other than North (Angola, South Africa) and Australia and Oceania (Australia). It is interesting to note that over the last three years quantities exported in East Europe has increased from 1816 thousand kgs in 1999-00 to 2115 kgs in 2004-05, while it was 16 thousand kgs to 84 thousand kgs during the period in America. There was fall in exports from 207 thousand kgs to 106 thousand kgs in West Asia and North Africa.

Exports of Instant Teas

Indian instant tea is exported to 23 countries. Among those countries, USA accounts for about 71 per cent of the total followed by Switzerland 9 per cent, Canada 6 per cent, Italy

5 per cent, etc. It is interesting to note that instant tea is gaining popularity in United Kingdom, France, Austria, Netherlands, UAE, Japan etc.

As regards instant tea, India is still on the threshold of product development. With the gradual acceptance of instant tea by the consumer, its demand is bound to rise gradually in the near future. Instant tea is processed in two forms, the cold-water soluble (CWS) and hot water soluble (HWS). These are manufactured both from the green leaf and from the black tea or from a combination of both types. HWS has limited market in the UK, Australia, etc. While CWS has markets in USA, Tata Finlay, is specializing in CWS and food specialties in HWS. Both the products are manufactured in South India. The data relating to export of instant tea from India is given in the Table 1.10 below:

Table 1.10: Export of Instant Tea from India during 1974-75 to 2004-05

Year	*Quantity (thousand kg)*	*Value (thousand Rs.)*	*Unit value (Rs/kg)*
1973-74	295	9217	31.24
1974-75	255	8563	33.58
1975-76	478	19162	40.09
1976-77	584	25066	42.92
1977-78	598	31533	52.73
1978-79	686	35500	51.75
1979-80	656	30509	46.51
1980-81	761	36608	48.11
1981-82	832	41712	50.13
1982-83	799	43185	54.05
1983-84	1049	66874	63.75
1984-85	1138	95538	83.95
1985-86	938	80428	85.74
1986-87	1134	94896	83.68
1987-88	861	66611	77.36
1988-89	733	66909	89.92
1989-90	1147	100986	88.05
1990-91	925	90068	97.37
1991-92	1283	158039	123.18
1992-93	1740	270592	155.51

1993-94	1121	221463	197.56
1994-95	1320	228667	173.23
1995-96	1230	260940	212.15
1996-97	1868	446403	238.97
1997-98	2483	578336	232.92
1998-99	2428	629703	259.35
1999-00	2602	653770	251.26
2000-01	2783	831013	298.60
2001-02	2594	741979	286.04
2002-03	3054	881347	288.66
2003-04	3463	995689	287.70
2004-05	3724	111892	300.49

Source : Various issues of Tea Statistics, Tea Board, Kolkata.

It will be seen from the above table that the export of instant tea increased from 295000 kgs in 1973-74 to 3724000 kgs in 2004-05 showing an improvement of 13 times. Similarly, in value terms it was Rs. 92.17 lakh in 1973-74 and Rs 1118.92 lakh in 2004-05.

Tea Powder

Although commercial production of instant tea began in the 1940s, little information is available as to what sort of process is suitable, as these techniques been kept a secret by patent rights over the manufactured products. Generally, tea powder, the basic material is derived from the fermented leaf. The usual steps adopted in the preparation of powder are extraction of tea solids followed by concentration of extracts and finally drying of these concentrates, to convert them into powder. Recovering the solids in water generally carries out extraction. Concentration of extracts is effected by evaporation of the water at low temperature and under reduced pressure. The final step of drying the concentrated leaf is achieved by subjecting the concentrate to low temperature, spray, fridge or foam drying. The solid thus obtained is brown in colour and amorphous in nature but on breeding, it turns into brown powder.

One such study was conducted in the tea research laboratory in Himachal Pradesh Krishi Vishwa Vidhyalaya, Palampur. The yield of powder from the fermented tea was generally better than that of made tea. At present a number of laboratories are set up which invented the technologies for preparation of tea powder.

Price Differentials of Value Added Tea

The of value added which could be seen from the price differentials in respect of packet teas and tea bags as compared to bulk teas is shown below:

Table 1.11: Price differentials of Tea in India during 1966-67 to 2004-05

(fob Rs./kg)

Year	*Packet tea*	*Tea bag*	*Bulk tea*	*Percentage of value addition in packet tea/ tea bag over bulk tea*	
1966-67	9.88	—	8.21	20.34	—
1971-72	9.48	20.39	7.51	26:24	172
1973-74	10.58	24.[illegible]0	7.61	27.90	225
1974-75	13.76	25.48	9.93	38.56	157
1975-76	15.99	37.67	11.27	41.88	234
1976-77	15.36	37.05	12.19	26.01	204
1977-78	20.64	47.49	25.45	18.90	86
1978-79	20.40	44.41	20.25	0.70	35
1979-80	19.34	41.13	18.08	6.70	77
1980-81	21.65	43.22	18.75	15.28	130
1981-82	22.85	43.15	18.15	25.90	138
1982-83	26.06	37.50	19.03	36.94	97
1983-84	30.01	47.20	27.56	8.88	71
1984-85	42.61	57.93	35.48	20.10	63
1985-86	38.69	64.13	30.25	27.70	112
1986-87	35.36	68.19	29.53	19.70	131
1987-88	37.18	65.11	31.10	19.50	109
1988-89	34.45	70.94	31.13	10.60	128
1989-90	46.80	85.85	42.97	8.90	100
1990-91	54.64	89.21	53.58	3.50	69
1991-92	57.72	147.84	55.61	3.80	62
1992-93	61.92	139.49	57.65	7.41	142
1993-94	72.18	100.75	67.78	6.50	33
1994-95	68.75	143.05	63.88	7.62	121
1995-96	73.39	146.15	73.30	0.12	99
1996-97	70.53	147.13	75.18	-6.18	97
1997-98	97.89	207.45	93.18	5.05	123
1998-99	108.57	206.29	104.64	3.76	97

1999-00	106.16	241.74	98.30	7.90	145
2000-01	103.81	200.96	80.96	28.23	148
2001-02	121.99	234.89	73.21	66.63	221
2002-03	121.54	210.37	76.20	59.50	176
2003-04	119.31	192.46	73.72	61.84	161
2004-05	114.23	195.53	76.69	48.90	155

Source : Various issues of Tea Statistics, Tea Board, Kolkata.

The data presented in the above table showed that packet tea and tea bags added more value approximately 26 per cent and 173 per cent respectively than the bulk tea during 1971-72. Value addition in respect of packet tea and tea bags stood at 66 per cent and 221 per cent respectively in 2001-02. Value addition for packet tea ranged from 3 per cent to 62 per cent during the period from 1966-67 to 2001-02, while it ranged from 30 per cent to 221 per cent during the same period in respect of tea bags. Value addition was reduced to minimum during 1990-91 and 1992-93 in respect of packet tea and tea bags as compared to bulk tea because of increase in the price per kg of bulk tea.

Packet tea can offer a dependable and standardized product to a consumer while tea bags standardization simplifies the process of brewing. In the second stage, by marketing tea under a brand name, although being a costly process in terms of high costs of distribution and consumer promotion, the exporter gets an easy access to preferences and some command over the market, together with increase in profitability comparatively higher than the returns available from the export of loose tea.

Incentives to Value Added Teas of Indian Tea

In order to encourage value added teas, the Central Government has been providing various incentives as under:

A. Package Tea

	Rate of Duty Rs/Kg
(a) Tea packed in unit containers of content not exceeding 25 grams and ordinarily intended to sell to consumers in those pack.	Rs. 0.44 + duty for the time being leviable for loose tea which has not already been paid (w.e.f. 11.3.86)
(b) Tea packed in unit containers of content exceeding 25 grams	Rs. 1.10 + duty for the time being leviable for loose tea which has

but not exceeding 20 kgs whether or not ordinarily intended for sale to consumers in that pack.	not already been paid (w.e.f. 11.3.86)
(c) The packed in bags for retail consumption known as "Tea Bags".	There is no excise duty on Tea Bags, but duty leviable for loose tea should be paid if such loose tea is used for manufacture of tea bags (w.e.f. 15.5.86) 11per cent + duty for the time being leviable for loose tea (w.e.f. 11.3.86)

B. Instant Tea

Rebate Allowed on Export (w.e.f. 9.9.86)

a. Loose Tea:

A rebate on excise duty @ 50 paisa per kg on loose un-blended per blended tea exported out of India is granted w.e.f 9.9.1986

With effect from 4.12.1986 the rebate is granted on export @ 50 paise per kg on loose un- blendedper blended tea exported out of India provided the duty of excise so paid is not less than 50 paisa per kg.

Full rebate of excise duty has been granted on loose tea exported out of India w.e.f. 27.4.1988.

b. Package Tea :

(i) A rebate on Excise Duty @ 50 paisa per kg on loose un-blended tea which is used in the manufacture of blended tea and packet tea exported out of India is granted w.e.f. 9.9.1986.

(ii) A rebate of additional excise duty on export of packet tea at the following rates are also granted w.e.f. 9.9.1986

(a) Tea packed in any kind of container not more than 25 grams net of tea — Rs. 0.44 per kg

(b) Tea packed in any kind of container more than 25 grams but not more than 1kg net of tea — Rs. 1.10 per kg.

c. Instant Tea

The whole of the duty of excise leviable on instant tea provided that the duty of excise has already been paid on loose tea used in the manufacture of such instant tea w.e.f. 1.3.1986.

W.e.f. 27.4.1988 the whole of the duty of excise leviable on instant tea.

C. Loose Tea

Rebate of Excise Duty granted on exports of Bulk tea w.e.f. 23.7.1983 has been withdrawn w.e.f. 1.2.1985.

D. Cash Compensatory support : W.e.f. 1.4.1989 the C.C. S. Has been granted at the following rates on f.o.b. Value of exports (valid upto 31.3.1992.).

Description of the product	Rates of C.C.S.
(a) Tea Bags	8 per cent (Eight)

(b) Packet Tea caddies and Tea chestlets	18 per cent (Eighteen)
(c) Instant	8 per cent (Eight)
(d) Quick Brewing Black Tea	12 per cent (Twelve)

Long Term Marketing Strategy for Value Added Items of Indian Tea

For expansion of exports of value added items of Tea, India is facing various problems. These are: *(i)* Dearth of indigenous know how in international market, *(ii)* inadequate production capacity of tea bags, *(iii)* lack of investment for establishment of firm's brand name and entry into the super markets in foreign countries, and *(iv)* imposition of various tariff as well as non-tariff barriers created by developed countries against the entry of Indian tea in consumer packs. The following long-term strategies have been evolved:

- For evolving a long term strategy for marketing of value added items, the "Committee on Tea Marketing "set up by the GoI recommended in its report a three phased approach which is quoted below:
- In the first phase packet tea export should be confined to our neighbouring countries through local collaboration particularly in those cases where there are no packeting facilities and tea is imported in packages especially in premium range. This would mean less investment, no clash of interest among own customers and a price advantage on account of lower freight. On both sides of India up to Africa and South East Asia, there is great demand for imported packet teas where our exported tea could successfully compete with others.
- The second phase would be collaborating with existing packers in Europe and supplying the blends in bulk and part of their profits.
- The third phase could be independent marketing efforts in value added, medium priced tea in major markets of UK and Ireland. Over riding all these phases, there are atleast two considerations to ponder over.
- First, research into new tea products and tea entente.

Second, to support export of value added tea abroad in the form of packets, bags and instant tea, we should first encourage and organize markets at home. It was noted by the Committee that exact strategy would depend on three factors like creating favourable market conditions, increasing investment on export promotion and building of organizational marketing strengths.

- As regards tea bags, the Committee has recommended that the facilities for manufacturing units in India with tea bagging facilities should be carefully examined and maximum encouragements may be given. It has also been observed that to acquire market facilities and skills abroad, the cost will be high and will to be standardized. The public sector agencies like Tea Trading Corporation and State Trading Corporation will be able to work on the problem of external marketing of value added items of tea. As regards instant tea, the Committee recommended that the existing companies in the field as well as new entrants should be encouraged. The company should invest capital in promoting technical and marketing skills by encouraging only or part acquisition of R&D equipments and international promotion expenditure on time bounds that must be result oriented and monitored against expected returns.

Long Term Perspectives— Production and Productivity

Viewed from long-term perspectives, the Indian Tea Industry has several constraints that are directly affecting both production and productivity. The following are some of the important constraints.

1 Old age of tea bushes—Nearly 40 per cent of present tea plants in India exceeded the economic threshold age limit of 40 years. This has been affecting productivity.

2 Limited availability of land for extension in traditional areas of tea cultivation.

3 Slower pace of replantation, the rate of replantation is less than 0.4 per cent as against the desired level of 2 per cent

4 Fluctuations in tea prices.
5 Higher rate of taxation on income from tea.
6 The dual structure (agriculture and industry) of Tea Industry has resulted in the incidence of high taxes, some of which are not applicable to non-plantation agriculture.
7 Stiff competition from soft drinks is needed to position tea as a health drink.
8 Poor drainage and lack of irrigation when needed greatly reduces yield.
9 There is considerable gap between potential and current tea yields.
10 Low productivity and high cost of production on account of high input cost particularly wages and the social benefits that always with wages, reduce attractiveness of tea production.
11 Untrammeled growth of small growers and poor adherence to quality production norms.

Rise in Production Cost

Labour cost accounts for a major part of the total cost of production of tea, which has been rising sharply. The stagnation in productivity levels is compounded by high land labour ratios. The productivity and cost of production matters the most in determining the profitability of tea estate. Considering the high cost and inadequate resources, the owners of tea gardens prefer to continue with the existing tea bushes for reasons of economy.

Skewness in Production

India's Tea production is skewed towards black tea, especially the CTC variety that accounts for 98 per cent of production. Within black tea, CTC variety is dominant for reasons of strong flavour and higher cuppage and productivity. What counts in the Indian domestic market are strength, affordability, cuppage and availability? Orthodox tea constitutes a significant portion of the world tea trade and fetches higher price realisation than CTC variety. Sri Lanka dominates in supply of orthodox tea. Lower cost CTC tea producers like Kenya, etc. are competing against Indian tea for market share and has displaced Indian Tea in key export market cities like UK.

Domestic production of orthodox tea has dropped by 40 per cent during the nineties; however, orthodox tea has significance in the World trade. Indian Tea Industry lags behind Kenya, Malawi in terms of yield per hectare mainly due to old age of tea bushes. The aging bushes are pulling down gains from adoption of improved cultural practices and increase in areas under tea. Domestic production of green tea is marginal; China dominates the global market for green tea.

Issues Affecting India's Export Performance

There are various issues that some impacts on the performance of Indian exports. If these issues are addressed squarely, there are hopes of increasing India's exports. These are as follows:

1 Inadequate efforts made in respect of marketing and brand building of Indian tea in overseas market.

2 Exposing India's tea exports to concentration of risk arising out of over-dependence on Commonwealth of Independant States (CIS), UK and UAE.

3 For CIS and UK markets, growth rates have been slower as compared to other import destinations.

4 Indian teas are getting edged out of emerging higher growth markets by competing produce from Sri Lanka, Kenya and China.

5 A large market like Pakistan that accounts for 9 per cent of world imports remains closed to India. Black CTC tea from Kenya dominates consumption in Pakistan. Though Indian Tea would work out cheaper on landed cost basis in Pakistan, trade in tea remains marginal because of political sensitivities.

6 Stagnant export realisation.

7 Limited presence in emerging markets.

8 Market share depleting in matured markets.

9 Tea exports constitute less than 2 percent of India's export revenues and hence it has not been covered under the priority list.

10 Given policies and regulations are oriented towards

protection of domestic market; availability of tea in domestic market and price stability are the over riding concerns dictating policy formulation.

India's Competitive Position in the World Tea Trade

India's competitive position has weakened in the world tea trade due to various reasons that are discussed in various interaction meets, workshops, seminars etc of national and international natures. The following factors are held responsible for such weakness:-

1 India's tea exports are facing a double crunch with a production slow down and loss of share in major markets served and inability to make significant headway in exploring the potential of the emerging markets.

2 World export growth @ 5.3 per cent Compound Annual Growth Rate (CAGR) was higher than India's export growth @ 3.4 per cent—CAGR during the period 1995-99.

3 Export realisations in dollar terms been stagnant during the 1990's.

4 Region-wise trends indicate that other than the CIS countries, India's share has been declining (in North America, India continues to be a marginal player).

5 In UK, the second largest importer after the CIS group, Indian tea has lost significant market share to Kenyan produce.

6 In green tea China has registered a much higher growth rate @ 15.3 per cent CAGR than Indian tea exports @3.4 per cent CAGR during 1995-99.

7 Even in India's traditional strongholds, CIS, Sri Lanka has made significant inroads since 1993 following the disbanding of the centralized marketing system. The main reasons attributed to Sri Lanka's success are better and more organised marketing efforts.

Indian Tea Industry—Supply Side Constraints

The Indian tea industry is facing various supply side constraints. The rate of growth of land under tea cultivation dropped from the level of 15 per cent + during the 1970's and the 1980's to about 6-7 per cent during the 1990's. Growth in land under tea cultivation was much higher in Kenya and Indonesia during the 1990's. India already has the second highest area under tea cultivation after China and further scope for expansion is limited.

India's cost of production is higher than that of Kenya and Sri Lanka essentially due to the higher production overheads, besides labour costs. Thus, Indian CTC tea is less competitive than Kenyan produced tea on the issue of pricing alone. With the opening up of the Indian market post WTO; a possible scenario is that cheaper imports may cater to the domestic demand while finer quality tea could be diverted to export markets.

The inward-looking nature of the tea industry has resulted in a lack of innovation and genuine value creation efforts and the result is a rather diluted export focus due to lack of competitiveness in international markets. Consumer satisfaction more than production efficiency is the key to long-term survival and growth The Indian tea industry thus has to move towards *'productising' Indian tea into a 'consumer product'*. It needs to shift away from the commodities, nature of exports in order to move up the value-curve.

The industry needs to address the issue of value creation through a concerted effort that addresses the product form and the delivery system (with the accent on convenience and innovation in packaging). Focused brand building and marketing campaign that positions tea as a 'healthy alternative to other beverages' and reinforces the superior value of Indian tea, are critical. The industry also needs to establish strategic alliances in its major markets.

Remedial Measures

For effectively dealing with the constraints, the following remedial measures relating to introduction of five schemes been taken up for the Xth Plan period (2002-07).

Plantation Development Scheme— Under this Scheme, extension of loans will be continued for undertaking extension planting, replanting, replacement planting and procuring irrigation equipments. Similarly, subsidy support for replanting, replacement planting, rejuvenation pruning and consolidation will also be continued. Renovation of the existing field assets rather than expansion would be the thrust area during the X Plan. Further, subsidy for irrigation and subsidy for new planting at different scales is possible under the scheme.

Quality Upgradation and Product Diversification Scheme— Under this scheme, loan will be advanced for procuring tea processing machinery, tractors, light commercial vehicles, packaging machinery and setting up of cooperative factories. During the X Plan period, thrust would be on more value realisation. For this purpose, the factories are required to be equipped with adequate machinery for undertaking dual manufacture of orthodox or CTC type as the market demands. Further, proper infrastructure needs to be created for improving the volume of value added teas and specialties such as green teas, flavoured teas, ready to drink teas, etc. In order to ensure quality of tea, the process of manufacture needs to undergo changes to suit the emerging new markets. To facilitate this tea growers and manufacturers may participate in the quality improvement programmes such as capital HACCP and ISO certification.

Market Promotion Scheme—The scheme would continue to support activities such as market research survey, uninational campaign for Indian tea in selected markets, brand promotion support to Indian companies for launching the brands in international markets, genetic campaign for tea in new markets and setting up of an umbrella unit in India to meet the requirements of product and packaging standards in international markets. There is an all round realisation that the growth rate of the domestic markets need a step up for sustainability of the tea industry. Towards this end, there is a need to make special provisions for launching domestic schemes under the scheme.

The market for tea is changing. Tea is now facing increased competition from soft drinks. In view of this, tea needs to protect its carefully nurtured market. It also needs to make forays into soft drink markets with a view to creating competition rather than merely reacting to it. This can be done through further value addition and development of new products

The system of auction will to be strengthened and technologically improved by moving to appropriate electronic formats modifying the existing systems. Accordingly, it is proposed to extend financial support for creating suitable database, information collection, dissemination system and electronic auction system.

Research and Development Scheme—Research and development scheme may expand the extension services of the research institutes so that the gap between lab and land is narrowed down and all the growers are able to ensure interface with the research institutes through a network of advisory centres. Further, research institutes may be directed to focus attention on productivity improvement, cost reduction in field operations, quality manufacturing process, value addition, product diversification, etc. Greater awareness about environmental issues for emphasizing the ecofriendliness of tea has to be created. Organic tea is emerging as a special product and demand for it is likely to increase. Therefore, there is an urgent need for research intervention for developing appropriate package of practices. Health benefits of tea been rediscovered recently through scientific research. Awareness campaigns will make tea "*the new age drink*" that is beneficial for physical health.

Human Resource Development Scheme—The scheme will aim at achieving overall improvement of the skills of persons associated with tea plantations at all levels (workers to managers) through extensive and intensive training. For this, the services of: *(i)* Indian Institute of Plantation Management, *(ii)* Training Centre for Small Growers and Manufacturers, *(iii)* Comprehensive labour welfare schemes implemented by Indian Tea Association (ITA) and United Planters Association of Southern India (UPASI), and *(iv)* Imparting technical training by Tea Research Association and UPASI may be availed of.

Introduction of Mother Club—The innovative idea of a Mothers Club being tested in Dooars region provides a new model for improving workers' health at the estate level. This model needs to be extended to all other tea growing regions for which additional funds need to be earmarked under this scheme. A new approach is required to tap local talent and internal training in estate management. In addition, continuing development of the managerial skills of existing managers is also required. The existing status of small and marginal farmers and identifying their basic needs for development of these sub sectors and evolving strategies to make them more active participants in overall development may be given priority. Organizing training programmes on modern aspects of tea growing and manufacture, establishment of demonstration plots in the important areas of small growers concentration and supply of high yielding planting materials at subsidized rates.

Demonstration Plots and Trial Plantations—Demonstration plots and trial plantations in important areas with concentration of small growers in collaboration with UPASI and CSIR in Himachal Pradesh may be explored Further training of small tea growers by UPASI, Assam Agricultural University, North Bengal University, etc.may be conducted. In addition, study tours to small tea farmers in North Eastern States, West Bengal, etc. to learn improved cultural practices being adopted by them are to be organized. Visit to Cooperative Tea Factories in Nilgiris to study their devotions, etc.is another area that requires to be looked into. Quality upgradation scheme that aims at creating awareness among the small growers and manufacturers as to the importance of adopting finer plucking standards and improvement of manufacturing process of tea are to be launched.

Quality Awareness, Upgradation-cum-Demonstration, Seminars/Conferences, Publicity etc.

Tea Board implemented the programmes like: *(a)* Quality awareness campaign in different villages, *(b)* Quality upgradation experiment cum demonstration in different regions, *(c)* publicity including advertisements, film posters, notices, etc. *(d)* Quality awareness seminars/conferences/ farmers' meets for growers as well as bought leaf and industrial cooperative tea factories in different talukas during the current financial year.

While area for expansion of tea in the estate sector is getting exhausted, there is distinct scope for bringing additional area under tea in the small growers sector. The land policy of the Government is also conducive to this development. Growing of tea especially in the North Eastern region would help in generation of sufficient income to sustain rural households, creation of employment opportunities for unemployed youth and landless labourers, conservation of natural resources through control of shifting cultivation and degradation of forest areas, and providing a means of living by minimizing the social unrest in the rural areas

Multi-Dimensional Welfare Measures

The Tenth Plan has adopted multi-dimentional measures for the welfare of the small tea growers who are concentrated in some parts of Assam, Tamil Nadu, and Karnataka etc. and constitute a major share in total tea estates of the country. Some of the measures are:-

* Setting up of demonstration plots in each of the North East States for demonstrating all aspects of tea growing, in a more comprehensive manner,
* Formation of central nurseries for supply of right kind of planting material to the small growers,
* Arranging training programmes to all the participating farmers on all aspects of tea growing in collaboration with TRA, Assam Agricultural University and North Bengal University,
* Launching of advisory services in each State for periodic field visits and advising on practical aspects of cultivation and providing soil analytical survey,
* Arranging study tours for the growers to visit the developed areas especially in south India as well as foreign countries such as Kenya and Indonesia where considerable work has been done for the benefit of small tea growers. The Tea Board through its regional offices and in collaboration with respective State Governments will carry out all activities.

Recent Technologies in Tea Cultivation

In recent times, micro-propagation, hybrid seed production and seedlings, hi-density planting, integrated nutrient management, use of bio-fertilizers, micro irrigation, fertigation, protected cultivation, organic farming, integrated pest management and use of bio-pesticides, mobecular diagnostics, pesticides residues, etc. are some of the techniques in tea cultivation.

Propagation of tea includes release of high yielding clones, bi-clonal seed stock and grafted plants. These planting materials had shown extremely satisfactory results. However, existing materials and techniques need to be improved. Standardisation of package for cultivation of organic tea is yet to be made. High density planting is sufficient for obtaining higher yield from a unit area. Any further increase in the density would only lead to uneconomic production in the end.

With introduction of stringent Minimum Residual Limits (MRLs), integrated post harvest management, techniques required to be further researched. More research and development efforts are called for in the areas of micronutrient management.

Thurst Areas of Tenth Five-Year Plan

According to the "Approach to Tenth Five Year Plan", targets should no longer be production oriented, but shall aim at improving productivity, value addition and marketability. It further states that one must concentrate on increasing the productivity of existing gardens rather than establishing new plantations with huge investments. There should be continued efforts towards further increasing the profitability of tea gardens through replanting/rejuvenation and mechanization of operations.

The main thrust would be on quality to make our teas competitive in the light of opening up of the economy under the WTO agreement on agriculture. Thrust is to be given on improving marketing capabilities as well as substantially improving packaging and value addition. Conversion to organic methods of tea growing is required to be encouraged.

Information technology needs to be given due consideration for making available ready information to the tea industry and for promotion of our produce in other markets

There must be continued efforts towards further increasing

the profitability of tea gardens through replanting/rejuvenation and mechanization of operations.

Strategies for the Tenth Plan Period

The strategies of the Tenth Five Year Plan are to:

* Enhance production through vertical development measures such as replantation, rejuvenation, pruning, infilling of vacancies with better varieties, etc.
* Improve the productivity of small tea gardens,
* Emphasize special attention on irrigation and drainage,
* Manufacture additional crop; augment tea processing facilities by construction of new tea factories,
* Modernize the existing tea factories for ensuring production of clean teas without any trace of foreign material in products,
* Encourage product diversification and creation of facilities for dual manufacture of tea (orthodox and CTC),
* Encourage value addition and production of instant, ready-to-drink tea, decaffeinated tea and specialty teas,
* Ensure adherence to the prescribed international and domestic SPS (Sanitary and Phyto-sanitary) standards for tea,
* Make higher investment on R&D and transfer of technology,
* Reach technological advances to smaller estates where potential for improvement is the best,
* Reduce packaging costs and use alternative and inexpensive packaging materials,
* Explore the possibility of setting up of modern packaging and blending units within India with foreign collaboration,
* Support for promotion of value added teas in overseas market by exporters, importers to take advantage of IT tools for promotion vigorously,
* Encourage organic tea cultivation and production of green teas,

* Initiate special promotional programmes in thrust countries,
* Need to continue an intensive generic promotion campaign within the country so as to increase per capita consumption and to arrest declining trend in domestic demand. A strong and vibrant internal market will create the necessary synergies for expanding the export market,
* Reduce the cost of production by improving productivity and minimizing wasteful expenditure to increase profits from the existing plantation.

The competitive advantage of tea industry depends primarily on quality of work force. Therefore, HRD inputs are critical to future development of the tea industry.

On the Production Front—On the production front, the strategies required to be adopted are:

* Implementation of HACCP and ISO standard,
* Launching of quality assurance scheme by Tea Board,
* Undertaking a planned programme to encourage shift in production from CTC to orthodox,
* Designing and launching of a separate scheme,
* Focusing on increasing yield of area under tea in order to contribute a higher per centage to world production and also increase exportable surplus,
* Reducing cost of production by educating workers at garden levels through workshops while maintaining targets for replanting, rejuvenation planting, etc.
* Narrowing down in number of grades produced which lead to confusion in importers' mind and
* Exploring the possibility of providing zero interest per low interest loans for purchase of rolling machines for orthodox, especially in the context of the crisis in South India.

On the Product Front—On the product front, continuous emphasis on value added forms of tea (tea bags followed by packet tea and instant tea) in order to maximize returns and foreign exchange earnings may be made. For this, there is a need to undertake specific activities to promote these forms of tea. These include:-

* Exemption of import duty on tea bagging machinery and filter papers,
* Arranging of workshops to help promote packaging standards in association with Indian Institute of Plantation Management (IIPM),
* On the bulk tea exports, focus on orthodox and Darjeeling as thrust areas while maintaining traditional markets,
* Improving packaging standards to meet world norms,
* Encouraging export of green tea with focus on specific markets like Morocco. Marketing an Indian green tea that is unique and not necessarily a replica of Chinese green tea, and
* Developing specific value added products i.e. flavoured tea and teas with herbal infusion while maintaining the brand equity of Indian tea.

On the Marketing Front—On the marketing front one must identify markets based on global predictions on demand and ability to pay premium demand by different types of Indian teas, develop specific strategies for focused markets, and allocate funds in these markets coinciding with penetration strategies.

There is need to build up value perceptions of Indian tea with Darjeeling as flagship and launch promotional campaign in major markets and provide legislative protection for teas of Indian origin alongwith Indian geographical indications such as Darjeeling, Assam and Nilgiris. Further attempts may be made to launch an Indian tea logo as a mark of quality and speciality tea register together with extensive promotion of speciality teas by way of using using website as a marketing tool to hasten the buying process. Emphasis may be shiftted from product to quality based on appearance, cuppage, ecology, and sensitivity to bio chemicals, health benefits and lifestyle. There is a need to project India as a stable, reliable producer and supplier that will honour commitments.

On the Infrastructure Front—Infrastructure is the key factor in sustaining development for any sector and tea is not an exception to this. Keeping this in view there is a need to

* Develop infrastructure for value addition,
* Provide duty free facility to exporters,
* Support the purchase of foreign brands/distribution arrangements/warehouses in foreign markets by Indian companies. Further traditional markets for primarily bulk tea must be retained. A drive to locate large growing segment of consumer markets across the globe has to be further launched and strengthened. We must promote our own global brands and secure a long term markets for Indian tea in origin.

On Government Front—Government may further consider duty free imports of capital equipments machinery for packaging of tea bags, instant tea, ready to drink tea and canned tea machinery and duty free imports of filter papers for tea bags and remove infrastructure bottlenecks and improve infrastructure facilities (ports, customs, banking, insurance, etc.). Provision of incentives for value added teas. Launching promotional campaigns for Indian teas in thrust markets, conducting market service to assist Indian exporters in their marketing efforts and deputation of delegations to prospective countries to enhance contract for exports as well as to study strategies followed by competing producer countries are some of the other areas to be strengthened.

In order to increase India's export potential, the option of importing tea for re-export will to be kept open, as world blends will require teas from other growing areas. A separate focus on tea bags is essential. One of the highest value added emerging markets is instant tea and ready to drink beverages. With a view to making India to a globally competitive position in value added teas, there is need for setting up of the blending, packaging and processing facilities at internationally competitive levels. Globally, competitive canning lines, processing equipment and branded, private level option needs to be organized. This is a highly technical field and an early edge would open up sophisticated markets in future.

Quality Upgradation and Product Diversification

One of the main reasons attributed to the price slump in South India during 2000, was the poor quality image. It is, therefore, proposed to pay more attention towards quality improvement of the basic product and on value addition. All the process related activities and quality upgradation and product diversification programmes would be covered under a new scheme viz. Quality Upgradation and Product Diversification Scheme.

Research and Development

Research areas covered during the Plan period are:-

(i) Integrated nutrient management,
(ii) Forecasting model for pest incidence,
(iii) Energy conservation,
(iv) Product diversification and value addition,
(iv) Tea and human health,
(v) Transfer of technology,
(vi) Establishment of chain of quality laboratories in the important tea growing regions,
(vi) Irrigation and drainage,
(vii) Biochemical analysis and quality improvement,
(viii) Soil management and organic cultivation of tea,
(ix) Packaging, eco-preservation and other related areas,
(x) Biotechnological aspects and
(xi) Pesticide residues, metals, myco-toxic and connected research work.

Development areas included:-

(a) Setting up of a training centre and advisory centres for the benefit of small tea growers in NE region,
(b) Opening of new Development offices of Tea Board for closer interface with the small growers in the non-traditional areas,
(c) Strengthening the existing field offices of the Board,
(d) Establishment of nurseries for supply of planting materials to the small growers,
(e) Setting up of demonstration plots,
(f) Organizing study tours, workshops, seminars etc. and
(f) Institution of productivity and quality awards.

Market Development

As a result of changes in the market scenario, the marketing orientation demands a new approach. Towards that end, it is necessary to make a specific provision for launching generic promotion campaign in the domestic market in joint collaboration with the tea industry. Besides, the regular promotion measures such as market research survey, uni-national campaign, brand promotion support, participation in fairs and tea festivals, exchange trade delegations etc. would be continued. The estimated funds requirement for the above activities is in the region of Rs. 300 crores to be equally shared by the Tea Board and the industry on 50:50 basis.

Financial assistance to be extended under this Scheme would be in the form of subsidies for various market developments and export promotional activities.

Conclusion

Tea is probably one of the most widely consumed beverages in the world and is accepted and acclaimed everywhere. The worldwide acceptance of tea is because of its zero alcohol content, stimulating effect and aroma etc. Many types like black, green, orange, flavoured, golden, pekoe, etc. grades of tea are available in the market. These types are mainly classified according to their manufacturing process, compiled with spices and other flavour rendering substances. Brewing of instant tea is a common and old practice. Black and green teas are only products obtained on a large scale from the tea bush and at present none of the other products mentioned above are being exploited on a commercial scale. Efforts will be made for developing and standardising suitable and effective technologies for tea industry to keep pace with other tea producing countries like China, Sri Lanka and Kenya who has already made their mark in the world export market for tea.

It is unlikely that with further liberalization of imports, the domestic market will be flooded with low- grade imported tea. For the Gresham's Law does not hold good in an open market. The law reacts in the opposite manner-good product drives away bad product. As far as India's domestic tea market is concerned, consumers here drink the best of CTCs. Not only that, they are prepared to pay a premium for quality. Because of the strong domestic demand Indian tea prices are generally higher than the world prices. And it is to be noted further that in volume terms India is the largest consumer. Evidently, in the perspective of the country's consumer behaviour it is doubtful that to what extent importers will be able to sell the low grade imported stuff to increase their profits and be able to exert dominant voice in the domestic market.

It was unwise to view that once India started buying of low priced tea, the price of its produce in the international market would fall. Some Asian sellers would be benefited out of this transaction. From the viewpoint of open market economy, however, it was felt that the aforesaid promise was not correct. In an open market mechanism only the appropriate substitute and its price played a dominant role in determining the demand of the principal product the vice-versa. Since Indian importers intended to import only cheap variety of teas, the price of Indian tea was likely too remain unaffected until now suppliers entered the market. And in this matter the only threat was likely to come from China- the Asian Dragon- having a large variety and quantity of tea at its disposal.

In the light of the above study it was viewed that there was no point of becoming shaky even though the Ministry of Commerce allowed free import of teas for re-exports in bulk as well. The only necessity is to remain alert against the unscrupulous traders who may take the advantage of import liberalization policy of the Government of India just to further their own interest.

2

Major Breakthrough of Indian Tea in UK

The Importance of Britain in the Tea World

The importance of Britain in the Tea World is acknowledged. When the Convention was announced, two questions came to mind. *Firstly,* "why was such a convention not held earlier?" *Secondly,* "why is the Convention necessary now?" The official answer to these questions is, "Change is the keyword. The time is auspicious. With change there comes opportunity. World trading patterns are changing. We are all becoming more aware of the need for healthier lifestyles. We are all more conscious of our environment and ecology. For Britain and Europe it was just around the corner and our neighbors across the Channel have acquired an unquenchable thirst for our favourite beverage. Tea is ideally poised to take advantage of opportunities worldwide and the tea trade is determined to ensure that these opportunities are grasped with both hands. It will not be daunted by the ever increasing competetion from all other drinks—for we drink a finite volume of fluids and the market place cannot accommodate every drink's grandiose expansion plans". Men and women from the world of tea invaded Eastbound. Delegates from Africa, Argentina, Canada, United States of America, Europe, India, Sri Lanka, and all points north, South, east and west signed in for the 'first ever UK Tea Convention. Participants included tea producers, brokers, traders, blenders, retailers, government officials, Tea Board personnel and industries connected with tea such as bankers, shipping companies and material suppliers. Some of the interesting findings of the Convention are listed below:

The First UK Tea Convention

The first ever UK Tea Convention was held in Eastbourne, East Sussex, and UK from Monday 21 May to Thursday 24 May 1990. The four day Convention, attended by over 400 delegates from 27 Countries, covered all aspects of tea—growing, production, new propagation, funding tea development projects, financing, generic advertising, communications, tea and health, the world tea market, catering, trends in the beverage market, the UK tea trade and its importance and role in relation to the world tea market. 'Never mix business with pleasure', is an old adage. However, the UK Tea Convention, ignoring this advice, chalked out an action packed programme in both the business and social fields. On the entertainment front, there were sports events and social evening every day. There were conducted tours to historic places and the wives attending had an integrated programme of sightseeing and shopping. Now about business, the British have been drinking and trading in tea for more than 300 years. They drink 70 million cups of tea each day. With the exception of water, tea accounts for approximately 44 per cent of all drinks. The UK imports around 18 per cent of tea producing countries annual tea exports. The London tea auctions conducted every Monday are the only International tea auctions in the world

Interesting Findings of the Convention

Supply Vs Demand: The demand for tea is rapidly increasing. Demand has been outstripping production. In 2007, supply and demand has become mismatched. However, over the years the market changed dramatically. While the UK remained the single biggest tea importing country, the share of London auctions fell to 3 per cent of World Supply from 24 per cent in 1952. Demand grew rapidly in India, the Soviet Union, the Middle East and other developing Countries; more than offsetting a decline in the UK market. India, the world's biggest producer, has been struggling to balance the demands from its domestic market and the export trade. Given the expected population growth, the potential demand is enormous. Assuming 3 per cent annual growth in World demand, the market would need and extra 750 million kgs by 2007.

However, if the recent 5 per cent growth rate continues, an extra 25 million kgs would be required. Looking at the future, 'lack of demand' does not appear to be a problem for tea. Production and productivity must receive due attention. New planting of tea assumes importance, as it may be difficult to match the improvements of the past from the existing areas. The Tea Industry should remain a profitable one in the years to come because of the supply and demand equation.

Tea and the British: The British drink a finite amount and every drink is conceivable. Tea is their favourite beverage and accounts for 44 per cent of every thing they drink. Sixty million Britons, on an average, drink four cups of tea a day each and are in the top league for tea drinking. Britain is perhaps the only country where they have a 'tea break'. The total consumption of tea in the UK is 200 million kgs per year. Kenyan teas are available in the UK àll through the year as, unlike North, East India, Kenya produces teas the year round. Gradually, the UK market has moved towards Kenyan teas. Indian teas are bought but Kenyans have overtaken them. The tea bag was introduced in the UK market about three decades ago and it accounted for more than 80 per cent of total tea consumed in the UK. One of the reasons for sustained tea consumption in the UK is the tea bag, which is a "very convenient way of brewing tea". However, for this 'Convenience', tea consumption in the UK could have been adversely affected. The fluid intake share (with the exception of water) and tea's share of the 'retail sale value' of the total drinks market are as follows:

	Fluid intake (per cent)	*Retail value of total soft drinks (per cent)*
Tea	44.6	2.5
Alcohol	17.8	77.0
Soft Drinks	16.3	17.4
Coffee	21.3	3.1
	100.0	100.0

Source: Compiled from *Assam Review* and *Tea News,* various issues.

It is observed the tea's share of the "retail sale value" of the total drinks market is reversed. Tea, thus, becomes the cheapest drink, even in the UK..

Multiple Captures: The average retail value of tea is $ 780 million pounds. Multiples capture 70 per cent of the total tea market, Coops 19 per cent and others 11 per cent. It is divided between four major branded producers and own labels. Brooke Bond has 29 per cent volume share, Premier 15 per cent, Lyons Tetley 19.5 per cent and Coops 12 per cent. Own label commands 19 per cent and others 5.5 per cent. Tradition and low price has meant that the tea drinking is most popular with Britons aged over 55; the beverage is less appealing to the younger generation.

Healthfulness of Tea: People, today, worry about what they eat and drink; they are increasingly becoming concerned with the environment. Every one wants a healthier lifestyle. Tea is a healthy, entirely natural, and free from artificial processing; colouring and calories. Tea growing does not harm the environment in any way. In fact, tea provides a secondary cover and helps to restore ecological balances. Soft drinks are marketed aggressively and are doing an excellent job in market place. Tea, however, is a much healthier drink, compared to all. A cup of tea, even today, costs a fraction over a penny to brew in a British home but it warms, cools, calms, cheers, brews all at once. It is a love all to everyone. There is a strong possibility; therefore, the tea is poised to be the drink of the new Millennium.

Retailers Returns: Tea is no longer used as a loss leader. The overheads having increased substantially, the retailers have to watch their margins very carefully. The retailer's return on tea does not match other drinks. Margins vary in accordance with the outlet. On an average, tea gives a retailer a margin of 10 per cent; specialty teas double the margin. Return of profit on an average of 10 years to retailers on tea was $ 55 million pounds compared to $ 120 million pounds for coffee and $ 800 million pounds for soft drinks. There is therefore, need for the industry to work towards a better return for the retailers on tea. This improves the image, product development, and by creating market place conditions for a more dynamic market.

Tea's Image and Promotion

The real potential of tea in the market place remains largely untapped. The magnitude of the present promotion programme is inadequate. Tea's image must be uplifted so that it is not seen only as a poor man's or old peoples drink. Special attention should be paid to the younger generation. Funds allocated for tea promotion are inadequate and certainly, other beverages spend a fraction of what. For example, tea with its dominant 44 per cent share of the total drinks market in the UK, takes up only 8 per cent share of the drinks advertising budget, soft drinks' share is 15 per cent and coffee is at 17.9 per cent. In the UK, the overall decline in tea consumption has been halted but to maintain its present share of the market and to increase it further, the money spent on advertising will have to be increased. A generic campaign, which can concentrate its message on the *'natural elements of tea as well as the value for money and distinctiveness of tea'*, will reappraise tea, which has so far been taken for granted.

Specialty Tea: In the UK the growth markets is *specialty teas,* which include Assam, Darjeeling, Ceylon and herbal teas. Premium teas, middle to good quality, account for 71 per cent of value share of the market followed by popular teas with 10 per cent. Specialty and herbals teas account for 4 per cent and at 2 per cent respectively.

Instant Tea: It represents only a small part of the overall tea market; 15 per cent in volume terms as opposed to 0.7 per cent in 1976. A strong point in favour of instant teas is that today there is knowledge available on 'instant' products. When coffee entered, the 'instant' field there was no previous knowledge. Instant teas make satisfactory progress.

Decaffeinated Tea: This is also showing exceptional growth, capitalizing on the trend experienced in coffee. Decaff coffee accounted for 24 per cent of instant coffee and 20 per cent of ground coffee sales in 2007. A consumer analysis clearly shows that they are prepared to pay more for tea. Infact, they expect to pay more, especially when one considers the cost of a cup of tea against any other drink. However, the consumers expect regular supplies of the quality they need. Presentation of tea must also be in a more appealing manner. The UK Tea Council feels that when the industry is next making a price increase; a small portion of this increase should be assigned for generic promotion of tea. An advertising campaign of a strong brand cannot do full justice to the cause of tea in general through its ads. While individual brands should continue with their promotional efforts, generic promotion should fill in the gaps in rebuilding the image of tea.

Other Uses of Tea: If one is a glamorous brown haired person, one can wash one's hair with tea – it gives it a lovely sheen! The tannin in tea is good for removing sunburn. There are useful applications of spent tea bags, in the garden. Like planting these are put in holes in lawn/ garden and are covered with seed first of all! The message of the UK Tea Convention was that while all seems to be going well for tea, "Pull your socks up".

Teas in the catering industry: Some 74 per cent of all teas now used in the catering industry are three star quality teas. According to their requirements, caterers can make their purchasing decisions confident that the quality of the blends is assured via the star rating system. Therefore, there is a solid quality base on which is built tea's image generically to the consumer via the catering trade. Assuming the quality teas are now being supplied to the caterer, job of Tea Council is to ensure that they are turned into high quality cuppas for the consumer. The Tea Council has again developed a promotional mechanic, which has proved very successful. It encourages the caterer to pay attention to good brewing practices while also alerting consumers to the fact that a catering cuppa is as good as the cuppa they can make at home. To do this the Council checks the quality of the cup served to the consumer in key catering areas where the council thinks the image of the tea may be particularly poor and where it can attract media attention. The target outlets are alerted, the mystery tea tasters move in and the winner is identified. The catering staffs in the outlets enjoy the hyper, the caterer loves the publicity and the consumer is alerted to the availability for good tea in these outlets. Areas covered include airports, airlines in and out of the UK, motorway service stations, railway station, tea places throughout the country—even London cabbies are becoming involved, telling their fares where they can get a good cuppa. The UK Tea Council left no stone unturned, even contacting new restaurant openings in the South East who did not serve tea. Even the council challenged them to tell why. Subsequently, they receive a special pack outlining tea's potential in their restaurant. Part of this pack offered them a "tea blending" kit which consisted of an attractive wooden tea caddy to give customers the opportunity to blend their own teas at the table. Tea is equivalent to the cigar box after a meal.

Education: Just as catering has a vital role in any market, so does the next generation of consumers—the school children. Here the council offered a comprehensive information service to schools, teachers and parents but with interesting and unusual elements. The council sponsored a publication that forms part of the biology syllabus in the UK's National GCSE examination. Its title "Finding out about Healthy Drinking" is self-explanatory; obviously, tea is featured wherever possible in the publication and constantly cited as the biggest drink in our life, always in the context of healthy drinking. Additional projects outlined within the publication allowed schools access into the database of the Healthy Drink Project, to compare the result of surveys and project work on the subject of healthy drinking.

Reappraisal of Teas: These programmes were just a small part of how the Council sought to provoke a re-appraised of tea. The re-appraisal should alert the public to the fact that the tea is a healthy drink free from additive and preservatives, an excellent way to take needed fluids, a product worth every penny we pay for it, and more; a story the can be told generically. With all these available possibilities, one must make effort to provide generic support for the product. Hardly any product is placed than tea to benefit from heavy generic support to the detriment of no one and to the advancement of all. The problem is funding. However, what is one really doing about it? This question has been asked again. Tea needs a contemporary image. A major element in achieving this should be generic advertising. The efficacy of generic advertising is proven. The question is not should we fund generic advertising, it is simply how!

Tea: A Health Drink

Tea accounts for 44 percent of all the British drinks in the UK. Fluid intake is in fact more important than solid food intake; yet most media concentration is on solid foods. Even

Government specialist reports only cover fluids in details in denouncing alcohol. In 1990s, the Tea Council moved to fill this vacuum by devising the Healthy Drinks Project. The concept is simple, flexible and infinitely exploitable. It consisted of a questionnaire, which consumers obtain as result of PR coverage of the project. This questionnaire covered all aspects of daily drinking habits; considered how habits were changed or might change in the future, and was compiled in association with a leading University in the UK. When the completed questionnaire was returned to The Tea Council, the data was fed into the computers where specially developed software allowed a personalized recommendation on fluid intake prepared for the respondent. The data was stored and used in various public relations activities throughout the year and finally summarized in the Annual Report on healthy drinking. It was important to note that the reports and Annual Report did not emphasize tea and perhaps forfeited credibility. Tea was featured by right and by default because it accounts for 44 per cent of all the drink. With the Healthy Drinks Project, the UK commandeered the ground of healthy drinking for tea, and Tea was seen as the representative on healthy drinking for the nation. The programme had considerable flexibility and the questionnaire was modified each year to build in topical aspects to add to media appeal and ensure the maximum coverage and exposure.

Catering Tea Grading Scheme

There have been many meetings of "image" and tea's inherent weakness in this area. In the UK's image, tea is cozy and familiar, it is reassuring and down market. In many instances it is so much a part of today's lifestyle that it goes virtually unnoticed. This aspect is nowhere bettered illustrated than in certain parts of the catering industry. Research indicates that only 7 per cent of restaurants offer the diner a choice of coffee or tea after dinner. The importance of the catering industry is that it must play a very important role in the consumers' re-appraisal of tea and indeed any product. The Tea Council undertook a bottom up, top down job on the catering trade. The foundation was their Catering Tea Grading Scheme. The panel of experts graded catering teas as plain, medium or quality against a sophisticated set of blend standards. Successful grading of blends allowed it to carry the badge of quality and the scheme was policed meticulously so that the quality of blend was always maintained.

Tea in Catering Establishments

The UK Tea Council reports tremendous strides in the quality of tea in catering establishments. It was found through the Council's Catering Tea Grading Scheme that the quality of hardly 16 per cent before the sudden Gulf Crisis struck the world; the Sri Lankan Tea Industry was filled with hope for the future. The market behaved most buoyantly. Other important factors for pushing up optimism were most aptly summed up by Forbes & Walker thus, "the weather had been exceptionally favourable so far—this year and normal patterns of rainfall had prevailed so as to facilitate the proper agricultural practices to be carried out. There had been neither prolonged droughts nor excess rainfall. Preplanned fertilizer programmes have been adhered to and pruned fields have recovered fast." What was significant was that a new trend emerged not only on the production front but also in the marketing of various categories of tea. Now the question asked is what the immediate future holds out. The overall position, according to Forbes & Walker is that a crop of 127.0 million kgs have already been harvested for the first six months, it is very likely that at the final reckoning, a crop of about 290 miilion kgs could result. Another very significant factor in Sri Lankan Tea Crop was enhancement of both production and exports. Of this increase, the biggest segment was concerned to packeted tea compared to bulk tea exports. A tea bag export was virtually double. The FOB unit value of all teas exported up to April 2005 registered a much-increased percentage.

Cent percent of the tea used in catering establishments is below that of tea consumed in homes throughout England. Naturally, the Council is yet to find out the reason as to why the amount of tea drank out of home should not be much higher than the 7.2 billion cups a year. Information indicates that although 21 per cent of all drinks are consumed out of home, only 9 per cent of this is tea. Forty (40) per cent of all restaurants do not have tea on their menu and the only 30 per cent of establishments offering specialty teas list them on the menu. The hotels and restaurants in England the do not serve tea say they don't because there is no demand.

The UK Beverage Market

Pergamon AGB Marketing is the largest European Market Research Agency covering most types of market research. It specializes in consumer panels, obtaining data on market sizes, brand shares and consumer dynamics through household purchases. Throughout its partnership in Europe, AGB is able to provide similar data from all West European countries. AGB is therefore able to give an outsider's view of the market and a quantification of the challenges and opportunities facing the tea industry. The British tea market is large with the domestic market alone. Almost three quarters of households took half a kilo of tea in a 4 week period. Eighty per cent of this market is expensive. Higher margin in tea bags represented a dramatic turn around in the last 25 years. These statistics establish tea as one of the very largest grocery markets. The bad news is that the market volume has been in a slow, steady decline over the last twenty-five years. In two decades tea price inflation has varied from 12 per cent to 43 per cent, the variance in volume has ranged only from 21 per cent to 4 per cent indicating price inelasticity. The growth in tea bags has contributed to loss of volume. More significant however, is the overall movement away from hot drinks towards cold in the western world.

Some Useful Lessons for Tea

Coffee, once believed to be the big threat, has only managed to average 10 per cent growth and actually declined by 4 per cent during the last five years. However, with this static picture there are some useful lessons for tea. While ground coffee has failed to make much impact, decaffeinated and premium priced instant coffees have been successful. The relative failure of ground and the success of decaffeinated and premium lines have one common link – branding. Branding for ground coffee is fragmented, weak while for instant coffee, the brands and sub brands are clearly positioned, and support is heavy. Few years back from now, there was a boom year for cold drink competetion . Nevertheless, even before that, cold drinks were booming. Fruit juice and mineral water have benefited from the health boom with the latter gaining from a fashionable image and increased concern about the quality of tap water.

Branding Innovation and Support

In most consumer markets, branding, innovation and support are important elements, and the importance of advertising is imperative to the health of the grocery markets. At first glance, the signs for tea are not encouraging. Total recorded advertising support in the last few years has been stable in money but declining sharply in real terms. One useful indicator of health is the private label. Originally, retailer brands had around 30 per cent of packaged groceries but in tea, the figure is considerably higher. In tea bags, the private label share is 36 per cent by volume and 31 per cent by value, which is in excess of the 20 per cent by value of instant coffee. In the one-cup sector, retailers are beginning to capitalize on the original manufacturer innovation. One cup was a good attempt at creating something distinctly different and fits well with the approach to the marketing advocated. They have not been wholly successful and have settled at below 55 per cent of the tea bag volume. Other innovations – in British terms – have included foil *packaging, tagged bags and, in particular, the introduction of the round bags which have benefited in volume and share terms*. But have these innovative products been able to attract new purchases? Tea volumes in general tend to be oriented down market and towards the middle aged. Round tea bags have an appeal with younger, up market families, with four in a household. One cup is slightly more up market still and finding a niche in a single person household. The fact is that such households now represent 23 per cent of the population may make the overall share performance look somewhat disappointing.

Challenge of the Sectors

The challenge within particular sectors of the population is to increase overall volumes of purchasing and share of total liquids consumed. Just about, everyone still buys tea and this represents an enormous strength compared to other traditional and declining markets. In continental Europe, there is little apparent buoyancy for coffee or tea, though France, Germany, Spain and Switzerland showed positive movement for tea. Some of the tea penetration levels in Europe are surprisingly high though there is plenty of room for growth. Unlike Britain, however, a significant proportion of a number of markets is taken up with herbal and fruit products. Thus, although there must be opportunities for tea in the rest of Europe, they are likely to be limited. The main challenges for the tea industry are domestic, innovation, and branding.

UK Tea Imports

The quantities of imports of tea in United Kingdom during the period from 1951 to 2007 are shown in the table below:

Table 2.1 : Import of Tea in United Kingdom during 1951 to 2006

(in thousand kgs.)

Name of the country/year	*1951*	*1961*	*1971*	*1991*	*1994*	*1997*	*2000*	*2003*	*2006*
India (a)	125224	127779	79409	27256	33593	32922	25919	25600	26800
Bangladesh (a)	15755	962	0	12	433	430	322	630	650
Sri Lanka	49987	72476	49200	11728	16284	8883	9356	7380	8450
Indonesia	7662	5671	6123	9924	10915	14034	16353	14200	17300
Kenya	1612	5740	5463	81952	72532	71977	54183	71845	72845
Uganda	235	1487	7632	446	330	168	164	287	560
Tanzania	287	2667	5848	6153	2536	3067	1836	897	2000
Malawi	5762	10638	28177	14156	13412	5560	25687	9831	10831
Mauritius	.31	670	502	2403	1487	363	-	—	-
Mozambique	336	6113	10591	255	192	-	27	-	-
Zaire	-	1319	1639	54	885	19	-	-	-
Malaya (b)	343	1300	315	—	257	481	35	—	-
China	72	4336	3639	7513	9318	8957	4242	4921	5921
Taiwan	887	4336	707	68	118	129	81	33	40
Japan	49	552	18	20	49	86	74	78	100
Vietnam (South)	-	1200	14	206	656	1520	536	755	800
Argentina	-	552	7963	2350	2437	8447	2410	4786	5470
Netherlands	1361	2336	9829	543	1374	937	50	279	289
USSR/ CIS	-	4638	-	40	-	86	16	-	-
Other countries	917	-	9221	13096	15981	23813	14616	27013	28650
Total	210520	252000	226290	178165	182789	181879	155907	168555	180706

(a) Prior to 1971 figures relate to Pakistan, (b) Figures relate to Malaysia and Singapore less than 500 kgs.

Source : International Tea Committee, London and *Tea Statistics*, Tea Board, India.

It is observed from the table that the UK imports from 19 countries besides "other countries". The total imports in 1951 were 210 million kgs, which was reduced to 181 million kgs in 2006. Import was maximum at 252 million kgs in 1961 and minimum at 156 million kgs in 2003. Over the years, imports declined, Imports from India with UK ranged from 125 million kgs to 27 million kgs during 1950 to 2006. From 1971 onwards i.e 1971 to 2003, it declined from 79 million kgs to 28 million kgs. UK is importing tea from Sri Lanka. It was in the range of 49 million kgs to 72 million kgs during 1951 to 1971. It however, declined from 11 million kgs to 8 million kgs during 1991 to 2006.

The monthly import of Indian tea to UK showed a fluctuating trend. In the initial months i.e. Jan-April there is an increasing trend. In May-August there is a shortfall and from September to December thre is enhanced trend. The details are shown in Table 2.2 ahead.

Data presented in the table brings out the fact taht quantum of import of Indian tea in UK varied over the month of each year. The quantum was appreciable from January to March all the years whereas it declined from April to August. The arrivals started increasing from September to December for all the years. Imports in the month of January, 1951 was 17.67 million kgs which reduced to 1.8 million kgs in 2004. Similarly in December of the same year the import stood at 18.04 million kgs which increased to 22.14 million kgs in 2004.

The UK imports huge quantum of instant tea. It enhanced from 331 million kgs in 1971 to 3105 million kgs in 2004. It is evident from the table that import of instant tea enhanced in all the years. Table 2.3 shows the details.

It is evident from the data that India's share to total import was highest during four points of time i.e. 1971, 1976, 1991 and 1994 followed by Sri Lanka, Kenya, Switzerland, Netherland and USA. From 1997 to 2004, import of instant tea by Kenya was maximum at 339 million kgs in 1997, followed by Germany, Sri Lanka, India, Netherlands etc. In 2004 the UK imported 463 million kg from USA followed by Germany, Netherlands etc.

Destination-wise export of instant tea (Table 2.4) displayed the fact that the UK in 1971 exported 317 million kgs which

Table 2.2: Monthly Import of Indian Tea into United Kingdom

(quantum in Thousand kgs)

Months	*1951*	*1961*	*1971*	*1991*	*1994*	*1997*	*1998*	*1999*	*2000*	*2001*	*2002*	*2003*	*2004*
January	17672	20418	10905	921	2934	1198	2633	1948	1425	1425	1568	2212	1780
Feberuary	14305	14150	12109	353	857	687	1160	1032	1071	1071	1149	951	870
March	11056	9796	4891	310	304	426	938	1714	1142	1142	880	617	985
April	10441	4917	2984	379	198	269	684	700	854	854	744	275	368
May	6623	4478	545	73	200	305	626	858	509	509	334	315	790
June	2263	2763	493	339	311	544	1690	295	601	601	294	860	643
July	3401	5607	2522	799	865	1322	1775	786	1429	1429	1477	622	1312
August	5306	7729	1860	2144	3521	3198	2061	1311	2740	2740	1771	1844	861
September	9007	14491	13287	5025	5376	5286	6454	3569	3559	3559	3180	2840	3409
October	13284	10595	7154	5463	6135	7552	4708	3995	4831	4831	5211	4890	3711
November	13829	17814	11875	4747	7622	6373	4500	4703	5476	5476	4019	4215	4098
December	18037	15021	10838	6704	5269	5762	2836	3165	2281	2281	2276	2801	3315
Total	125224	127779	79463	27257	33592	32922	30065	24076	25918	25918	22903	22442	22142

Source: ITC, London.

Table 2.3: Import of Instant Tea into United Kingdom

(quantum in Thousand kgs)

Name of the Country	*1971*	*1976*	*1991*	*1994*	*1997*	*1998*	*1999*	*2000*	*2001*	*2002*	*2003*	*2004*
India	84179	30100	31564	54000	28450	22001	31816	30806	1136	24325	2400	398
Sri Lanka	65383	103400	20584	227367	30754	32957	31740	21600	44013	56620	45200	0
Kenya	6743	75600	186300	54000	338610	261750	387128	330685	247800	219880	97922	103796
Denmark	42651	48258	54361	32835	86740	NA	10453	2976	NA	NA	NA	3670
Uganda	30837	35624	29112	278551	NA	NA	NA	NA	NA	NA	NA	--
France	457	265642	315860	486657	103668	287207	94872	82080	5557	1880	21850	114759
Germany	2124	2100	8491	183738	355545	243262	161729	163362	193804	207137	193949	282346
Switzerland	21500	24210	279260	2261	NA	11330	15	415	43021	237644	117218	115206
Netherland	20150	27100	8567	9423	140312	134222	194210	72649	186442	124919	231716	273732
USA	55425	143300	221449	87154	93379	41230	21438	118361	311216	418177	594166	462764
Other Countries	2398	4100	6400	9423	401754	1365702	325255	211015	679261	630698	1594305	1748755
Total	331843	520330	1161948	973561	1579209	2399661	1258656	1003143	1712250	1921280	3071915	3105446

Source: ITC, London.

went up to 1570 million kgs to various countries. Australia accounted for 177 million kgs followed by France (34 million kgs), Germany etc in 1971. The picture was somewhat different in 2004. Out of 1570 million kgs France shared 431 million kgs, Germany 260 million kgs, other European countries 511 million kgs etc. In 2002 the UK exported 770 million kgs to Ireland, 200 million kgs to Germany, 68 million kgs to France.

Europe and the UK: A Look to Tea Consumption

Tea consumption by the Europeans is not something very much remarkable—just 70 million kgs of tea per annum. The notable consumers in Europe are the Federal Republic of Germany, France and Netherlands. Federal Republic of Germany consumes, in particular, Darjeeling's rich quality of tea. The annual consumption is estimated at 16 million kgs. Netherlands consumption of tea is increasing. The consumption reached to 20 million kgs in 2006 from 9 million kgs in 1984. The other country in the Continent of Europe, France is also gradually increasing her consumption of teas. It has moved from 3.44 million kgs in 1984 to 16.5 million kgs in 2006. The three countries account for 55 per cent of the total European consumption of black tea. Contextually what is worth is mentioning that the United Kingdom (UK) alone consumes about 185 million kgs of tea per annum? In the UK, tea knows no social age or class boundaries. In recent years, *cordial reception to instant tea is a fascinating development in* the UK. It has been reported that total 195 million cups of tea are brewed daily, some 8 million cups are prepared with tea bag. In the opinion of the market experts this is just the beginning. However, there is no point of becoming glad at this event. It has been reported that in the UK's total drinks market both tea and coffee are currently suffering from soft drink pressure. The consumption of tea and coffee per person per day has fallen during 1985 to 2006, the decline rate was 6.4 per cent and 4.4 per cent respectively. Despite that, the future of tea in the UK and continent of Europe should not be considered as on the wane. Rather it can be made bright just by popularizing tea as a healthy drink, an important ingredient in our daily fluid requirements, market experts feel.

The latest UK Tea Council Report indicated tea accounts for 43 per cent of all beverages the British people drink. Eighty

Table 2.4: Destination-wise Export of Instant Tea from United Kingdom

(quantum in Thousand kgs)

Destination	*1971*	*1976*	*1980*	*1991*	*1997*	*1998*	*1999*	*2000*	*2001*	*2002*	*2003*	*2004*
Ireland	13005	9700	93905	61673	36772	65918	90416	749918	904236	77088	671796	12689
West Indies (a)	2947	2500	6348	288	--	--	--	--	--	--	--	50
West Africa (b)	10618	11700	22978	3034	1296	3993	7676	3451	1	3110	495	--
Australia	177554	5800	1515	--	1603	590	342	--	500	200	200	4165
Other America	9398	5600	2255	13236	13092	19287	21734	10349	9928	7971	8170	11085
Finland	4334	23300	8523	3164	5964	28232	1753	1036	1521	1230	690	1415
France	34038	33000	29674	127864	75429	830633	83749	85345	119962	66703	531239	430656
Germany	23369	17600	25097	1050236	851774	1024614	855117	789017	687728	199412	95757	259306
Sweden	8992	4200	1135	6373	9823	16561	633	78799	36290	30291	24646	508
Switzerland	8687	12500	17829	8590	1850	450	1711	1036	344	2398	2869	1635
Other Europe	17222	38400	66997	109156	111953	45763	59040	52913	34519	24638	22051	511436
Other Countries	6436	4700	8124	31556	335233	546012	490375	835111	624810	927602	704277	337965
Total	316600	169000	284380	1415170	1444789	2582053	1612546	2606975	2419839	2033723	2062077	1570910

Source: ITC, London.

(80) per cent of the population consumes around 170 million kgs of tea. In the hot drinks sector, tea occupies 62.8 per cent share. The Report adds instant tea accounts for only 2.2 per cent of all brewed tea, which is over double of its 1 per cent share in 2006. The trade circle, however, felt that there is abundant scope to develop in this sector. The use of tea bags came down from 84.4 per cent in 2006 to 84.1 per cent in 2007. The loose-leaf share of tea has remained steady at 13 per cent for the past few years. In UK specialty tea is becoming popular these days and the trade is growing in this area. Over 8 million kgs of "specialty tea" was sold in 2006. It may be interesting to note that 25 to 34 year old consuming group has been leaning too heavily on these teas.

The consumption of tea in the UK declined in the age group of 10 years and above from 84.1 per cent in 1995 to 78.1 percent in 2007, mentioned in Britain's National Drinks Survey. Probable reasons pulling down the consumption have been observed as—diminution of product quality, absence of product innovation, perception of tea as old fashioned drink, erosion of branded tea by own label, negligence in brand advertising, fierce competetion from other drinks, the preoccupation of major companies with short term profit. Besides, tea importers and sellers failed to utilize the beneficial aspects of tea in popularizing it as a health drink.

Re-exports of Tea

United Kingdom also endeavoured to re-export tea to 28 countries. Among them the major important in terms of re-export volume are Belgium, France, Ireland, Italy, Canada, Australia, USA, Japan, Germany, etc. In 1951 total quantum of re-exports from UK was 5.97 million kgs which enhanced to 274.44 million kgs in 2004. Re-exports attained record level at 32 million kgs in 1991 followed by 31 million kgs (each in 1997 and 2003) and 30 million kgs (each in 1998 and 2002). Table 2.5 gives the details.

Contemporary Drinks Market in the UK

Moving forward today, it is worth reviewing briefly the structure of total drinks market in the UK. The consumption pattern as emerged is as follows

Table 2.5: Destination-wise Re-Exports of Tea from United Kingdom

(quantum in Thousand kgs)

Destination	*1951*	*1961*	*1971*	*1991*	*1997*	*1998*	*1999*	*2000*	*2001*	*2002*	*2003*	*2004*
Austria	15	41	56	89	232	128	131	120	114	131	115	104
Belgium	106	196	274	442	475	270	312	267	4150	5419	4898	4022
Denmark	254	417	826	230	234	129	142	141	133	147	132	127
Finland	151	194	300	421	697	205	260	319	322	241	217	152
France	192	712	1407	2142	2451	3373	2562	2474	4987	5136	5095	3369
Germany	1170	1379	1258	2727	1144	1241	1274	774	802	745	855	782
Greece	*	*	68	60	48	33	47	57	49	122	161	52
Ireland	0	8	5	1293	1308	1336	2812	2778	2327	2951	2881	4040
Italy	98	172	578	1361	1061	893	993	1072	1134	1092	1165	1071
Netherlands	223	1384	1844	1041	134	250	55	82	78	19	44	88
Norway	123	252	544	413	432	387	413	399	432	449	566	423
Poland	0	30	31	344	205	122	109	163	152	74	238	193
Spain	*	*	398	470	468	212	270	269	384	383	445	409
Sweden	420	909	1544	1337	1207	806	911	852	777	867	66	563
Switzerland	151	249	405	806	363	271	277	240	262	620	502	566
Canada	166	2883	3227	4629	4265	4201	3864	3826	4090	4076	4158	4178

USA	171	2890	2921	2042	2057	2216	2716	2676	1627	1771	3549	1749
Chile	49	50	151	7	15	18	23	23	45	22	29	40
Israel	183	*	262	394	527	530	329	384	161	142	44	37
Japan	*	*	3377	1037	1990	1113	1069	1144	1359	1503	1321	1259
Kuwait	*	*	43	15	181	21	36	17	24	4	8	23
Lebanon	*	*	91	41	166	144	109	26	8	11	13	10
Saudi Arabia	*	*	68	2503	2881	2922	1046	51	78	80	37	43
A.R.E.	132	5	9	240	56	12	15	19	5	28	11	30
South Africa	*	38	854	26	42	55	28	31	35	18	14	20
Australia	*	*	144	1053	1253	938	1130	1261	1052	272	1076	1284
Other countries	2373	2578	2053	6901	7449	7740	4152	2966	2653	2600	3671	2910
Total	5977	14387	22889	32083	31341	29566	25085	22431	27240	29923	31311	27444

Source: ITC, London.

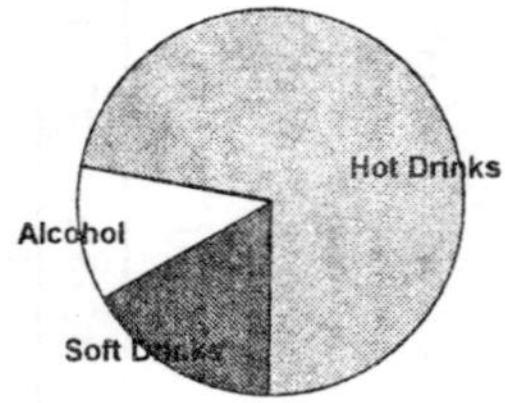

Currently, both tea and coffee are suffering from soft drink pressure. Tea consumption per head has come down to 3.15 cups in 2007 from 3.77 cups in 1995. Over the same period, coffee has seen its consumption per person per day to fall from 1.82 cups to 1.74 cups. Within the beverages market tea accounts for 63 per cent and coffee just 31 per cent. About with 80 to per cent of the population drink tea daily and 56 per cent drink coffee.

Conclusion

The tea trade is an excellent example of a complex multinational business involving several different types of specialists and companies each assisted by a variety of services, supplies and agencies, where the importance of information and communication is paramount. A good example of the use of information, communications and planning systems is in the supply and demand management. Such imbalances, if any, can be exploited in allocations to markets, product mix and price levels. These systems can be used and accessed by customers or suppliers using arbitrage and bargaining techniques and systems. One problem the industry faces is with the use of "standard" information tariffs, rate tables, price lists, delivery schedules, etc. The question is how to get this information to the people who need it, when they need it, and as reliably and economically as possible. Most information users, particularly cyclic or seasonal such as the tea industry, are intermittent users of much information, but it must be correct and easily available when it is needed. Paper based systems are difficult or even impossible to keep up to date and expensive in operation. In addition, the straightforward difficulty of the lack of common language often leads to confusion access to this information. Such problems are eliminated and the end user gets a better service at a less overall cost. One may see many uses of such systems within the Tea Trade. The "open" system contained information of no particular confidentiality. The 'closed" or "subscription" databases system cover information on companies or producer areas. It also takes into account future supply and demand of teas of different types, quality or origin.

3

Indian Tea in Poland

Poland's Trade with India

The polish People's Republic has an estimated total population of about 14 million 2006. Polish is the official language and Roman Catholicism is the major religion. The unit of currency is the Policy zloty. All foreign trade in Poland is a state monopoly and no duties are levied on the imports made by the state.

The major commodities of imports from India into Poland are primary products like de-oiled cakes, iron ore, mica and mica nite, hides and skins, jute-goods, black pepper, tea and coffee. Major commodities of exports from Poland to India are agricultural tractors, rolled steel products, capital goods, sulphur, organic and in-organic chemicals, urea, etc. In the past, India's imports of machinery and equipments covered a large field, but with the increasing industrialization in India, the composition of Indo-Polish trade has been adjusting to changing requirements of respective economies. The growth of trade with India may be seen from the table 3.1.

Table 3.1: Balance of Trade between India and Poland during 1956-57 to 2005-06

(in million Rs.)

Year	*Exports from India*	*Imports to India*	*Balance of trade with India*
1966-67	178.7	135.0	+43.7
1969-70	335.6	213.4	+22.2
1972-73	344.8	441.8	-97.0

1975-76	883.8	810.5	+73.3
1978-79	442.9	606.8	-163.9
1981-82	470.0	412.8	+57.2
1984-85	738.9	635.9	+103.0
1987-88	905.6	825.9	+79.7
1990-91	955.4	925.5	+29.9
1993-94	1201.5	1150.6	+50.9
1996-97	1326.0	1300.5	+26.5
1999-00	1560.5	1450.8	+109.7
2001-02	1630.4	1560.7	+69.9
2002-03	1685.6	1625.5	+60.1
2003-04	1761.6	1710.5	+51.1
2004-05	1915.4	1875.6	+39.8
2005-06	1995.6	1905.6	+51.0

Source: Director General of Intelligence and Statistics, Govt. of India.

Data presented in the table showed that almost all the years' exports from India were higher than imports to India resulting in favourable balance of trade. On a few occasions, exports were lower than imports. The Balance of trade was favourable and maximum at Rs. 109.7 million in 1999-2000 and minimum at Rs. 22.2 million in 1969-70.

Poland—Import Pattern of Tea

Amongst the countries in Eastern Europe, Poland is the second largest importer of tea after the USSR and total quantities imported increased since 1964. The Table 3.2 shows the details:

Tal.e 3.2: Import Pattern of Tea in Poland during 1964 to 2006

(in thousand kgs)

Year	*Imports for consumption*	*Exports from India*	*Sri Lanka*	*UK*	*Re-exports Netherlands*	*USSR*
1964	4712	1176	17	4	2	2146
1967	7309	1781	914	14	4	2725
1970	8097	1899	1461	21	4	1944
1975	15150	12096	300	110	174	2129
1978	18857	11542	659	126	227	2660
1981	24547	13775	204	86	554	2740
1984	25522	6313	103	1072	699	3481

1987	28165	9125	140	1250	752	3095
1991	28000	10450	488	666	344	459
1994	30100	19750	1499	183	352	54
1997	30300	10490	1806	906	205	62
2000	30450	12527	1920	1213	163	23
2001	33102	8269	2113	1834	152	82
2002	35452	9467	2310	2025	180	102
2003	36125	11150	2450	2215	200	150
2004	37102	12450	2550	2315	220	160
2005	37852	12850	2670	2420	240	171
2006	38200	12950	2790	2500	300	182

Source: Tea Statistics, Various Issues, Tea Board, Kolkata.

Poland imports about 37 million kgs of tea annually. The major suppliers to this market are India and Sri Lanka. Large quantities of teas are re-exported from the USSR. Small quantities are also re-exported to Poland from the UK and the Netherlands. Total imports of tea into Poland had gone up from 4.7 million kgs in 1964 to 38.20 million kgs in 2006. In other words, imports increased by 8.13 times. Although the share of India in this market did not exhibit appreciable increase between 1964 (25 per cent) and 2006 (34 per cent), but the quantum of exports, increased heavily. It was 1.2 million kgs in 1964 and 13 million kgs in 2006. The share of Poland market held by Sri Lanka started increasing from 1964 onwards. Sri Lanka, on an average, exports about 26 thousand kgs.annually. Export was very negligible in the year 1983.

Statistics of re-exports of tea from the UK, the Netherlands and the USSR showed that the quantum of re-exports from the UK to Poland was very less upto 1970. It, however, started improving after 1970 and continued up to 1990, except 1981. It again declined in 1991 and 1994. The increasing trend is noticed from 1997 onwards. On an average, the UK re-exports a little more than 2 million kgs per year. As regards the Netherlands, re-exports were negligible during the period from 1964 to 1975. It started improving from 1978. The Netherlands re-exports about 300 thousand kgs annually. Re-export from the USSR was more or less unchanged around 3.00 million kgs during the period from 1964 to 1987. It decreased afterwards.

Tea Exports from India to Poland

Exports of tea from India to Poland in 1979 were 5.1 million kgs, which increased to 8.9 million kgs in 2006 i.e. an increase to the extent of 75 per cent over 27-year period. It was maximum at 9.51 million kgs in 1999 and minimum at 5.10 million kgs in 1979. On an average, India exports 9 million kgs to Poland per year. The details of quantum, value of exports and unit price realization are shown in the Table 3.3.

Table 3.3: Exports of Tea from India to Poland during 1979 to 2006

Year	*Quantity (thousand kgs)*	*Value (thousand Rs.)*	*Unit Price (Rs./kg)*
1979	5110	79764	15.66
1980	11787	208778	17.71
1983	11715	276180	23.57
1986	7890	267471	33.90
1989	8250	539962	65.45
1992	8790	617496	70.25
1995	9385	684635	72.95
1999	9507	670244	70.50
2001	8269	520037	62.89
2004	8679	570210	65.70
2005	8845	320476	7015
2006	8945	672664	75.20

Source : Tea Statistics, Various Issues, Tea Board, Kolkata.

Instant tea at present is not exported to Poland. *Tea bags* were exported to Poland only in 1984-85. It was only 400 kgs valued at Rs.22 thousand. Packet teas, which were 1390 thousand kgs in 1979-80, increased to 1705 thousand kgs in 2005-06. The quantum of *Packet teas* exported was 1.94 million kgs in 1991-92 worth Rs. 146.74 million. Subsequently it declined to 1.45 million kgs valued at Rs. 111.12 million in 2001-02. Details of packet tea are shown in the Table 3.4.

Table 3.4: Exports of Packet Tea from India to Poland during 1979-80 to 2005-06

Year	*Quantity (thousand kgs)*	*Value (thousand Rs.)*	*Unit Price (Rs./kgs)*
1979-80	1390	26381	18.98
1982-83	1767	58536	33.12

1985-86	1415	49737	35.15
1988-89	1845	125736	68.15
1991-92	1945	146740	75.45
1994-95	7456	134630	77.12
1999-00	1578	112796	71.40
2001-02	1449	111119	76.68
2003-04	1575	118834	75.45
2004-05	1676	127544	76.10
2005-06	1705	133757	78.45

Source : Tea Statistics, Various Issues, Tea Board, Kolkata.

Conclusion

In order to boost exports of Indian tea to Poland the government of India is exploring further possibility of evolving a new scheme. For this both the governments must launch the strategy, which is based on the SMART (specific, measurable, attainable, and reasonable and time bound) principle. Since Poland's total requirement of tea for internal consumption is appreciably increasing over the periods under reference, there is a wide scope to expand India's share to Poland. Necessary steps are being geared to cope with the situation.

4

Popularity of Indian Tea in USA

Tea's Popularity is Skyrocketing

"Tea's popularity is skyrocketing", reports Mr. Joseph Simrany, the then President, Tea Council of the USA. "Americans are now drinking more than 48 billion cups and glasses of tea, or about 10 gallons per person, every year. Tea is becoming more and more the beverage of choice, because of its refreshing taste and its perfect 'fit' with our desire for healthier lifestyles. Served hot, tea is a soothing and relaxing cold weather beverage choice, perfect anytime". According to the observation of the Tea Council of the USA more than 127 million *Americans, almost half the population is now drinking tea on any given day. Spiced teas, scented teas, fruited teas, and decaffeinated teas* are all adding to the trend towards tea. However, what is more interesting to note that the younger generation, more health conscious people, driven by their increasing desire for quality, lighter all natural beverages, are contributing significantly to the growing popularity of tea. Mr. Simrary said : "Tea is one of the few all natural beverages that contains no sodium, fat, carbonation or sugar and is virtually calorie free." For all these reasons more and more consumers are turning to tea as the smart choice for the 90's.

Tea is fast becoming the coffee of the 90's in the United States of America. A newfound appreciation of tea led to a rush of smart tea bars and tea boutiques from coast to coast. Tea lovers were no longer content with indifferent mass-market tea from poor quality growing regions like Argentina, packed in skimpy tea bags. They graduated to good quality tea, better tea bags, and choice loose tea. Some of them even looked for select top quality invoices from a single estate. The Germans had done this for year – estate produced invoices are printed on the menu cards in the restaurants and price lists in the tea shops give full details of garden, its brief history, period of manufacture. *The consumer selects his cup of tea from his favourite garden. On the spot tasting facilities are also available in the shops.* On December 14, 1994 the Tea Council of the USA Inc. in conjunction with the American Health Foundation held an editors' forum presenting the exciting research currently being conducted on the potential health benefits of black tea. Editors from various media including Ladies' Home Journal, Longevity, Good House Keeping, Men's Health, Elle, and American Health crowded the hall of the New York Academy of Sciences, to listen to the panel of five scientists

Changing Consumer Needs

The American tea companies responded to the changing consumer needs by offering an ever-wider variety of tea. Says an analyst, "Given the passion for variety and expertise that already exists for wine, bear, coffee and even bottled water, perhaps it is inevitable that tea would be the next on the list". The newfound *interest in tea already paid rich dividends to importers, packers, sellers and people to sell tea-making equipment, publish books and newsletters on tea. In San Francisco, a newsletter titled 'Everyone's Cup of Tea' on tea etiquette and general information had found a ready audience.* A chain store in the New York region increased in demand for teapots. An importer of rare and expensive teas in Salisbury, Conn., converted a schoolhouse in nearby Ashley Falls, Mass., into a learning center and museum dedicated to tea. Even Seattle, with its high consumption of coffee, is changing. "Tea is big in Coffee country," says the owner of an Asian style tearoom in Seattle. "Tea, in fact, is popular all over the country these days. Over the last year tea sales have increased by 7.7 per cent", says Helen Bary, a Vice President of Beverage Marketing, a research company in New York. "This growth is likely to continue over the next few years, driven mainly by increased consumption of ready to drink iced tea and specialty tea".

"Republic of Tea" A Line of New Designer

Teas new found popularity has to do with its *soothing qualities, something to be craved for in this stressful era.* The Americans believed that tea is more subtle than coffee and it is meant to be sipper and not gulped. "Republic of Tea', a line of new designer teas pointed out that the tea is more satisfying and yet not expensive. A cup of tea can cost as little as a penny to make, with the very best tea costing not more than 25 cents a cup. Moreover, tea has less caffeine than a cup of coffee (half the amount or even less) makes attractive to the ever growing segment of the population concerned with health and fitness. The recent studies indicating the tea, green tea in particular, may possess disease-preventing qualities have also helped increase its sales. The consumption of ready to drink iced tea doubled the dollar sales of tea in retail stores from 1991 to 2006 when they topped 40 billion kgs of iced tea is popular with people who want a non alcoholic alternative at mealtimes. "Ready to drink is King" said Joseph P Simamy, the President of Tea Association. He adds, "Interest in the government side of the tea market is definitely increasing. The kind of teas sold in stylish new tea shops is estimated to account for 78 per cent of the market".

Connoisseurship Necessary to Appreciate Tea

It is worth noting that quality is taking over, where price dominated once. A tea merchant in Salisbury, Conn sold several varieties of expensive teas. They include those served at the Ritzto Carlton hotels and at Tea Box. The team says, "Like coffee, once people have a good tea, they do not want to go back to ordinary teas". Thomas J. Lipton, who holds more than 50 per cent of the market, anticipated a substantial crossover from better coffee to better tea. It may be mentioned here the Dean & Deluca is added to the store's line of teas after noticing the sales of better teas began to increase from 1993 on words. Dean & Deluca carried select brands like Kusmi and Mariage Freres teas from French, Jackson's of Piceadily from England and Royal Gardens from Fortbragg, Calif. A former perfume blender carried hundreds of teas, including own blends. Speecial imports and more than 30 from Mariage

Freres, a Parisian company known for its standards of excellence, asserted, "*Connoiseurship is necessary to appreciate tea,* 'but it's actually so simple because brewing a good pot of tea is so easy". Establishments at different placed nowadays offer a selection of unusual teas, including many green teas. These teashops and tea bar certainly reflect a shift in tea drinking toward better tea. Contextually it is referred to that English teas are typically black tea blends meant to be sturdy enough to stand up to the addition of milk and sugar. But as the interest grows in green teas and the more delicate teas like Darjeeling and fine Oolongs, tea is beginning to shed its English image, especially afternoon tea, the complicated, frilly Victorian ritual often mistakenly labeled "high tea".

Still tea has a long way to go. In most restaurants, even the finest ones the pride themselves on their ingredients, cuisine and tableware, tea service is essentially no better than it is in economy class on airplanes; a cup of water with a tea bag on the side. Our mission is to inspire a tea revolution in this country by encouraging tea made with good tea leaves", said the then President of Republic of tea in San Rafael, Calif. Republic of Tea combines good quality with clever and effective marketing, resulting in a fivefold increase in the company's sales in two years. In fine, however, the United States of America presents a grand opportunity for quality Indian teas. With their vast variety, the Indian teas can offer a tea for everyone from coast to coast.

Year 2006—Transition and Challenge

Presently USA is not a large market for Indian tea. There are various reasons for that. Now the India's set market in USSR has been unsettled, new markets have to be sought. Why not USA then? Various articles on US market were published in many leading and reputed journals. However, acute analysis of the US beverage markets, the pattern of which is not yet known in India, will be useful in two ways namely (a) by indicating a clear picture of the US market and (b) by suggesting to Indian producers and exporters a new method of study. 2006 was a year of transition and challenge. It was a year for change in the country's leadership and of the global bariers, which existed for decades. Tea had to be marketed in a very sluggish economic environment. If tea was not enough to contend with, experienced temperature declines throughout the year, especially during some of the prime convenience iced tea period. Despite the obstacles, the Tea category was able to maintain the level achieved in 2005 in supermarkets. This is encouraging, as the market experienced seven consecutive years of decline prior to the 2005 turnaround. Dolalr sales through the 3rd quarter of 2006 are projected to grow + 2 per cent while pound sales are flat. While the two largest segments, regular tea bags and iced tea mixed, were stagnant in few years back, there was a lot of excitement that generated in several other segments. The two growth areas are the result of changing consumer trends and new marketing alliances.

The Growth Areas: Consumers continue to exhibit an increasing trend towards purchasing products perceived as healthy, and tea manufacturers have apparently got their message across then that they too have products appropriately *positioned for this emerging lifestyle*. Decaffeinated tea bags experienced a + 10 per cent increase in both dollar and tonnage sales. Herbal tea bags saw dollars grow + 18 per cent and tonnage increase by + 12 per cent. Liquid tea continued the great growth. One has observed since 1989, experiencing a + 35 per cent increase in tonnage at supermarkets. Dolalr sales surged + 53.9 per cent. The major tea manufacturers with the giant of carbonated beverage forged the marketing alliances to expand liquid beverage. Ready to drink teas now represent 15.5 per cent of total category dollars. Another change in consumer purchasing habits relative to that Tea category is the importance of *non-grocery outlets* to category sales. Warehouse clubs, Mass Merchandisers and Drug Stores became more important to the category in 1992 (at the expense of supermarkets and small food stores). These three outlets combined now represent more than 10 per cent of total sales. The manufacturers who develop the best marketing and sales strategies to capitalize on these areas of opportunities will be most successful in the changing world of 2005 and beyond.

US Tea Sales Top $ 3 Billion: Consumption of tea in the United States climbed above $ 3 billion for the second consecutive year, according to Joseph P Simrany, that then

Executive Director of the Tea Council of the USA. Simrany said that, on any given day, a record 140 million Americans, almost half the population is drinking tea, consuming more than 65 billion six ounce servings annually. This report from the Tea Council based on research conducted by Nielsen Marketing Research and Price Waterhouse showed that away from home tea consumption in restaurants and other food service outlets grew 14.5 per cent over 2005 to al least 18.7 billion servings. This is an almost 30 per cent increase over the prior two year period. Consumer supermarkets purchases of tea surpassed a record $ 3 billion for the second consecutive year, while sales at non-food retail outlets jumped by at least 46 per cent to 5.3 billion servings. *The new ready to drink canned, bottled or aseptically packaged liquid is leading the industry as the fastest growing tea product.* Ready to drink tea represents fifteen per cent of total US tea sales. Last year, liquid tea sales in supermarkets alone, accounting or 3.67 million gallons or 457.7 million servings, represented a 64 per cent dollar increase to $ 104.4 million from $ 78.9 million in 2005.

US Tea Sales Top 10 Billion: "US Tea Sales top $1 billion for the second consecutive year 2006"—the headline came from the Tea Council of the USA Inc. According to information collected and analysed by Thenielson Marketing Research and Price Waterhouse for the Tea Council, tea sales are growing rapidly in restaurants and other foodservice outlets. The increase is almost by 20 per cent in two years. Consumer supermarket purchases of tea were more than $ 1 billion for the second year. The consumption of ready to drink liquid tea in bottles, cans, etc. is growing very fast. According to available report, liquid tea sales in supermarkets alone accounted for 32.5 million gallons in 2006. And this represents a 44 per cent increase from 117.8 million gallons in 2005 to 169.6 million gallons in 2006. It has been felt that the growing consumption of tea is due to the fact that more and more people in USA are accepting tea as a drink beneficial to health. A few years back, the Tea Associations of the *US, the UK and Canada initiated the first cooperative multi national project to encourage and fund scientific and medical research on the health benefits of tea.* A Steering Committee with representatives from all these three countries was constituted to administer this multi million-dollar project, which aims at researching the potential protective effects of tea in inhibiting Cancer and Cardiovascular disease. The committee presented the report indicating the health aspects of tea.

Steady Growth in Consumer Demand for Tea

In supermarkets, the steady growth in consumer *demand for tea bags, decaffeinated teas, herbal tea bags, and iced tea mixes* was focused, according to the Nielsen study. Consumer purchases of tea bags were steady, accounting for 60 per cent of tea in terms of pound sales and posting two per cent increases, in terms of gallon sales, in the east and South. Purchases of decaffeinated tea bags increased four per cent to 100 million gallon or 106 million iced tea mixes advanced three per cent on the year ago period, topping 356 million gallons or 295 Herbal tea bags, recovering from one per cent loss in 2007 posted a five per cent increase to 58.7 million gallon or $ 104 million.

USA Liquid Consumption Trends (Shares of Stomach) Although tea consumption ranks second to coffee in USA, more people consume the beverage worldwide and in greater quantity than any beverage. In the USA, 127 million people, almost 50 per cent of the population drinks tea every day, and a full 80 per cent have tea in their kitchen cupboards. Since 1990, tea consumption outside the home has increased almost 20 per cent. Much of this growth has come from the increased demand for speciality teas. US Liquid Consumption trends during 1981 to 2007 is depicted in the table below.

Table 4.1: US Liquid Consumption Trends (Shares of Stomach) During 1981 to 2007

(In percentage)

	1981	*1984*	*1987*	*1990*	*1993*	*1996*	*2000*	*2003*	*2006*	*2007@*
Soft Drinks	19.1	21.3	24.2	26.1	26.2	26.3	19.5	20.3	22.4	23.1
Coffee*	14.8	14.4	14.8	14.5	14.5	14.3	14.4	14.3	14.7	14.8
Beer	13.5	13.1	13.1	13.2	12.8	12.7	13.4	13.3	13.0	13.2
Milk	11.1	10.8	10.9	10.8	10.6	10.5	10.8	10.7	10.8	10.9
Tea*	4.1	3.9	4.0	3.8	3.7	3.7	4.1	3.9	4.0	4.0
Bottled Water	1.8	2.2	3.5	5.0	5.3	5.4	1.8	1.9	2.8	3.1

Juices	3.7	3.6	3.8	3.4	3.5	3.6	3.7	4.3	4.1	4.0
Powd. Drinks	3.3	3.5	3.0	3.1	3.2	3.1	3.3	3.6	3.4	3.3
Wine**	1.2	1.3	1.3	1.1	1.0	1.0	1.2	1.2	1.3	1.3
Dist. spirits	1.0	1.0	0.9	0.8	0.8	0.7	1.0	1.0	1.0	0.9
Subtotal	73.6	75.1	79.5	81.8	81.6	81.3	73.2	74.5	77.5	78.7
Impounded Consumption***	26.4	24.9	21.5	18.2	18.4	18.7	26.8	25.5	22.5	21.3

Source: World Coffee and Tea. Note: *Coffee and tea data are based on the three year moving average to counter balance inventory swings, thereby portraying consumption more realistically, ** Includes wine coolers beginning in 1984, ***Includes all other and @ : Estimated.

The percentage of the shares of stomach compiled by John Maxwell, Jr uses 182.5 gallons as the average per capita intake of liquids during a year. After subtracting per capita for ten beverages remaining gallons are listed as imputed water. Maxwall's tea data is based on three year moving average to counter balance inventory swings. This should thereby portray consumption more realistically. Consequently higher numbers has not yet translated into the tea excitement over the ready to drink products any significant. After hitting 7.5 gallons, tea per capita consumption has slipped. Maxwell's estimates put tea at 6.8 gallons, on an average. While overall tea gallonage has not changed significantly, more than a decade long shift from hot tea to iced tea has occurred. Accordingly Beverage Industry Iced teas, on an average, comprise about 80 per cent of volume compared to 72.9 per cent.

Maxwell's categories claimed the following estimated per capita gallon consumption:

Table 4.2: Category-wise Liquid Consumption per capita

Category	*Gallons*	*Category*	*Gallons*
1. Soft drinks	48.0	2. Coffee	26.1
3. Beer	23.1	4. Milk	19.2
5. Bottled Water	9.9	6. Tea	6.8
7. Juices	6.6	8. Powdered Drinks	5.6
9. Wine	1.8	10. Distilled Spirits	1.3
11. Imputes Water	34.1	- -	

Source : World Coffee and Tea.

Maxwell was quoted in 'Beverage Industry as saying the move of the younger generation to alternative beverages specifically coffee, teas and fruit flavoured drinks. This will continue a slow but steady impact on the traditional soft drink market'.

Ready To Drink Tea in USA: In US tea industry the year 1993 is considered as one of the most important years since the invention of the tea bag and iced tea were made in 1904. In 1993, many new ready to drink (R to D) iced tea products were introduced and the consumers were readily accepting these products. With the development of ready to drink teas, World Coffee and Tea reported that the iced tea has become even more the beverage of choice for a whole new generation of Americans. In 1993, approximately two billion glasses of iced tea were consumed in the country and today the business circle views that the sales of the new ready to drink teas will top $ 1 billion, in effect doubling the size of the traditional tea market in the United Sales. From all indications, however, it appeared that the future of tea in America is very promising. "Iced tea is 'hot' in the USA and hot tea is likely to get 'hotter' in the future. Iced tea is fast becoming an all American beverage and taking its rightful place next to apple pie!"

Features of the US Market

There are various key features of the US Market and these are summarized below:

- ✓ Trends in the Tea category are promising. This is especially true given the slowdown in retail food outlet sales over the past few years.
- ✓ The total tea market maintained the level attained in 2006. This is encouraging, as the market had declined for seven consecutive years prior to 2006's turnaround.
- ✓ Dollar sales of tea in supermarkets exceeded 3 billion dollars for the second consecutive year, growing at a 2.5 per cent rate. Pound sales remained at basically the same level for the fourth consecutive year.
- ✓ Only shelf stable juices and drinks and carbonated beverages exhibited tonnage growth among the beverage categories. Tea's flat performance actually

outpaced coffee, powdered soft drinks and frozen juices and drinks.

- ✓ Liquid Tea continues to show very strong growth, while iced tea mix and Herbal tea also grew across all regions.
- ✓ Tea volume increased in 3 of the 4 regions. The East, which leads the country in per capita consumption, led the way with increases of 4 per cent and 6 per cent for pounds and dollars respectively.
- ✓ Liquid Tea's importance on a dollar basis is almost 9 per cent of the entire category. Similarly, Herbal Tea and iced mix also are quite important on a dollar basis.
- ✓ Tea bags, by far the dominant form representing 80 per cent of pounds sales, account for less than half the category dollar volume.
- ✓ Iced Tea Mix continues to increase its relative importance to the category. Most of the gain appears to be at the expense of Instant Tea, which may be losing shelf presence as Iced Tea Mixes expand.
- ✓ Non-Food outlets, importance to the Tea Category has increased at the expense of Supermarkets and Small Food Stores. Drug Stores, Mass merchandisers, and Warehouse Clubs now account for more than 15 per cent of Category sales.
- ✓ Tea Bags dominate in the South. Iced Tea Mix and Tea Bags share importance in the East. Instant Tea is important in the Central. Herbal's importance continues strong in the West.
- ✓ The Tea category performance is highlighted by substantial growth from 3 segments, such as Liquid Tea, Herbal Tea Mix, and Iced Tea Mix etc.
- ✓ Tea Bags performance was flat following growth in the last few decades. Instant Tea and Loose Tea continued their declining trends.
- ✓ The American consumer has become more health conscious and more aware of what they are eating and drinking. Salt content, cholesterol and fat content and calories can be as important as the product itself. The increase in sales of products perceived as healthy by consumers has been evident throughout the

supermarket. Both herbal and decaf teas have posted strong sales gains and may be benefiting from the increased consumer awareness.

Tea Import and Consumption into USA

A disquieting feature of the tea trend in the USA is that, in spite of all that has been done by the producing nations, the Tea Council and the Tea Association of the USA, import of tea into the USA and consumption has been slowly but surely going down. It is now apparent that soft drinks and coffee have steadily made inroads into tea consumption. According to a 2006 winter survey, per capita coffee consumption in the USA during the winter of 2006 was estimated at 1.75 cups per day. On the other hand, tea consumption was reported to be only 0.30 per cent. The coffee consumption represents an increase over 2005 with the consumption then at 1.67. It has been estimated that the number of cups of coffee consumed by coffee drinkers per day has remained more or less steady during the past five years and presently it is 3.34 cups per day, similar to 2005.

The winter coffee drinking survey financed by the Promotion Fund of the International coffee organization also claims that with more than half of the population drinking coffee it is the second most popular beverage in the US after soft drinks. However, curiously enough milk and juices on grounds of health consciousness are now aggressively assailing this second place. It is no doubt true that the Americans are highly health conscious and insist on qualitative drinks. One wonders what has happened to the propaganda long carried on behalf of Tea that it is a healthy drink more preferable to coffee and soft drinks. The efforts made by the Tea Industry and the Tea Council and Associations have to make much headway, as imports and consumption keep on sliding. In this alarming context, the USA Tea Association organized a Tea Convention in the past fall. A large number of international tea experts including a number of them from the producing countries attended the convention. A variety *of opinions were expressed and according to the editorial page of the Tea & Coffee Journal, "the dynamic speeches all thundered the same order—Change"*.

Dynamic Approach for Increasing Tea Consumption

The speeches indeed underlined the need for a dynamic approach to the problem of increasing tea consumption in the USA. Soon a dynamic campaign was launched in the USA for enabling tea to pick up consumption. In this, the tea producing countries like India and Sri Lanka played a notable part. Based on the information available, Kenya is already in the second place among the largest exporter to USA. It has been spending large sums of money for promotional campaigns in the USA. According to statistics released by the Tea Board of Kenya, *the Board's generic promotional funding* increased by 42 per cent from 624 Kenya pounds in 2005-06 to 890 Kenya pounds in 2006-07. The UK Tea Council received the largest share of 67 per cent of the Tea Board's promotion funding, followed by the USA and Canadian Tea Councils in the order. The strategy of the Kenyan Board is to concentrate its promotional campaigns in a few selected places and it has obviously succeeded in its efforts. In the UK, it is the largest exporter of Tea and in the USA it is the second and China being the first in 2005.

According to statistics available, 95 million kgs of China mainland Tea was passed for entry into USA from January to November end 2007 followed by Kenya with 33 million kgs. But it would also be significant to note that both China and Kenya have also slided down slightly with their exports compared to the same period in 2006 when they exported 85 million kgs and 40 million kgs respectively. The gainer in this regard has been Argentina, which advanced to 102 million kgs during the period under review compared to 90 million kgs during the same period in 2006. India could only manage to export 210 million kgs in 2007 as against 200 million kgs in 2006. In spite of all its troubles, Sri Lanka managed to send 30.5 million kgs, a marginal increase compared to 31.5 million kgs in 2006. Sri Lanka also made a policy of aggressive salesmanship in select places and one for the places obviously selected was the USA.

It has been a matter for concern to *front ranking global tea producers the consumption of tea in the United States in recent years has shown an alarming trend of significantly falling*. In spite of the fact, the efforts have been made to stress the health, nutritional and medicine aspects of tea, consumption continues to fall. The question is being increasingly asked in this country as to why there should be such fall especially when affluent Americans are in search of really a healthy good drink and tea fits in admirably with all their requirements.

India to Chalk Out Well Coordinated Campaign

The India Tea Board, which has set a higher export target, would do well to consult and confabulate with the Tea interests. The Tea Council and the Tea Association of the USA chalk out a *further well-coordinated campaign in the USA to bring home to the people the concept the Tea is a healthy drink. It can be taken either hot or cold.* Attempts have also been made to improve the quality standards of Tea served in the teashops and restaurants. Very often it is noticed that while prepared cups of coffee are served in establishments, in the case of tea, the customers themselves will have to mix milk and sugar and tea water to get a cup of tea. In the hury bury complex of the present day America, customers have little time to devote to such things. In addition, the large number of brands of tea offered to him invariably baffles the customer. It would be indeed helpful if only a lesser number is offered and attempts are made to educate the public at large on qualitative teas. It is noted in Tea circles here that there is a similar threat to the consumption in the UK. *The UK Tea Council and producing countries must make a further concerted campaign to push forward Tea as a healthy drink. A sustained campaign would arrest a further slide. Something on the lines of the UK Campaign of the USA will have to make propaganda aggressively if tea is to retain its place in the country.*

Steady Sailing in USA

Food Store Sales both in retail and in volume have shown marginal increase in the USA for the year 2006. All the same, tea has to face brave competitors such as soft drinks, fruit juices, and alcoholic liquors, as efforts to expand its consumption from its present use in iced form (80 per cent) are continuing. Recently, there have been a few agreements between tea manufacturers and major soft drink producers to market liquid teas with the help of the latter. These are extensive and popular distribution chain. Liquid tea for a large part water, recorded a mere one per cent in tea to leaf sales in 2006, although more than five per cent (above $ 50 m) of the entire sales was its actual value gained as a result of costly packaging.

Retail Food Store Sales and Tea Sales

Retail food store sales increased by five per cent over sales in 2006 at over $ 2 billion. Volume sales, too, have risen by more than 3.5 per cent to above 70 million kgs. Tea bags still dominate US tea sales, making up about 60 per cent of the volume and just below 50 per cent of the total value in 2006. However, herbal tea has lost its high profile of the eighties, and a leading mineral water distributor is probably to infuse fresh vitality in this particular variety by distributing its multiple flavours after brewing and bottling. Import of herbal teas to the USA mainly from China, Taiwan, Germany and the Republic of Korea was dropped marginally to approximately 2.80 million kgs. On the other hand, almost $ 25.5 million worth of herbal teas were exported, with a marked rise in sales to Canada, Spain, Hong Kong, etc. Regular, non-herbal tea exports – principally to the UK, Japan, Canada and Mexico – also grew in both value and volume. Exports of instant tea by the US have also nearly raised twofolds to almost 2.40 million kgs at a value approximating to $ 9.3 million. China, as always, topped the list of suppliers of herbal, not to instant teas of the US. The other chief sources have been Argentina and Indonesia. Of the total, more than 84 million kgs of tea was imported on an average. Out of which over 80 per cent were black, and the rest green teas. Though a nearly 10 per cent rise in volume was perceived, prices came down by about 2.3 per cent to about $ 123.5 million.

Canadian Involved in US Tea Growing Enterprise

Two men, William Barclay Hall, a Canadian from St. Boniface, Manitoba and Mack Fleming had a unique combination of skills to bring the US tea-growing industry back to life. They operated a tea plantation near Charleston, South Carolina. There they grew, packaged and marketed their own tea, which they called American Classic. The Charleston Tea Plantation, Inc., on Wadmalaw, a barier island 20 miles from Charleston, South Carolina, deliver its homegrown, American Classic Tea from the field to the store in approximately one week. All other tea sold in the USA can be about 9 months old or more before consumed, and Tea does not improve with age. Freshness gives tea its smoothness and delicacy of flavour. The Charleston Tea Plantation is a streamlined operation, able to accomplish drying, grading and packaging all within the same 10000 sq. ft. facility at the center of the plantation. Mack Fleming is a horticulturist and researcher who have grown tea for eight years, and William Hall is a professional tea taster. "Three are only about eight tea tasters in the whole United States", says Hal, who worked for a time with Brooke Bond in Montreal then did a four-year apprenticeship as a tea taster with a British tea company. As part of his training he had to sample 800 to 1000 teas per day. In London he worked for Van Rees, a Netherlands tea trader. After that he worked for a tea company in Argentina, then came to the United States. His tea industry experience and tea tasting training helped him select the blends used in American Classic. Even though tea has been an integral part of US history since Colonial times (The Boston Tea Party American Revolution), tea has not been grown commercially in America for nearly 100 years.

Light Bright Gourmet Tea: An American Classic

It is a combination of ancestral tea bushes from China, India and Ceylon, together with the advanced American technology. All these natural freshness put American Classic, a category by itself. The tea is described as being a "light bright gourmet tea". "American Classic will hold its own among world teas" says Fleming, who put his product up against any tea grown in China, India, Sri Lanka and other tea countries, Fleming and Hall have 150000 healthy tea plants. They launched the product in selected areas. "We started locally in stores in South Carolina, but were aiming for the whole Eastern Seabord", said Hall. A box of 25 teabags costs about $ 2.50 the equivalent of the popular British tea Earl Gray. Fleming and Hall have pooled their talents and finances to produce the only home grown tea in the United States, which imported 193 million pounds of tea in 1986, up from 170 million pounds in 1985.

Growing Tea Plants in America

People ask us if growing tea in America is such a good idea how come no one else is doing it?" Fleming says. It's not a matter of climate, he insisted. Tea plants require warm weather and bout 60 inches of rainfall a year, which is what Charleston Country usually gets. The real obstacle to American tea growing has been labour costs, says Fleming and he thinks he has eliminated the problem. His solution is a piece of equipment that makes harvesting economical. A simple machine looks like a modified tractor and picks tea plants at a rate of two miles per hour. Fleming designed the harvester and had it made in South Carolina. It does the work of 500 people picking tealeaves, he says. Labour costs have been the downfall of two centuries of efforts to make the US self sufficient in tea. However, the United States is far behind many other countries in tea consumption. In England, the per capita tea consumption is eight pounds a year, compared with seventeenth of a pound in the US. In Canada, per capita consumption is 0.81 kgs.

Tea—A Popular Beverage Gaining Market in USA

The USA Tea Convention held in October 1993, reported that the demand of tea, as a popular beverage, in the country is growing fast. Consumers of beverages, in recent years, have leaned too heavily on tea—a clean, refreshing and healthy drink. This demand is, in fact, the outcome of additional advertising budgets and increased publicity. A recent study of the market indicates the bottled water and tea were the fastest growing beverages between 1987 and 1990. There is some indication that the soft drinks and carbonated beverages are losing popularity. During the said period consumption of tea at hotels and bars, etc. increased by 17 per cent. It appears that tea as a healthy drink is gaining wide acceptance throughout the country although for many years it has been perceived that tea as a drink helps to banish fatigue, stimulates mental power and enhances energy levels.

Medicinal and Health Properties of Tea

USA Tea Association's Report for autumn 2006, states: "Consumers answered the latest question with a resounding vote for tea as the smart beverage alternative for 2000's. *Tea out- performed several competing beverage categories in 2006.* The gains have been so much impressive because of the combined efforts of Lipton (Perpsi) and Nestle (Coke) along with Snapple, Celestial Seasonings (Perrier) and Tetly (A & W) the some beverage industry consultants expect sales of ready to drink tea to touch $ 2 billion. The Report adds: "Another testament to the popularity of iced tea was that 6 per cent growth set by iced tea mixes in 2006. Also joining the growth ranks were two "healthy" segments, herbal and decaffeinated tea bags. Herbals posted a 4 per cent gain in pound sales—this on top of the 10 per cent growth rate in 2005 while decaffeinated tea bag tonnage increased 5 per cent equal to last year's pace". *The recent revitalization of tea sales is, however, due to its healthy image and appeal, industry circles feel.* To quote the words of a teahouse proprietor in London in 1770: *"Tea is a beverage of relax the brain, settle the stomach, relieve headaches and strengthen mental acquity, to list only a few of its benefits".*

With a view to making tea more popular, the United States Tea Association highlighted the *medicinal and health properties of tea. Good grounds were advanced for claims being repeatedly made in recent years that the tea has a positive preventive effect on some types of cancer.* A vigorous campaign was launched for tea and in this campaign it is anticipated that the world's leading producers of tea would cooperate wholeheartedly. To act as a spur to the campaign world meet on tea was fixed by FAO's inter governmental group of tea and take place in the USA in March 1991. In the meet India took a leading part in that it provided a common forum for the leading producers to act in concert for tea. It was recalled that Mr. Alan Davies of the the United States Tea Association, who represented a paper in the international convention on tea held in UK stated that the Association had been attempting to scientifically document the traditionally held belief that *the tea is good for the people. He said the funds were approved for an international Tea Symposium held in late 1990 early 1991 under the auspices of the New York Academy of Science with Scientists from around the world. Scientists were invited to present the papers on the health benefits of tea with emphasis on cholesterol reduction and cancer prevention. "The benefits to the consumer and to the world tea industry of such a symposium will be significant."* The Association believes the credible and responsible health claims for tea have the potential to increase sales faster than any other vehicle. "We ask for the help and encouragement from the tea industry at large in an effort which has an inherent potential to usher an era of growth of us all"

Imports of Black Tea by US between 2007 and 2005

Black tea imports into the United States for consumption during 2006 totaled about 111 million kgs while re- exports from India was 10 million kgs as reported by the Tea Association and corelated by the US Department of Commerce. Imports from the Mainland China showed 24.4 per cent imports in quantity and 18.2 per cent in value terms. However, the distinction of first place for most volume and value belongs to Argentina. Argentine teas accounted for 27.2 per cent of the country's imported black tea with a striking 40 million kgs. In the same grouping was Indonesia with an impressive 18 per cent of the black tea imports and 14.6 per cent of the Rupee. The three countries, namely, Argentina (27.2 per cent) China (24.4 per cent) and Indonesia (18.00 per cent) in a combination claim 69 per cent of kgs and 54 per cent of the rupee. Further, Malawi accounted for 4.0 per cent, Sri Lanka 4.5 per cent, India 3 per cent, Germany 5.1 per cent, Brazil 3.4 per cent, Kenya 5.0 per cent and other countries 5.4 per cent.

Table 4.3: Tea Passed for Entry in USA in July 2007 and 2005

(in kgs)

	July 2007	*July 2005*	*Absolute increase/decrease*	*Percentage increase/decrease*
Black Teas				
North India	30112	39611	-9495	-3.98
South India	54169	60151	-5985	-9.95
Total India	*84281*	*199765*	*-15484*	*-15.53*
Argentina	719832	8245632	-104720	-12.7
Australia	0	0	0	0
Bangladesh	0	0	0	0

Brazil	2204070	2222687	-18617	0-0.85
Burundi	0	0	0	0
Cameroons	0	0	0	0
Ceylon & India	10776	13457	-2680	-19.92
China	5354567	6365450	-1010893	-15.88
Earl Gray	12050	17441	-535	-30.90
Earl Gray (Decaf)	360	1384	-1024	-73.99
Ecuador	264570	89944	+174596	+194.22
Formosa	18232	0	+18238	+100.00
Guatemala	0	0	0	0
Indonesia	5733232	5645594	+87638	+1.55
Kenya	821954	720250	+101704	+14.12
Lapsang Souchong	4162	1388	+2772	+199.77
Malawi	1912122	1970072	-57950	+2.95
Mauritius	0	79898	0	0
Misc. Black Blends	855972	495354	+360618	+72.80
Mi. Bl. Blds. Decaf	3356050	2725358	+630698	+23.15
Mozambique	0	0	0	0
Nepal	0	0	0	0
New Guinea	158732	254852	-96120	-37.22
Peru	0	0	0	0
Rwanda	193948	100940	+93088	+92.14
Scented Black	169334	247180	-77842	-31.49
Scented Black Decaf	11934	6614	+5320	+80.43
Sikkim	0	0	0	0
Sri Lanka	1440578	1021276	+419302	+41.06
Tanzania	88184	0	0	0
Thailand	0	0	0	0
Turkey	0	0	0	0
Uganda	0	0	0	0
Zaire	0	76296	0	0+48.92
Zimbabwe	98766	66320	+32448	+28.92
Total Black Teas	22217199	17317212	+4899897	+7.11
Total Green Teas	301290	281290	+20000	-2.28
Total Mixed Teas	349050	357206	-8155	+27.35
Grand Total	22867538	17955708	+4911830	+27.40
By Districts				
New York	11552942	9067633	+2426521	+27.30
New Orleans	11314596	8888075	+15688170	+87.37
Total Kgs	22867538	17955708	-	-

Source : Tea Association of USA.

Black Tea, Passed for Entry into USA during 2006-07

Tea entered into USA as a whole in 2006 was 19.65 million kgs, which enhanced to 22.53 million kgs. Variety wise, quantum of block tea was 18 million kgs in 2006 and 21 million kgs in 2007. Green Tea in 2006 recorded at 1.30 million kgs, which went up to 1.40 million kgs. Table 4.4 below shows the details. The share of Oolong tea was very negligible. It was higher in 2006 compared to 2007.

Table 4.4: Tea for Entry into USA during 2006 and 2007

(million kgs)

Variety	*2007*	*2006*	*Absolute inc/dec. in 2007 over 2006*	*Percentage inc./dec. in 2007 over 2006*
I. Black Teas	21.0	18.0	+3.00	+16.66
II. Green Teas	1.4	1.30	+0.10	+7.69
III. Oolong Teas	0.06	0.15	-0.05	-60..00
IV. Mixed Teas	0.07	0.20	-0.13	-65.00
Grand Total:	22.53	19.65	-2.88	-14.66

Source: Tea Association of the USA-65.00.

Conclusion

Tea is increasingly traded as a global commodity. It often binds price movements in one auction center triggering off a sympathetic reaction in others. Evidently, the international tea community would definitely view the recent unexpected withdrawal of large volumes of tea in Jakarta closely. Industry circle feels the heavy withdrawals in Indonesia at the Jakarta auction during the first week of December 2006 was snapped up ex auction, probably to fulfill a large order to the CIS. The size of the order has necessitated further withdrawals in subsequent auctions. Therefore, it would be now worth observing that regular international buyers at this center are compelled to seek alternative sources of supply.

5

Export Potentials of Indian Tea in Canada

Import Pattern of Tea into Canada

Canada is mainly a coffee drinking country. A Canadian drinks more coffee than any one in the world. On an average, a Canadian drinks 3 cups of coffee a day while it is 1.5 cups a day in the case of tea. In other words, per capita consumption of tea in Canada is only 1.40 kgs as against about 5 kgs in the case of coffee. Nevertheless, Canada occupies the fifth position among tea importing countries.

Canada's imports of tea fluctuated during the period from 1951 to 2007. In quantitative terms total imports of tea into Canada over the last five years, on an average, was about 19 million kgs. It was, however, maximum at 24 million kgs in 1975 and minimum at 13 million kgs in 1991. Prior to 1961, India was the major supplier of tea to Canada followed by Sri Lanka, East Africa, U.K., etc. In 1961, Sri Lanka became the major supplier of tea followed by India U.K., East Africa, and Indonesia. Countries like China and Hong Kong, Japan, etc. started supplying teas to Canada. In the year 2007, Canada's imports were 21 million kgs.Out of this total, India supplied about 1.3 million kgs , Sri Lanka 4 million kgs , Indonesia 1.5 million kgs, East Africa 3.2 million kgs, U.K.4 million kgsand other countries 4.8 million kgs.Canada also re-exported tea to the U.K and Netherlands. A study of the trend of tea imports into Canada is brought out in Table 5.1.

Table 5.1: Import Pattern of Indian Tea in Canada during 1951 to 2007

(in thousand kgs)

Year	*Total Imports @*	*India*	*Sri Lanka*	*Indonesia*	*East Africa*	*U.K.*	*Japan*	*China & Hong Kong*	*Other countries*
1951	19258	9384	7283	175	1310	233	118	125	560
1961	20570	7129	8327	86	1060	2952	117	166	853
1971	23512	3710	8802	367	3773	2991	117	587	5165
1975	24369	3890	4791	1682	5503	3066	100	563	4053
1980	23187	2208	5547	1795	4589	3604	37	634	4773
1985	18018	873	3635	1316	2298	4085	62	1064	4785
1991	13314	477	1634	440	3305	4321	123	912	2102
1997	16913	1049	1518	667	3445	4646	165	1046	4377
2000	15656	1133	1657	900	NA	5013	78	766	6109
2003	17088	1213	2154	1015	1245	5413	102	954	4992
2004	18018	873	3535	1316	2298	4085	62	1064	4785
2005	19838	1179	3574	1735	3346	3802	62	1367	4598
2006	19736	1205	3470	1835	3046	3902	152	1468	4658
2007*	20534	1306	3570	1925	3245	4012	162	1564	4750

*@ Includes Other Countries, * Provisional, Various Issues of Tea Statistics, Tea Board, Kolkata, India, N. A. = Not Available.*

India's and Sri Lanka's share to total imports started declining from 1971 to 1985. In the case of India, it was 15.78 per cent in 1971, 9.21 per cent in 1984 and 4.84 per cent in 1985 compared to Sri Lanka's share of 28.93 per cent, 16.69 per cent and 19.61 percent respectively. The share of India and Indonesia started declining from 1986 to 2007. East Africa's share was improving during the said period. The UK.'s share was almost double, while it was more than twice in the case of China & Hong Kong. In the year 1951, India constituted 48.73 per cent of total imports, followed by Sri Lanka (37.82 per cent) and East Africa (6.80 per cent), while other countries shared the balance. The picture was different in 2007, U.K. accounted for a major share (19.74 per cent) followed by Sri Lanka (17.39 per cent) East Africa (15.80 per cent) and India (4.84 per cent). The other countries shared the balance.

Table 5.2: Country-wise Total Import of Tea into Canada during 1950 to 2007

(in Percentage)

Year	*Total Imports @*	*India*	*Sri Lanka*	*Indonesia*	*East Africa*	*U.K.*	*Japan*	*China & Hong Kong*	*Other countries*
1951	100.00	48.73	37.82	0.91	6.80	1.21	0.61	0.65	3.27
1961	100.00	34.70	39.90	0.41	5.15	14.34	0.56	0.80	4.14
1971	100.00	15.78	28.93	1.56	16.05	12.72	0.50	2.50	21.96
1975	100.00	15.16	23.88	6.57	25.52	11.39	0.39	1.22	16.37
1980	100.00	9.52	23.92	7.74	19.79	15.54	0.16	2.73	20.58
1985	100.00	4.84	16.69	7.30	12.75	22.67	0.34	5.90	26.56
1991	100.00	3.52	12.27	3.30	24.82	32.46	0.92	6.84	15.78
1997	100.00	6.20	8.95	3.94	20.37	27.47	0.98	6.18	25.89
2000	100.00	7.24	10.58	5.74	-	32.02	0.50	4.89	39.03
2003	100.00	7.09	12.63	5.94	7.29	31.69	0.60	5.60	29.16
2005	100.00	4.84	16.67	7.32	12.75	22.65	0.36	5.92	26.54
2006	100.00	6.11	17.58	9.30	15.43	19.77	0.77	7.44	23.60
2007*	100.00	6.36	17.39	9.37	15.80	19.54	0.79	7.62	23.13

@ Includes Other Countries, * Provisional

Source : Tea Statistics, Tea Board, Kolkata, India, Various Issues

Re-Exports of Tea into Canada

The U.K. and the Netherlands reexported sizeable quantities of tea to Canada. Total re-exports were about 0.17 million kgs in 951 and 3.02 million kgs in 2007. Re-exports showed an increasing trend during the period under study. During the last five years total re exports were about 4.5 million kgs a year. Out of which the U.K. re-exports were about 3.6 million kgs.and the Netherlands about 0.9 million kgs to Canada. In terms of percentage, the U.K. accounted for 80 per cent and the Netherlands about 20 per cent of total re-exports. The pattern of total tea re exports by the U.K. and the Netherlands to Canada is given in Table 5.3.

Table 5.3: Re-export of Tea to Canada during 1951 to 2006

(in thousand kgs)

Year	*Total re-exports @*	*U.K.*	*Netherlands*	*Percentage to Total*		
				U.K.	*Netherlands*	*Total*
1951	166	166	@	100.00	-	100.00
1961	2883	2883	-	100.00	-	100.00
1971	3391	3227	164	95.16	4.84	100.00
1975	4954	3219	1735	64.97	35.02	100.00
1980	3908	2995	913	76.64	23.36	100.00
1985	4600	4050	550	88.05	11.95	100.00
1990	5084	4260	824	83.79	16.21	100.00
1995	5439	4544	895	83.56	16.44	100.00
2000	4174	3065	1106	73.48	26.52	100.00
2003	5002	3861	1141	77.19	22.81	100.00
2004	4775	3951	824	82.74	17.26	100.00
2005	4200	3650	750	82.15	17.85	100.00
2006	3900	2910	990	74.62	25.38	100.00
2007*	3025	1825	1200	60.33	39.67	100.00

@ Includes Other Countries, * Provisional

Source of Tea Statistics, Tea Board, Kolkata, India, Various Issues

Exports of Black Tea from India to Canada

India exports black tea to Canada in bulk form. India's exports to Canada showed a declining trend. It was 9 million kgs in 1951 and 1.21 million kgs in 2007. Maximum quantity of tea exported to Canada was recorded in 1951 while the minimum (0.93 million kgs.) was attained in 1997. During the last five years, India exported nearly 1.40 million kgs of tea to Canada valued at Rs.12.67 crore. A statement showing exports of black tea from India to Canada is given in Table 5.4:

Table 5.4: Exports of Black Tea from India to Canada during 1951 to 2007

Year	*Quantity (thousand kgs)*	*Value (thousand Rs)*	*Unit price (Rs. per kg)*
1951	9165	449932	4.90
1961	6354	38768	6.10
1971	3815	28040	7.35
1974	3520	33376	9.48
1979	2063	30737	14.90
1980	2358	39949	16.94

1984	2407	76542	31.80
1990	1412	62735	44.43
1997	932	69778	74.87
2000	974	92728	95.20
2003	1328	120184	90.50
2004	1225	113251	92.45
2005	1420	128751	90.67
2006	1567	143224	91.40
2007*	1430	128228	89.67

* Provisional.

Source : Various Issues of Tea Statistics, Tea Board, Kolkata, India.

Exports of Value Added Teas from India in Canada

India's exports of packet teas to Canada increased from 6 thousand kgs in 1980-81 to 90 thousand kgs in 2006 -07. India also exported tea bags to Canada. Exports of tea bag started declining from 206 thousand kgs to 10 thousand kgs during 1995-96 to 2006-07. On an average, India exported 7.75 thousand kgs of tea bags a year valued at Rs. 15.50 lakh with a unit price of Rs. 172.50 per kg. Exports of instant tea to Canada showed fluctuating trend. It was highest at 55 thousand kgs valued at Rs. 35.0 lakh in 1980-81 and lowest at 10 thousand kgs valued at Rs. 26.80 lakh in 2006-07. Instant tea exported annually to Canada was 13.75 thousand kgs valued at Rs. 36.64 lakh with the unit price of Rs. 266 per kg. The details of value added items exported to Canada are presented in Table 5.5.

Table 5.5: Exports of Value Added Teas in Canada during 1980-81 to 2006-07

Year	*Exports of Packet Tea*			*Tea Bags*			*Instant Tea*		
	Qty. thousand kgs.	*Value thousand Rs.*	*Unit value Rs. per kg.*	*Qty. thousand kgs.*	*Value thousand Rs.*	*Unit value Rs. per kg.*	*Qty. thousand kgs.*	*Value thousand Rs.*	*Unit value Rs. per kg.*
1980-81	6	206	34	206	14794	74	55	3486	64
1985-86	10	325	33	685	53436	78	45	2970	66
1990-91	6	468	47	180	15463	86	45	4050	90
1995-96	9	648	72	205	38700	140	50	10050	201
2000-01	86	11286	131	15	2400	160	40	9600	240
2003-04	75	11700	156	10	1650	165	10	2600	260

2004-05	80	12800	160	5	850	170	15	3975	265
2005-06	85	13685	161	6	1050	175	20	5400	270
2006-07	90	14850	165	10	1800	180	10	2680	268

* *Provisional, Source: Tea Statistics, Tea Board,* Kolkata, India, Various Issues.

Taxes & Duties

There is no import duty on tea in Canada. There are also no other tariff or non tariff barriers on tea.

Tea Board, India—Promotional Measures

The Tea Board has an office in New York, with a director of Tea Promotion as its head. This office has been functioning since the last 45 years and has jurisdiction over the USA, Canada, Latin American Countries and the West Indies. The main function of this office is to take promotional measures for popularizing Indian tea for this purpose. The Board's office at New York used to participate in various fairs and exhibitions in the USA. The fairs and exhibitions cover Internal Fancy Food & Confection Show, Washington DC; Oklahoma State Fair; Indian week Sanjun, Puret Rico & Ann Arbor, Michigan; and International Fancy Food and Confection Show, Los Angeles. Store demonstrations are organized regularly in several departmental stores. Tea sampling and services are undertaken on important occasions like Indian Food Festival, U.N. Women's Guild Church Bazar, Indian Dance Programme of Asia Society, Indian Independence Day, Indian Republic Day, and Reception of Asia Society on a regular basis.

India is a member of the Tea Council of Canada along with Sri Lanka, Indonesia and East African countries as well as the local trade. The promotional activities of the Tea Council are concentrated on media publicity through TV commercials. Tea Council of Canada launches successful programme targeted at the Consumer as well as Food Service Industry. While consumer programmes were mainly through food editor release seasonal mailing, the educational programme was through production and distribution of teachers guide and poster of schools. The food service or tea grading programme launched by Canadian Tea Council is not only successfully implemented but has own appreciation from the members of

Tea Council as well as the media. As regards 'Unilateral Promotion', a joint promotion scheme with a Canadian Firm namely Messrs Nabob Foods Inc., Vancouver, Canada, for promotion of Indian tea is in operation. The scheme relates to the promotion of a premier Indian blend with 60 per cent Indian tea packed in bags. The Tea Board's share of expenditure for promoting Indian Tea is of the order of $30,765 through Radio programme.

Conclusions

India is facing a problem to compete with Sri Lanka and East Africa. To over come the situation both internal and external climate of the industry are required to be more suitable. For growth of such commodity, India may go for further value addition of tea. More stress may be given for exports of instant tea and tea bags to Canada.

6

Exports of Indian Tea in South American Countries

South American Countries—An Overview

India is the leading exporter of tea in the World and at present, she is exporting around 200 million kgs of tea. Major markets of Indian teas are West Europe, East Europe, America, West Asia and North Africa, Asia other than West, Africa other than North as well as Australia and Oceania. Among these countries, West & East Europe as well as West Asia and North Africa constitute major importers of Indian teas. Many discussions been made regarding export possibility of Indian tea in those markets, but there has been hardly any endeavour to study the tea market situation of South American countries. Attempt has been made to outline the tea marketing possibilities and potentials in South American countries. South America is predominantly a coffee growing region. Besides Brazil and Columbia, which accounts for 50 per cent of World's total production of coffee, the other leading coffee producing countries in this region are Mexico, Guatemala, Salvador, Equador, Peru, Honduras, Costaria, Dominican Republic, and others. Naturally, coffee is the predominant beverage in the South American countries. Tea is occupying a secondary position. Argentina, Brazil and Peru are the three important teas to producing countries in South America, of which Argentina is the largest producer. These three countries together produce about 80 million kgs, which accounts for about 5 per cent of the total World's production of tea a year. Out of 80 million kgs, Argentina alone constitutes 64 million kgs or 80 per cent of South American production. South American countries are exporters of tea. Out of 80 million kgs about 65 million kgs are exported mainly to neighbouring countries. They also import 20 million kgs for internal consumption. Therefore, the total consumption of tea in this region is about 35 million kgs. Considering the vast area covered under this region, the total market for tea is comparatively small.

Chile

The only importer of tea for consumption in the entire South America is Chile. She imports about 35 million kgs of tea for consumption, most of which come from Argentina. Other suppliers are Sri Lanka, Brazil and India. Chile is the largest tea consuming country in South American region accounting for about 15 million kgs The other important consuming countries are Bolivia (0.4 million kgs) and Uruguay (0.7 million kgs). Most of the countries in the South American region are members of LAFTA and preferential treatment is given to the member countries for trade amongst themselves. As far as tea is concerned the import tariff is an inhabiting factor for expanding export from India, e.g. in Chile importers were required to make their deposits, which were as high as 100 per cent of CIF value. Moreover, Chile used to levy an import duty of 30 per cent ad valorem on imports from countries other than those who are members of LAFTA. Although these levies are no longer in force now, there still exists a 10 per cent duty on imports from non-LAFTA countries. Similarly, in the Caribean countries preferential treatment is given for members of the CARIFTA. In some of the CARIFTA they set up countries packaging factories and as a result there is a total ban on products like packet tea and tea bags.

Non-availability of suitable shipping facilities on a regular basis is also a deterrent factor. In addition, the distance from India, high freight rates and longer voyage time also stand on the way in offering competitive quotation. As per information collected from Shipping Corporation of India and Scindias, there have been some improvements in providing shipping services to this region. Scindias stated the following services are currently being provided for South American ports:

Every month one selling covered by US Atlantic vessels of Scindias.

1.	a) Mexican Port	: Veracruz
	b) Direct Caribbean Port	: Kingston (Jamaica)
	c) Through Caribbean Ports with	: Port of Spain (Trinidad), Plysouth (Monteserat),
transshipment at Kingston		: St. Johns (Antigua), Bassetere (St Kitts), Georgetown (Guana or Damerera), St. Georges (Greneda), Paramaribo (Surinam), Roseau (Dominica), Bridgetown (St. Vincent), Castries (St. Lucia).
d) Latin America Port with		: Port au Prince (Haiti) Puerto Cortez (Honduras) Curacao
Transshipment at Kingston		(Willemested)

2. Kolkata per Argentina with transshipment: On Scindia's US Pacific loaders, at Singapore Alternate month between Scindia per S.C.I

It is understood that some private lines like Everette and Bank Line operate between India Chile and other destinations. These services are depending on availability of cargo. The consignments are also accepted more than one transshipment at Singapore and Hongkong. The country wise position is reviewed briefly below:

Argentina—Area, Production, Yield and Exports of Tea

As stated earlier, Argentina produces about 61 million kgs of tea annually and exports about an equal quantum of tea (54 million kgs). The quantity retained for domestic consumption is very negligible. Table 6.1 shows the position.

Table 6.1: Production and Export of Tea in Argentina during 1971 to 2007

Year	*Area hectares*	*Production (million kgs)*	*Yield (kgs/ hectare)*	*Export (million kgs)*	*Consumption (million kgs.)*	*Percentage of export to production*
1971	33750	27	800	22	5	81.48
1974	40000	34	850	24	10	70.59
1977	36361	30	825	26	4	86.67
1981	34115	29	850	25	4	86.20
1984	37222	36	970	34	0	94.40
1985	37115	37	940	32	1	97.00
1986	40640	39	935	31	2	93.94
1989	41278	40	969	39	2	97.50
1992	41406	42	1042	36	3	85.70
1995	41500	53	1277	51	3	96.20
1998	39000	55	1410	52	4	94.50
2002	36000	62	1722	54	3	87.10
2005	36200	63	1740	55	3	87.30
2006	36300	63	1735	55	4	87.30
2007*	36340	64	1761	56	5	87.50

* Provisional.

Source : Tea Statistics, Various Issues, Tea Board, Kolkata, India.

Mexico

Mexico is a coffee producing and exporting country. The tea import for consumption in Mexico is quite insignificant. Annual average imports are slightly more than 100 thousand kgs. The import requirements in Mexico are presumably met by way of re-exports from the UK, Exports from India are virtually insignificant. It was, however, in the order of 1 thousand kgs only. Since the size of the market is very small, there is hardly any scope for increasing exports of tea from India to this country.

Guyana

Guyana is a very small market for tea because of its small population, which is less than 3 million. Figures of total tea imports of Guyana are not available. Purchases from India are irregular and no exports have been recorded in some of the years. However, there has been a rise in exports from 25 thousand kgs in 1973 to 48 thousand kgs in 1976 and 100 thousand kgs in 1986. It further increased from 300 thousand kgs in 2000 and 350 thousand kgs in 2006. Guyana also purchases, on an average, 100 thousand kgs annually in the form of re- exports. Guyana is a coffee producing and exporting country and tea occupies only a secondary position in the beverage market. India used to supply some quantities of packet teas and tea bags to Guyana, but since 1976- 77, these supplies were tapered off, presumably because of the setting up of packaging unit in Guyana. It was also understood that the Guyana imposed a ban on the import of packet tea and tea bags from outside. Another inhibiting factor for promoting the export of Indian tea to this market was the Guyana was a member of CRAFTA and the trade policy of this country provided preferential treatment to import from CARIFTA members, At present, Govt. is exploring the possibility of exporting value added tea mainly packet tea from the producers country. Since 1990 onwards the exports of packet tea is negligible. In 2006, however, India exports small quantity of packet tea to this country.

Venezuela

No statistics for import of tea are available. Presumably, tea consumption is insignificant. Venezuela is a coffee producing and exporting country. India, however, exports a negligible quantity of tea to Venezuela. This country also imports tea from the U.K. It is estimated that about 150 thousand kgs of tea per annum are purchased from the U.K. It was ascertained the Venezuela has a demand for a specific type of tea viz., McCormic tea bags that is said to be a popular brand and this is being imported from the U.K. In the initial stage, India attempted to supply this sort of tea bags and at present, it is being exported occasionally. To explore the possibility of this type of tea market, a dialogue between Indian and Venezuela is required to be strengthened. This could be pursued provided the importer is impressed upon to buy tea bags and tea in loose and packet forms.

Trinidad and Tobago

This country is a producer and exporter of coffee. The total import of tea to this country is estimated at about 600 thousand kgs annually. India exports less than 100 thousand kgs. and the U.K. in the form of re-exports is meeting the balance quantum of tea. There are certain leading companies like TM & MC, etc. who are supplying teas in small quantities to Trinidad and Tobago on a regular basis. It was understood that sometime in two decades back, the Trinidad Government was interested to purchase substantial quantities of tea on Government-to-Government basis and this was passed to Public Sector Undertaking, Tea Trading Corporation of India (TTCI). With the passage of time, the TTCI has been offering teas to Trinidad and Tobago.

Brazil—Area, Production, Yield and Exports of Tea

Brazil is one of the largest producers of coffee in the World. It is also tea producing and exporting country. On an average, Brazil produces about 9 million kgs of tea a year and also exports more than 7 million kgs of tea. The net consumption is about 2 million kgs. Table 6.2 shows the figures of area, production, yield, quantity retained for consumption and exports of tea in Brazil.

Table 6.2: Area, Production, yield and Export of Tea in Brazil during 1971 to 2007

Year	*Area (hectares)*	*Production (thousand kgs)*	*Yield (kgs / hectare)*	*Export (thousand kgs)*	*Consumption (thousand kgs)*	*Percentage of export to production*
1971	4675	6547	1400	5530	1017	84.47
1974	4624	6544	1415	5211	1233	79.63
1977	4747	6741	1420	5191	2550	77.01
1980	5138	8000	1557	7888	1919	98.60
1981	4930	8000	1625	7900	1872	98.75
1982	5120	8506	1650	8200	2303	96.41
1983	5212	8600	1690	7798	3082	90.67
1984	5214	8550	1640	8305	1395	97.13
1985	5454	9000	1650	8807	2026	97.85

1986	5506	9650	1752	8945	1463	92.78
1987	5470	9600	1755	9000	1500	93.75
1989	5000	10000	2000	9000	1800	90.00
1992	5500	9500	1727	7500	2000	78.94
1995	5500	9500	1727	4000	2400	42.11
1998	5500	7500	1363	4200	2600	56.00
2002	5500	7200	1310	4500	3000	62.50
2005	5000	8000	1600	5000	35000	62.50
2006	5050	8500	1683	5500	3600	64.70
2007*	5050	9000	1780	6000	3700	66.66

*Estimated.

Source : Tea Statistics, Various Issues, Tea Board, Kolkata, India.

Peru and Columbia

Peru is another coffee producing country in the South American region. Peru is also a tea producing country, harvesting about 3 million kgs a year. Almost the entire quantity is consumed within the country itself. The quantity of tea imported for consumption is about 12 thousand kgs annually, which is said to be very negligible. During the period from 1974 to 2006, the average annual quantum of production was about 3 million kgs, while imports for consumption for the said period were 15 thousand kgs. There has not been any change of this trend. Columbia is another coffee producing and exporting country in the South American region. Columbia imports very negligible quantity of tea.

Conclusion

The market situations for tea in South America countries reveal the fact that there is comparatively a small market for marketing of tea. The analysis, however, suggests that there are certain possibilities for promoting Indian teas in the countries like Chile, Bolivia, Uruguay, Venezuela and Trinidad & Tobago. To explore these possibilities, a comprehensive study is again to be undertaken to locate potential areas for Indian teas. It is expected that the Tea Board may conduct surveys in some of these countries through its Nu York Office. Meanwhile, it would be helpful if Indian Embassies in all these countries were requested to cary out detailed study on the prospects of Indian teas in these markets and keep the Tea Board informed. The quantity of teas entering into the South American market is obviously of Argentinean or Brazilian origin, which could hardly be quality teas. Apparently there are some scopes for quality teas of Indian origin, which can cater to the needs of high income bracket people. The entry of our quality teas could obviously be in the form of packets and bags. Better shipping facilities could perhaps generate more interest amongst the Indian exporters to enter into the South American markets.

7

Export Possibility of Indian Tea in the Arab Republic of Egypt (ARE)

Although India is the largest producer and exporter of tea in world market, its share has been declining day by day in view of the various countries' entry into the global market. Keeping this in view, an attempt has been made to examine the export possibility of Indian tea in the Arab Republic of Egypt (ARE). Thus, focus is being concentrated on the geographical location of the ARE, its economic feature, its pattern of trade with India, its nature of tea imports, exports of tea and value added tea from India, type of taxes, duties etc. on tea and conclusions.

Location and Economy

The ARE occupies the north-eastern corner of Africa with an extension across the Gulf of Suez into the Sinai region which is usually regarded as lying in Asia. It is bounded on the North by Mediterranean sea, on the North-East by Israel, on the East by Red Sea, on the South by the Sudan and on the West by Libya. Cairo is the Capital and Alexandria, Tanter, Damietta, Assout and Aswan are other important cities. Alexandria, Port Said and Safaga are the major harbours. The A R E's population is said to be projected at 62 million. Arabic is the official language, but English and French are also spoken. Major religions are Islam and Christianity. National Income in million US dollar was estimated at 39760 in 2006 and per capita income was US dollar 950. The unit of currency is Egyptian pound.

In local currency 1 Egyptian pound = 100 plasters = 1000 milliems. More than 90 per cent of the country is desert. Agriculture is the largest single sector of the economy contributing over 25 per cent of the National Product. Cotton is the largest cash crop and main item of export. It accounts for more than 60 per cent of foreign exchange earnings. The ARE is rich in minerals and also has some crude petroleumillion.

Arab's Trade with India during 1969-70 to 2005-06

Major commodities of imports from India are jute manufactures, machinery, tea, etc. Major commodities of exports from the ARE to India are raw cotton, rice and rock phosphate. The trade balance of the last few years is shown in Table 7.1.

Table 7.1: Balance of Trade between India and ARE during 1969-70 to 2005-6

(in million Rs)

Year	*Imports to India*	*Exports from India*	*Balance of Trade with India*
1969-70	346.3	216.9	- 129.40
1970-71	563.7	398.4	- 165.30
1971-72	230.5	332.2	+ 101.70
1972-73	317.1	288.7	- 28.40
1973-74	148.2	259.0	+ 110.780
1975-76		—— Negligible ——	
1979-80	2087.96	1307.63	- 780.33
1980-81	3499.67	1523.08	- 1976.88
1981-82	4705.01	2106.98	- 2598.03
1982-83	5308.25	2807.23	- 2501.02
1983-84	6205.29	3802.15	- 2403.14
1990-91	6705.45	5020.24	- 1685.20
1995-00	7005.15	5845.17	- 1159.98
2000-01	7405.25	6275.15	- 1130.10
2001-02	7506.75	6406.75	- 1100.00
2002-03	7606.25	6806.25	- 800.00
2003-04	7705.75	7026.75	- 679.00
2004-05	7890.45	7245.25	- 564.20
2005-06	7950.25	7545.75	- 404.50

Source: Director General of Intelligence and Statistics, Govt of India.

Pattern of Tea Import into A.R.E.

The import pattern of tea into the ARE may be divided into six phases. *The first phase* relates to 1951 to 1961, *the second phase* covers 1962 to 1970, the *third phase* includes 1971 to 1980, *fourth phase refers to* 1981 to 1990, *fifth phase* incorporates 1991 to 2000, and the *sixth phase* incorporates 2001 to 2007. During the first phase, total imports of tea increased from 16 million kgs to 21 million kgs representing an improvement of 33 per cent over the 11-year period. In the second phase, there was only an increase of total imports by 3 million kgs from 27 million kgs in 1962 to 30 million kgs in 1970. The trend is, however, upward in *the third phase*. It was 15 million kgs in 1971 and 54 million kgs in 1980. During the *fourth phase*, tea imports sharply enhanced from 53 million kgs in 1981 to 69 million kgs in 1990. In the fifth phase i.e. from 1991 to 2000 onwards, it was 69 million kgs and 63 million kgs. The tea import pattern is brought out in Table 7.2.

Table 7.2: Imports of Tea into the A.R.E. during 1951 to 2007

(in thousand kgs)

Year	*Imports from*						
	India	*Sri Lanka*	*Indonesia*	*China*	*Kenya*	*Other Countries*	*Total*
1951	1884	10730	3104	29	–	317	16084
1961	13794	1149	$	6449	–	5	21397
1962	18670	1388	–	6300	–	293	26651
1963	15273	2336	–	5676	–	4	23289
1964	17069	2927	–	6236	–	11	26243
1965	17785	3591	–	7299	–	54	28729
1966	19502	317	–	8773	–	63	28655
1967	19909	5407	–	6103	–	665	32084
1968	7129	8074	–	7168	–	950	23321
1969	16012	8514	–	-	–	374	24900
1970	17778	9385	–	334	–	2346	29843
1971	6751	8150	–	100	–	2359	15002
1972	5841	3947	–	1640	–	2358	13786
1973	4264	2220	–	2648	–	680	9802
1974	6775	4700	–	939	–	1997	14411
1975	12500	13700	–	2100	400	11800	40500

1979	15900	14800	6900	2000	7400	6900	53900
1980	17200	16400	8700	2000	2900	7200	54400
1981	18700	17400	10800	–	2600	3500	53000
1982	13600	24200	8400	1400	4600	5100	57300
1983	14900	31000	2100	1600	7100	9000	65700
1984	17200	32400	10100	1500	8700	5800	75700
1985	16300	32200	9100	1500	7500	8250	74850
1990	7500	19000	15590	305	7250	4300	70120
1991	7800	20400	15000	300	21000	4400	68900
1997	5633	4581	2499	26	52993	4754	77890
2000	475	2440	342	299	56623	1035	63355
2001	128	2040	312	114	52268	1141	56403
2002	450	2550	400	150	53250	1714	58514
2003	470	2610	500	200	54650	1840	60270
2004	400	2750	600	300	55450	1950	61450
2005	423	2800	700	400	56750	2050	62700
2006	420	2900	800	500	54650	2500	61770
2007*	1450	2700	1200	800	53000	3500	61650
Average	12298	11505	4533	2415	30657	2875	42953

Note : $ Indicates below 500 kgs, * Provisional

Source : Tea Statistics, various issues, Tea Board, India, Kolkata.

India is, however, the major supplier of tea to the ARE. The supplies of tea from India, on an average, remained at 12 million kgs per year. The quantum of tea supplied from India varied from 4 million kgs to 20 million kgs with the exception of 1951 and 2000 to 2007. Next to India, Sri Lanka supplied, on an average, 11 million kgs annually. During the last four years, Sri Lanka's supply of tea to the ARE was more than that of India's supply. Indonesia started supplying tea to that country virtually from 1980. Her average supply was 7 million kgs per annum. China was also supplying tea to the A R E. Her supply was to the level of 3 million kgs. Kenya started supplying tea from 1975. The average quantum of supply per year was to the level of 3 million kgs. "other countries" which include mainly Bangladesh, UK, Netherlands, Turkey also supplied tea and they, on an average, constitute 5 million kgs annually.

India's share to total imports varied widely during the period from 1951-2007. It was maximum at 70.06 per cent in 1962 and minimum at 0.67 per cent in 2006. Sri Lanka's share has been improving appreciably except a few intervening years. The share of tea imports of various countries into the ARE is given in Table 7.3.

Table 7.3: Imports of Tea to the A.R.E. during 1951 to 2006

(in percentage)

Year	*Imports from*						
	India	*Sri Lanka*	*Indonesia*	*China*	*Kenya*	*Other Countries*	*Total*
1951	11.71	66.71	19.29	0.19	–	2.10	100.00
1961	64.47	5.37	–	30.14	–	0.02	100.00
1962	70.06	5.21	–	23.64	–	1.09	100.00
1963	65.58	10.03	–	24.31	–	0.02	100.00
1964	65.04	11.15	–	23.76	–	0.05	100.00
1965	61.91	12.50	–	25.41	–	0.18	100.00
1966	68.06	1.11	–	30.62	–	0.21	100.00
1967	62.05	116.85	–	19.02	–	2.08	100.00
1968	30.57	34.62	–	34.74	–	4.07	100.00
1969	64.31	34.19	–	–	–	1.50	100.00
1970	59.57	31.45	–	1.12	–	7.86	100.00
1971	45.00	54.33	–	0.67	–	–	100.00
1972	42.37	28.63	–	11.90	–	17.10	100.00
1974	47.01	32.61	–	6.52	13.85	0.01	100.00
1975	30.85	33.85	–	5.19	0.99	29.12	100.00
1980	31.62	30.14	15.99	3.67	5.34	13.24	100.00
1981	35.28	32.83	20.37	-	4.90	6.62	100.00
1982	23.74	42.23	14.66	2.44	8.03	8.90	100.00
1983	22.68	47.18	3.20	2.43	10.81	13.70	100.00
1984	22.72	42.80	13.34	1.98	11.49	7.67	100.00
1985	21.78	43.02	12.16	2.00	10.02	11.02	100.00
1991	11.32	29.61	21.78	0.43	30.48	6.38	100.00
1997	7.24	15.40	3.20	Neg.	68.05	6.11	100.00
2000	0.20	7.23	0.53	0.47	89.37	2.22	100.00
2003	0.77	4.33	0.82	0.33	90.67	3.08	100.00
2006	0.67	4.69	1.30	0.80	88.45	4.09	100.00
2007	2.30	4.30	1.91	0.80	84.59	6.10	100.00
Wt. Av.	31.26	25.32	16.90	7.80	11.76	6.96	100.00

Source : Tea Statistics, various issues, Tea Board, India, Kolkata.

India's share in total tea imports into the ARE varied between 60 and 70 per cent during the period under reference except 1951 and 1968. The share, thereafter, started declining. This was because of increase in the share of Sri Lanka during the same period. It was learnt that the ARE placed orders to Kenya. This was the first time the ARE purchased tea from Kenya. Besides, the ARE entered into trade agreement with China. The ARE negotiated for import of large quantities of tea from Indonesia also. This is the first time Indonesia entered into this market.

Tea Exports from India to A.R.E. during 1951-52 to 2006-07

Exports of tea from India to the ARE exhibited a fluctuating trend. During the period between 1951-52 and 19061-62, exports increased substantially from 2 million kgs to 17 million kgs over the two points of time. In 1971-72 it, however, dropped to 11 million kgs which maintained upto kgs in 1975-76. It again rose to 21 million kgs in 1980-81. During the last three years, the exports of tea from India to the A. R. E declined drastically. It ranged from 0.99 million kgs to 1.04 million kgs. On an average, India exported 15 million kgs of tea valued at Rs.34 crore annually. The details are brought out in Table 7.4.

Table 7.4: Tea Exports from India to the A.R.E. during 1951 to 2006-07

Year	*Quantity (thousand kgs)*	*Value (thousand Rs.)*	*Unit Value (Rs/kg)*
1951-52	1622	7104	4.39
1961-62	16996	85154	5.01
1971-72	11196	72296	6.45
1975-76	11301	110718	9.80
1980-81	21071	287064	13.62
1981-82	14834	210320	14.18
1990-91	7777	319950	41.15
1997-98	5742	275615	48.00
2000-01	1040	48148	46.30
2003-04	850	42075	49.50
2004-05	990	496485	50.15
2005-06	1100	59675	54.25
2006-07	1420	79023	55.65

Exports of Green Tea from India

Besides, green teas were also exported from India to the A.R.E. Data available from the "Tea Statistics", Tea Board revealed that India could export green tea to the A.R.E. only in the year 1979-80 and 1980-81 to the tune of 21 thousand kgs valued at Rs.4 lakh and 61 thousand kgs at Rs.11 lakh, respectively. Exports pf green tea was very negligible during 1990-91 and

2000-01. During 2006-07, about 35 thousand kgs of green tea worth Rs. 30.00 lakh was exported.

Exports of Value Added Teas from India

India did not export any instant tea to the A.R.E. Tea bags and packet teas are exported from India to the A.R.E. During the last seven years exports of tea bags increased from 6 million kgs in 2000-01 to 1.40 million kgs in 2006-07. On an average, India exported 18 million kgs valued at Rs.103 crore. Export statistics further revealed that there was a fluctuating trend. It was less than one million kgs in 2005-06 and maximum at 40 million kgs in 1985-86. Exports of packet tea more or less remained static at 4 million kgs over the period from 1985-86 to 2006-07. On an average, it was 2 million kgs valued at Rs.5 crore annually. Details are exhibited in Table 7.5.

Table 7.5: Export of Value Added Teas from India during 1979-80 to 2006-07

(Qty. in thousand kgs and Value in thousand Rs.)

Year	*Tea Bags*			*Packet Tea*			*Total Value Added Teas*		
	Qty.	*Value*	*Unit Price (Rs./kg)*	*Qty.*	*Value*	*Unit Value (Rs./kg)*	*Qty.*	*Value*	*Unit Value (Rs./kg)*
1979-80	22065	784948	35.57	1243	24563	19.76	23309	809511	34.73
1980-81	12062	420320	34.85	1472	31779	18.44	13785	452099	35.49
1981-82	22752	863505	37.95	1437	24835	17.30	24189	888358	36.73
1982-83	8464	406411	49.02	1346	28242	20.98	9810	434653	44.31
1983-84	3484	221627	63.63	2211	58366	26.40	5695	279993	49.16
1984-85	18978	1315206	69.31	3140	106111	33.79	22118	1421317	64.26
1985-86	39975	3201003	80.08	3098	100498	32.44	43073	3301501	76.71
1990-91	10425	859541	82.45	3242	202400	62.45	42850	1061941	67.32
2000-01	6000	505080	84.18	3300	211800	64.18	9300	716880	77.08
2005-06	900	80000	88.88	3545	231878	65.41	4445	311878	70.16
2006-07	1450	1297033	89.45	3742	255051	68.15	5192	384750	74.12

Taxes, Duties & Marketing

The State Trading Company is handling the import, wholesale trading and packing of tea wholly. The import duty at present levied by the Government of the A.R.E. on import of tea is as follows:

For all kinds of tea other than instant tea: 50 per cent Ad Valorem with a minimum of 200 millerries per kg net

Duty on tea extract, essence or concentrates: 60 per cent Ad Valorem

Additional duties and taxes:

1. Statistical Duty	1 per cent of c.i.f. value
2. Consolidation Tax	10 per cent of c.i.f. value
3. Municipal Duty	collected according to kind of goods
4. Porterage Duty	collected according to kind of goods
5. Marine Duty	collected on goods imported through Marine Ports (0.002 per cent of c.i.f. value)
6. State Tax	Egyptian pound 1.17 per kg on packeted, bulk and instant teas

Regulations

The private sector is permitted to import pre-packed teas. Bulk tea imports by the private sector to be packed by the State Packing Organisation or any other licenced packer in the Free Trade Zones of Egypt. In the case of private sector teas packed by the State packer, the retail prices, gram weight of tea to be clearly stated on the pack.

All imported pre-packed teas should the gram weight, name of the importer, shipper and grade of tea, clearly printed on the label.

Conclusion

Inspite of the fact that there are certain taxes and duties levied by the Government of the A.R.E on imports of tea, the total imports of tea has been increasing day by day. India may explore the possibility of exporting more teas to the A.R.E. and should compete with teas supplied by Sri Lanka. For this, certain strategies between India and the A.R.E. are to be evolved so that Indian teas are available in large quantities in the A.R.E.

8

Export Possibility of Indian Tea in Syria

Introduction

The Syrian Arab Republic is one of the countries of Asia. It lies in the eastern shore of the Mediterranean Sea with Turkey to the north, Iraq to the east and Jordan to the South Lebanon and Israel are to the south and west. The Capital is Damascus. The chief ports are Banias and Latakia. The population is estimated at 26 million in 2006. National Income in million US @ was estimated at 8950 and per capita income was US @ 657. The unit of currency is the Syrian Pound.

Economy

More than half of the working population is engaged in agriculture, forestry and fishing. Wheat and cotton are the chief crops, which are also exported. Oil was discovered in northeast and oil exports began in 1968. The Iraq Petroleum Company's Oil pipeline from Iraq crosses Syria to Banias. The Arab American Oil Company Pipe Line from Saudi Arabia crosses Syria to Sidon in Lebanon. Syria earned a substantial income from exports of oil. Besides, Syria is a tourist spot. The town Bazaars and antiquities of Damascus and Palmyra are tourist's attractions.

Syria's Trade with India

The major commodities imported from India to Syria are jute manufactures, iron and steel, machinery and transport equipments etc. The exports from Syria to India are negligible.

The growth of trade between India and Syria is given in Table 8.1.

Table 8.1: Balance of Trade between India and Syria during 1969-70 to 2005-06

(in million Rs.)

Year	*Imports to India*	*Exports from India*	*Balance of trade with India*
1969-70	24.2	Negl.	-24.2
1970-71	19.8	Negl.	-19.8
1971-72	17.8	Negl.	-17.8
1972-73	26.4	Negl.	-26.4
1973-74	25.4	Negl.	-25.4
1975-76	19.87	0.01	-19.86
1978-79	22.75	0.01	-21.74
1980-81	9.15	Negl.	-9.15
1981-82	12.82	0.07	-12.75
1991-92	24.15	0.85	-23.30
2001-02	34.25	1.52	-32.73
2003-04	33.15	1.62	-31.53
2004-05	34.65	1.75	-32.90
2005-06	36.50	2.45	-34.05

Source: Director General of Intelligence and Statistics, Govt. of India.

It would be seen from the table that exports from Syria to India was negligible during the period from 1969-70 to 1973-74. Very small quantities of exports to India however, started from 1975-76 and onwards. It was Rs. 2.45 million in 2006, while imports from India were Rs. 36.50 million, showing a favorable balance of trade with India.

Tea Imports for Consumption in Syria

The Syrian Arab Republic has a centrally managed economy and almost all manufacturing companies and importers of basic food- stuff and commodities are state controlled. The principal hot beverage consumed in the Syrian Arab Republic is tea. Per capita consumption of tea is 1.24 kgs compared to 0.4 kgs for coffee. While carbonated and soft drinks are also consumed in the urban areas, milk based drinks are also available in most retail outlets in which tea is sold. However, their importance, both in terms of volume, and value, is reported to be very limited. The imports of tea into Syrian Arab Republic have been very erratic in the recent past. During

Table 8.2
Imports of Tea into Syria from various Countries during 1970 to 2006

(Qty. in thousand kgs.)

Country/ Year	*1970*	*1972*	*1975*	*1977*	*1979*	*1981*	*1983*	*1985*	*1990*	*1995*	*2000*	*2001*	*2002*	*2003*	*2004*	*2005*	*2006*
India	–	0	404	91	549	835	–	758	800	1000	1200	1210	1270	1315	1450	1500	1500
Sri Lanka	2360	972	2241	4299	7061	8325	10521	14251	16850	18500	18000	18500	19000	19500	20000	20500	21200
China	538	1400	241	344	–	248	348	402	750	1095	1250	1020	1050	1230	1200	1175	1100
Indonesia	–	61	6	2	–	4	3	5	6	7	9	1020	15	12	13	10	11
Kenya	–	–	–	–	350	450	652	749	980	1050	1100	1290	1250	1350	1360	1400	1410
Malaysia	–	–	–	–	2538	3526	4125	4729	5800	6570	7000	7050	7500	8000	8500	9000	9400
Others	–	–	124	1	26	32	42	53	73	80	90	1001	700	300	400	450	400
Total	7312	2435	3016	4737	10524	13430	19331	24055	25259	26502	28748	27971	30225	31207	32923	34035	35021

Source : *Various Issues of Tea Statistics*, Tea Board, Kolkata, India and *The Planters' Chronicle*.

the last five years, imports ranged from a low over just 2 million kgs in 1972 to a high of 35 million kgs in 2006. Presently the state organization handling imports of tea—TAFCO—imports about 3 million kgs a month with a 50 per cent increase in the monthly order in the months immediately before Ramzan Id. While the current levels of imports through official channels is in the region of 13 million kgs per annum, another 22 thousand kgs per year is estimated to reach the market through personal imports from neighbouring countries.

The principal supplier of tea to the Syrian Arab Republic is Sri Lanka, followed by India, China and Indonesia, Malaysia and Kenya entered into the market in a big way since 1978 and 1979 respectively. Details of imports of tea into the Syrian Arab Republic are given in the Table 8.2.

Total imports of tea to Syrian Arab Republic varied between 7 million kgs and 35 million kgs during the period from 1970 to 2006. Total imports were maximum at 35 million kgs in 2006 and minimum at 2 million kgs 1972. Sri Lanka accounted for major share in total imports. It was 2 million kgs in 1970 and 21 million kgs in 2006. Indonesia, Malaysia and Kenya as a whole contributed less than 1 million kgs during the period. China also constituted a little more than 1 million kgs except the year 1972.

Exports of Tea from India to Syria

The quantum of tea exports from India to Syrian Arab Republic was very fluctuated during 1979-80 to 2005-06. It varied between 205 thousand kgs and 105 million kgs during the said period. Small quantum of teas [less than 500 kgs] was also exported in 1985-86. Quantum of tea exports and value realized are shown in Table 8.3.

Table 8.3: Exports and Value of Teas from India to Syria during 1979-80 to 2005-06

(Qty. in thousand kgs and value in thousand Rs.)

Year	*Quantity*	*Value*	*Unit value (Rs/kg)*
1979-80	205	2918	14.23
1980-81	96	2020	21.04
1981-82	99	2495	25.21

1982-83	109	2686	24.65
1983-84	400	8968	22.42
1985-86	0	8	0
1990-91	80	3612	45.15
1995-00	105	4315	60.15
2000-01	125	8768	70.75
2003-04	100	7515	75.15
2004-05	95	7243	76.25
2005-06	105	8174	77.50

Source: Various Issues of Tea Statistics, Tea Board, Kolkata.

NB : 'O' Indicates less than 500 kgs.

India exported tea bags to the level of 10 thousand kgs valued at Rs.4.51 lakhs in 1979-80. Thereafter there were no exports of tea bags upto 1984-85. A small quantum of tea bags to region of only 58 kgs valued at Rs. 8 thousand was exported in 1985-86. As regards packet tea, India managed to export about 50 thousand kgs valued at Rs. 2 million in 1979-80. It was however doubled in 1980-81 when packet tea was about 150 thousand kgs valued at Rs. 3 million. Packet tea exported in 2006 is very negligible.

Market Structure of Tea in Syria

All tea is imported by TAFCO in bulk and the preferred type of tea is long leaf orthodox tea of the FBOP type. Tea is distributed though another state organization called "The General Consumption Institution". Imports of tea by private trade are prohibited. There is only one brand of tea on the market—Picnic brand—and its current retail price is around L s 55 per kg. TAFCO takes 5 per cent of the import price as a commission and the retailer takes the margin of Ls 0.5. The standard distribution channel for tea in Syria is from TAFCO to GCI to the retailer. There are no official wholesalers operating in the market. Other subsidized food items show a similar distribution pattern. Tea is virtually a universal beverage, but no research has been carried out to identify or to define the profile of tea or consumer attitude towards tea and other beverages. According to TAFCO, tea is consumed with the first meal of the day and then regularly every two to three hours by most of the population.

Duties and Taxes

An import duty is levied @ Syrian Pounds 1.25 per kg on all teas packed and bulk. Besides, the following additional duties and taxes are levied.

a.	Import Licence Tax-		4.6 per cent advalorem
b.	Consumption Tax	-	4 per cent advalorem
c.	Statistical Tax	-	4 per cent advalorem
d.	Transit	-	Levied at a rate varying from 0.2 per cent. Advalorem to 5 per cent advalorem
e.	School Tax	-	10 per cent of consumption tax and 2 per cent custom duty.
f.	Port Tax	-	3 per cent of custom duty.
g.	Defence Tax	-	15 per cent of custom duty.

Conclusion

There is no promotion of tea in Syrian Arab Republic at present. The official policy is that the supplies to the market are strictly controlled to prevent the smuggling of subsidized tea out of the country. Since any increase in tea consumption would cost the state Ls 2-3 per kg in the subsidy scheme, there is no likelihood that tea promotion will be permitted. Thus, sufficient resource will be made available to maintain an appropriate level of imports. Tea consumption in Syria, with rise in the rate of growth of population is increasing. This has given an added advantage to India. She must ensure to capture the market by way exporting tea to Syrian Republic of Arab.

9

Indian Tea in Jordan

Introduction

Jordan is an almost landlocked country in the Middle East. Israel separating it from the Mediterranean Sea with Syria to the North, Iraq to the East and Saudi Arabia to the South, the port of Aquiba in the far south gives Jordan a narrow outlet to the Red Sea. The capital is Amman. The population of this country was estimated at 10.45 million in 2006. More than 90 per cent of the population is Muslim and the rest Christian. The official language is Arabic. The unit of currency is the Jordanian Dinnar. In local currency 1 Dinnar is equal to 1 thousand fills.

Loss of Jerusalem and the West Bank in 1967 completely ruined Jordan's economic position, which was improving rapidly. Almost half of the population lives in areas now occupied by Israel that contained the most fertile land and 25 per cent of Jordan's cultivable area. Places of interest to tourists that provided most of the country's foreign exchange earnings also been lost. Phosphates are now the country's biggest natural resource.

Trade with India

The major commodities imported from India to Jordan are tea, fruits and vegetables, jute manufactures, iron etc. Jordan's export to India is phosphate. The growth of trade between the two countries is indicated in Table 9.1.

Table 9.1: Balance of Trade between India and Jordan during 1969-70 to 2006-07

(in million Rs.)

Year	Imports to India	Exports from India	Balance of trade with India
1969-70	32.0	40.2	+8.1
1970-71	23.6	8.2	-15.5
1971-72	26.2	43.6	+17.1
1972-73	25.0	43.1	+18.1
1973-74	36.9	89.2	+52.3
1974-75	46.3	94.3	+48.0
1975-76	106.9	61.8	-45.1
1979-80	35.9	204.8	+168.9
1980-81	65.7	328.0	+262.3
1981-82	99.9	379.5	+279.6
1982-83	105.8	395.6	+289.8
1983-84	148.7	402.5	+258.8
1990-91	208.5	514.6	+306.1
1995-00	312.7	643.5	+330.8
2001-02	405.6	800.6	+395.0
2002-03	420.5	805.5	+385.0
2003-04	415.8	790.5	+374.5
2004-05	420.9	780.6	+359.7
2005-06	428.7	795.2	+366.5
2006-07	430.6	770.5	+339.9

Source: Director General of Intelligence and Statistics, Govt. of India.

Figures relating to 'Imports to India' in value terms increased from Rs. 32.0 million in 1969-70 to Rs. 430.6 million in 2006-07 while 'exports from India' in value terms enhanced from Rs. 40.2 million to Rs. 770.5 million. The latter, however, increased on the high side as compared to the former. This has resulted in a favourable balance of trade almost in all the years under review except the years 1970-71 and 1975-76. During the five years, ended 2005-06, imports and exports were Rs. 423.80 million and Rs. 788.50 million respectively per annum. Thus, there was a favourable balance of trade to the tune of Rs. 364.60 million annually.

Tea Imports to Jordan by India, Sri Lanka and Other Countries

Imports of tea into Jordan are 2 to 3 million kgs , on an average. India is the major supplier of tea followed by Sri Lanka. 'Other Countries' like Lebanon, the United Kingdom, Kuwait, etc.

Table 9.2: Imports of Tea to Jordan during 1971 to 2006

(*Qty in thousand kgs.*)

Year/ Country	*1971-72*	*1972-73*	*1973-74*	*1974-75*	*1975-76*	*1976-77*	*1977-78*	*1978-79*	*1979-80*	*1990-91*	*2000-01*	*2004-05*	*2005-06*	*2006-07*
India	2426	2147	1912	2326	1628	1511	1286	994	822	1050	1250	1150	1020	975
	(81.32)	(82.58)	(62.28)	(72.37)	(57.67)	(54.47)	(40.40)	(28.73)	(25.41)	(26.9)	(33.2)	(30.2)	(26.63)	(24.5)
Sri Lanka	462	414	400	816	983	1117	1806	228	2162	2430	2050	2160	2320	2465
	(15.49)	(15.92)	(13.02)	(25.38)	(34.82)	(40.26)	(56.75)	(65.93)	(66.81)	(62.1)	(54.3)	(56.7)	(60.6)	(61.9)
Others*	95	39	758	72	212	146	91	185	252	430	470	500	490	540
	(3.19)	(1.50)	(24.70)	(2.26)	(7.51)	(5.27)	(2.85)	(5.34)	(7.78)	(11.0)	(12.5)	(13.1)	(12.8)	(13.6)
Total	2982	2600	3070	3214	2823	2774	3183	3460	3200	3910	3770	3810	3830	3980
	(100.0)	(100.0)	(100.0)	(100.0)	(100.0)	(100.0)	(100.0)	(100.0)	(100.0)	(100.0)	(100.0)	(100.0)	(100.0)	(100.0)

Source : Various Issues of Tea Statistics, Tea Board, India.

Note – Figures in parentheses show percentage to column total.

* 'Others' include Lebanon, the United Kingdom, Kuwait, Indonesia, Hongkong, Japan, Taiwan Province (China), Federal Republic of German, Singapore, United States, China, Malaysia and Czechoslovakia.

Total tea imports to Jordan shows appreciable increase except the years 1972-73, 1975-76 to 1976-77. It varied between 2.77 million kgs to 3.98 million kgs over the years. It was 2.98 million kgs in 1971-72 and 3.98 million kgs in 2006-07 also supply meager quantities of tea to Jordan. The details of import of tea to Jordan are given in Table 5.2.

Market Structure of Tea in Jordan

While importers of tea must obtain prior approval from the Ministry of Supply, Jordan is a relatively free market for tea. No government control or restrictions other than the duties and taxes limit trade in tea. The tea trade in Jordan has two categories. *The fist comprises* established business marketing branded tea. These enterprises are well off and maintain constant supplies of their brands to wholesalers and retailers. *The second category* includes a variety of traders in other products who enter the tea market speculatively when an opportunity for profit is detected. The number of enterprises of this type active in the market varies considerably from year to year depending on the market factors operating at the time. However, they are reported to account for a very small amount of tea traded in Jordan. Major importers maintain their offices and principal distribution points in Amman, Tea must be imported through the Port of Aqua where majority of importers maintain some storage or warehousing facilities. Small importers may deal through intending agents with the sources of supply but the major importers deal direct with exporters in the country of origin.

Exports of Teas

Jordan is principally a market for OP and BOP teas and in general orthodox long leaf types are preferred to CTC blends. In this market, there are no blending facilities and as such, bulk teas sold here are pre-blended and pre-packed. All types of tea are available in the market but OP and BOP teas are mainly supplied to the retailers. There is still substantial amount of loose tea imported into Jordan and this is distributed mainly to rural areas. The details of exports of tea from India to Jordan are shown in Table 9.3.

Table 9.3: Exports of Teas from India to Jordan during 1971-72 to 2006-07

Year	*Quantity (thousand Kgs)*	*Value (thousand Rs)*	*Unit Value (Rs./Kg)*
1971-72	3014	14912	4.95
1975-76	1432	14436	10.08
1980-81	452	9446	20.89
1981-82	115	2736	23.79
1982-83	105	2351	22.39
1983-84	413	10114	24.56
1984-85	156	5377	34.46
1985-86	183	7512	41.04
1990-91	277	10500	37.90
1998-99	130	14705	78.56
2001-02	146	13089	89.57
2002-03	150	12847	85.69
2003-04	145	12833	88.46
2004-05	152	13672	89.90
2005-06	155	13973	90.14
2006-07	160	14878	93.20

Source : Tea Statistics, Various Issues, Tea Board, Kolkata, India.

Exports of Value-added (Packet and Tea Bags) Teas from India to Jordan

Exports of packet tea from India to Jordan showed a declining trend during 1971-72 to 2006-07. It was reduced from 2.25 million kgs to 0.07 million kgs. This is because of the fact that Sri Lanka supplied more teas to Jordan as compared to India. The total imports of packet tea into Jordan are about 2 lakh kgs per annum and these are about 21 thousand kgs for tea bags. The table 5.4 shows exports of packet tea and tea bags from India to Jordan.

Table 9.4: Exports of Packet Tea and Tea Bags to Jordan during 1971-72 to 2006-07

(Quantity in thous. kgs and Value in thousand Rs.)

Year	*Packet Teas*			*Tea Bags*		
	Quantity	*Value*	*Unit value (Rs./kg)*	*Quantity*	*Value*	*Unit value (Rs./kg)*
1971-72	2250	33750	15.0	-	-	-
1981-82	106	2389	22.54	9	347	38.56
1982-83	55	1308	23.78	45	1806	40.15
1983-84	324	7577	23.38	4	1625	39.65
1984-85	151	5123	33.92	-	-	-
1985-86	160	6095	38.09	24	9612	41.05
1990-91	140	13370	95.5	20	1950	97.50
1995-96	80	8120	101.5	15	1538	92.5
2000-01	50	5782	115.6	10	1176	117.6
2005-06	60	7200	120.0	8	1004	125.5
2006-07	65	8125	125.0	5	653	130.6

Source : Tea Statistics, Various Issues, Tea Board, Kolkata, India.

Distribution Channels of Tea in Jordan

The conventional distribution channel for tea in Jordan is from the merchent importer direct to large retailers. Tea is also distributed to small retailers through wholesalers. The major importers maintain close contact with the major retailers and principal wholesalers. The traders who represent the second category of importers do not close liaison with the tea trade and may face difficulty during the period of low demand.

Duties and Tariffs in Jordan

The following duties and tariffs apply to Jordan are given below :

* Tea in packages not exceeding 5 kgs: JD 0.070 per 55 g.
* Tea in package exceeding 1 kgs: JD 0.063 per kg.
* Extracts of tea essences etc. are taxed at a duty rate of 23 per cent ad valorem c.i.f. Inaddition to the above, all imports are taxed at a rate of 11 per cent ad valorem c.i.f. A fine equivalent to 20 per cent of the value is imposed on goods imported through a port other than Aquiba.

* Import licences are required for most imported goods and are delivered for a fee of 4 per cent ad valorem of c.i.f. value. These licences are valid for 12 months; a fine of one quarter percent of the value is levied on goods arriving before the licence is issued.
* An import licence carries the right to acquire the relevant foreign currency. The Ministry of supply must approve imports of tea, but such approval is normally forthcoming.

Generic and Brand Promotion of Tea in Jordan

Tea promotion is carried out in Jordan in support of brand by tea producing countries. In practice, there is an overlap between generic promotion and brand promotion.

Brand Promotion: Television is the major medium for promotion of tea in Jordan Television campaigns are usually supported with extensive below-the-line activities designed to change the favourable attitudes created by advertising into actual practice.

Generic Promotion: In the first quarter of 1981, the only visible generic promotion of tea was a brief advertising campaign organized by Tea Board, India. This consisted of 8′ x 30″ commercials at a total cost of JD 510 ($2515). This is said to be the only part of the Indian promotional efforts on the market, where the share of Indian tea has fallen markedly. Other activities of the Tea Board, India has public relations and dealer support. The Tea Board Office in Kuwait supervises such activities.

Conclusion

The preparation of consumption forecasts for tea in Jordan is complicated because of absence of any reliable data. Recorded imports do not provide an accurate measurement of market demand as they include an element of transit trade for other markets. In view of this, it is clear that consumption of tea in Jordan and the surrounding areas served through Jordan is showing a healthy upward trend. Apparent consumption increased by 35 per cent during 2002-06. The latest available data on tea imports to Jordan for 2006 suggested a marked increase in volume. Imports from the two major supplying countries, Sri Lanka and India totaled 15 million kg suggesting 70 per cent increase in consumption. Similarly, during the year 2006, the total imports were estimated at 20 million kgs.

The underlying trend in consumption in Jordanian domestic market is clearly upwards. Per capita consumption at present is 0.90 kgs (in 2006), which is still comparatively low for a market in which tea drinking is well established and where there is little and no competition from other hot beverages. The current level of consumption is only 60 per cent of the average per capita consumption level throughout the Middle East Region. A reasonable target figure for per capita tea consumption in Jordan could be 1.5 kgs representing imports of 5 million kgs. This could be achieved with appropriate generic promotion. India may now explore the possibility of supplying more tea to Jordan and thereby capture the Jordanian market.

10

Libyan Arab Republic: Scope for Indian Tea Exports

Introduction

The Libyan Arab Republic is one of the countries of North Africa. It is situated on the Mediterranean sea of North Africa and is bordered by Arab Republic of Egypt (ARE), Sudan, Chad, Niger, Algeria and Tunisia. Tripoli and Benghazi were its joint capital. A new capital has been constructed at El Beida. The major important cities are Miswrata, Homs-Kussabat Zavia, Zlitan, Derno and Tobruk. The major harbours are Tripoli, Benghazi and Port Brega. Libya's population is estimated at about 4 million. Arabic is the official language and Islam is the major religion. The National income in million US $ (dollar) was estimated at 9675 in 2006 while the per capita income was US $ (dollar) 4381. The unit of currency is the Dinar being equivalent to about Rs. 39. In local currency, Dinar is equal to 100 milliemes.

The major part of the country is covered under barren desert. As a result, the country finds it difficult to produce food crops. More than half of the food requirements are imported. Since 1955, Libya has been yielding returns on oil and at present it has become the largest crude oil producers in the world. Oil constitutes 99 per cent of Libya's total exports.

Libya's Trade with India

Major commodities of imports from India into Libya are textiles, tobacco, manufactures of metals, etc. Libya's exports to India were negligible up to 1975-76. Trade with India for the last few years is shown in Table 10.1.

Table 10.1: Balance of Trade between India and Libya Arab Republic during 1969-70 to 2006-07

(in million Rs)

Year	*Imports to India*	*Exports from India*	*Balance of trade with India*
1969-70	12.4	Negl	(-) 12.4
1972-73	35.5	Negl	(-) 35.5
1975-76	43.1	Negl	(-) 43.1
1978-79	19.1	169.9	(+) 150.8
1981-82	81.0	61.3	(-) 19.7
1983-84	46.6	72.5	(+) 25.9
1986-87	70.5	83.4	(+) 12.9
1989-90	80.4	120.4	(+) 40
1992-93	85.4	128.5	(+) 43.1
1995-96	75.5	110.3	(+) 34.8
1999-200(	76.5	120.4	(+) 43.9
2003-04	80.5	125.6	(+) 45.1
2004-05	85.6	130.5	(+) 33.3
2005-06	90.7	125.6	(+) 34.9
2006-07*	98.5	132.5	(+) 33.0

* Estimated, *Source:* Director General of Intelligence and Statistics, Govt. of India.

Data presented in the table 10.1 brought out the fact that imports from India to Libya has shown an increasing trend. In 1969-70, the import was Rs. 12.4 million that increased to Rs. 35.5 million in 1972-73, Rs. 43.1 million in 1975-76 and Rs 81.0 million in 1981-82. However, in the year 1983-84, it declined to Rs. 46.6 million, which sought up to Rs. 70.5 million in 1986-87; Rs. 80.4 million in 1989-90 and Rs 85.4 million in 1992-93. Import to India declined to Rs. 75.5 million kgs in 1995-96 and Rs. 76.5 million in 1999-2000. During 2003-04 to 2006-07 onwards it started improving from Rs. 80.5 million to Rs. 98.5 million. Imports were highest at Rs. 98.5 million in 2006-07 compared to Rs. 90.7 kgs in 2005-06. It was Rs. 12.4 million in 1972-73. Libya's balance of trade with India was unfavourable in 1969-70, 1972-73 and 1975-76 at Rs.12.4 million, Rs. 35.5 million and Rs. 43.1 million respectively. It was favourable in all the years except 1981-82 at Rs. 19.70 million.

Total Import and Exports of Tea in Libya

Until the 1930's Libya was basically a green tea drinking country and huge unsorted green teas were received mainly from China. The Second World War brought out a new dimension in the tea map of Libya. During this period, Libya was facing shipping difficulties in obtaining green teas from China and thus there was a shift to black tea. During and immediately after the Second World War, tea trading remained a government monopoly and imports were largely confined to Sri Lanka. With the lifting of government controls in 1952, Sri Lanka teas became popular. The popularity of Sri Lanka teas continued throughout the postwar years and at present, Sri Lanka exports more than three fourths of total black tea imports into Libya. Next to Sri Lanka, Japan was the second regular supplier to this market and she supplies, on an average, 2 to 3 million kgs annually. India's share was negligible up to 1951. It got momentum from 1984 onwards. Libya's tea imports substantially increased over the last five decades. In 1980, the total imports of tea into Libya stood at 13 million kgscompared to only 8 million kgs in 1970 and 2.8 million kgs in 1960. The total imports of tea, however, started declining from 12 million kgs in 1981 to 12 million kgs in 1985. The details are shown in Table 10.2.

Table 10.2: Total Imports and Exports of Tea to Libya during 1961 to 2005

(in thousand kgs)

Year	*Total imports*	*Exports of tea from*				*Total*
		Sri Lanka	*India*	*China*	*Japan*	
1961	6214	5214	2	1480	18	6714
1968	8466	6285	2	2200	21	8508
1971	10180	7618	8	1685	17	9328
1973	12784	12347	5	1006	10	13368
1976	10660	9058	14	2175	30	11270

1979	11784	10347	709	1000	1000	13056
1981	11900	9461	701	1100	2961	14223
1984	12000	6695	4891	1000	2581	15167
1987	11900	7500	3500	1500	2481	14981
1990	11000	6500	4500	2000	2366	15366
1993	9500	7274	4000	1600	1946	14770
1996	8500	8441	2316	1400	2164	14321
1999	9000	9500	4570	2000	2400	18470
2003	11000	9700	4400	1500	1800	17400
2004	12000	9850	4250	1600	1800	17500
2005	11500	9650	4000	1550	1850	17050
2006	11700	9500	4150	1700	1900	17250
Average	10520	8525	2472	1558	1490	14045

Source : Tea Statistics, Various Issues, Tea Board, Kolkata, India.

During the twenty-five years ending 2006, the total imports of tea to Libya was to the tune of 14 million kgs annually. Sri Lanka was the main supplier accounting for 61 per cent of the total tea imports followed by India and Japan, respectively. China supplied teas to Libya and her share accounted fro 10.6 per cent.

Tea trading in Libya was in the hands of the private sector until the first quarter of 1972. The situation, however, changed from April 1972 and the National Supplier Corporation of Libya (NASCO) was established for progressively canalizing imports. The entire tea trade in Libya at present is dealt with by this organization.

Exports of Tea and Value Added Tea from India to Libya during 1969-70 to 2006-07

Exports of tea from India to Libya increased from 2 thousand kgs in 1969-70 to 2750 thousand kgs in 2006-07. The details are shown in Table 10.3.

Table 10.3: Exports of Tea from India to Libya during 1969-70 to 2006-07

Year	Quantity (thousand kgs)	Value (thousand Rs.)	Unit Value (Rs./kg)
1969-70	2	22	11.00
1972-73	5	47	9.76
1975-76	502	5146	10.25
1978-79	5811	107630	18.52
1981-82	828	25429	30.71
1984-85	2488	92069	37.01
1987-88	4600	179860	39.10
1990-91	4500	190710	42.38
1993-94	4000	193800	48.45
1996-97	3050	158536	59.15
1999-2000	2500	169000	67.60
2001-02	1900	132050	69.50
2002-03	1700	119255	70.15
2003-04	1950	141375	72.5
2004-05	2250	165150	73.4
2005-06	2560	189696	74.1
2006-07	2750	206525	75.1
Average	2416	122135	50.34

*Provisional

Source : Tea Statistics, Various Issues, Tea Board, Kolkata, India.

India, on an average, exports about 2.4 million kgs of tea to Libya valued at Rs.12.2 crore with unit value realization of Rs.50.34 per kg. Exports of tea from India recorded at 5.8 million kgs in 1978-79 valued at Rs.10.76 crore. Figures relating to exports of *packet tea* to Libya showed the fact that during the last twenty-five years; India has been exporting packet tea. The quantum of packet tea exports was to the level of 5 million kgs in 1979-80 and 4.8 million kgs in 1989-90. Exports of *packet tea* drastically reduced from 2004-05 to 2006-07. As regards tea bags, India was able to export only 50 thousand kgs of tea valued at Rs.1.91 million in 1979-80. Thereafter, there was no export of *tea bags* from India to Libya. Exports of packet tea from India are given in Table 10.4.

Table 10.4: Exports of Packet Tea from India to Libya during 1979-80 to 2006-07

Year	*Quantity (thousand kgs)*	*Value (thousand Rs.)*	*Unit Value (Rs./kg)*
1979-80	5107	96822	18.96
1980-81	3300	7293	22.10
1983-84	828	25430	30.17
1986-87	4347	137462	31.62
1989-90	4826	192943	39.98
1992-93	4956	215586	43.50
1995-96	5057	230599	45.60
1998-99	4345	223768	51.50
2001-02	2085	113841	54.60
2004-05	1900	122664	64.56
2005-06	1850	125615	67.90
2006-07	1950	145763	74.75
Average	3379	136482	2577

Source : Tea Statistics, Various Issues, Tea Board, Kolkata, India.

Taxes, Duties and Marketing

Any import duty is not levied on teas other than instant tea supplied by the Corporation. There is a 30 per cent advalorem duty on the c.i.f. value for instant tea and 20 per cent ad valorem duty on the c.i.f value for teas other than instant tea. Besides, there are two types of taxes viz., charity tax, @ 5 per cent and municipal tax @ 5 per cent of import duty. An import licence is required which is obtainable from the National Consumer Products Organisation (NCPO). Prepared tea in containers is restricted. The Libyan Government has banned certain British Consumer goods and tea as well as tea extracts in the list of such goods.

Promotional Efforts of Tea by Tea Board in Libya

During eighties, the then Chairman of the Tea Board, led a Tea Delegation comprising three members to the countries of North Africa viz., Morocco, Tunisia, Algeria & Libya. The aim of the delegation was to make an indepth study of these markets in order to assess the nature of demand for tea and the likely quantum of teas required. The delegation was also interested to explore the possibility of production potentiality and to see how best the production can be adjusted to meet the supply needs of these countries. The delegation enquired into the high level of import of tea for the population of the country. They came to know informally that a large number of workers from the A.R.E. and Tunisia were employed in Libya and when they go home, they always take with them some tea from Libya. Another reason, which make taking of tea from Libya attractive, was the fact that duties and taxes on tea in Libya were lower compared to neighbouring countries of the A.R.E and Tunisia. Besides, lots of tea got to the desert markets on the Southern borders of Libya in chhad, Niger, Sudan, etc. The delegations arrived at the following conclusions:

a) Libyan market is a market for black tea in packets, the demand is going higher and higher because of re-exports to neighbouring countries.
b) Import of tea into Libya is a state monopoly but the distribution in wholesale and retail is done through private agents. The State Monopoly Organization is willing to deal with private trade from India.
c) Although Libya is a market primarily for black tea, there is also some demand for green tea of the Chinese variety as also of tea bags.
d) *The Libyan Government has already established a tea-packing factory.*

Conclusion

It is, therefore, inferred that further initiatives may be strengthened by the Government of India to export more value-added teas to Libyan market, where there is a better demand for packet tea. The government should also utilize the opportunity to export more loose tea in order to feed the tea Export Possibility of Indian Tea to Libya.

11

Tea Economy of Iran

Backdrop

Iran is bounded by the USSR and Caspian Sea in the north; Afganistan and Pakistan in the east; the Arabian Sea and Persian Gulf in the south, south-west respectively, Iraq, and Turkey to the west. Most of the country consists of a high plateau surrounded by mountain range. The Capital is Tehran that is 125 km south of Caspian Sea, in the foothills of Alborzrange and 1250 miles above sea level. The principal ports on the Persian Gulf are Bushira, Lingah, Bandar Abbes Khorranser and Bandarsherer. Ports on the Caspian Sea are Bandarsherer and Pahlavi. Iran has an area of 628 thousand sq. miles with a population of about 65 million and the majority is Muslims. The official language is Persian (Farsi), but various dialects of Rurdish and Turki are spoken. The unit of currency is Rial.

Iran is the world's largest producer and exporter of oil. Petroleum provides most of its foreign exchange and government income. The climate of the area, which is of sub-tropical in nature, helps in production of rice, tobacco, tea, jute and citrus fruits. Agriculture is the main single economic activity employing about 42 per cent of country's labour force 4.5 million and contributing about 14 per cent of gross National Product. It, however, remains the least developed part of the economy due to proliferation of smallholding. Iran is making progress in the tertiary sector. Tobacco, raw silks, gums are manufactured and processed. The country is popular for the tourist. The chief attraction of the tourists is the wealth of historical sites and its museum of Persian Art and Culture.

Iran's Trade with India during 1975-76 to 2006-07

Principal products imported by Iran from India are cotton manufactures, jute manufactures, transport equipments, tea, iron and steel, metal manufactures, etc. The most important items of export from Iran to India are petroleum, petroleum products, crude sulphur, fruits and vegetables, crude vegetable materials. The growth of trade between India and Iran revealed that the balance of trade was favourable for the first six years commencing from 1969-70 to 1974-75. It was, however, unfavourable from 1975-76 to 1983-84. During the first six years period the balance of trade was favourable at Rs. 2249 million in 1973-74 and at Rs.590 million in 1969-70. During the second six-year period, the balance of trade was unfavourable. In terms of value the year 1975-76 showed lower negative figures at Rs. 1857 million, while the figure was high at Rs. 12869 million in 1983-84. From 1984-85 onwards the balance of trade was not favourable. Even during 2006-07 total value of imports from India was less than import value showing unfavourable balance of trade to the tune of Rs. 25,750 million.

Tea Economy of Iran—Area, Production and Yield of Tea

Iran is a tea producing country. On an average, she owns 34664 hectares under tea with an annual production of 51 million kgs. During the last twenty years, the area and production of tea increased. It was 30000 hectares in 1985 while the same increased to about 36500 hectares in 2006. In 1985, production was 45 million kgs, which enhanced to 50 million kgs in 2006. Tea production was as high as 60 million kgs in 1999 followed by 48.5 million kgs in 2006. Iran's share to global production of tea was 1.78 per cent in 2006. The yield is 1424 kgs per hectare, on an average. Area, production and exports of tea for the 21 years ending 2006 are given in Table 11.1.

Table 11.1: Area, Production and Yield of Tea in Iran during 1985 to 2006

Year	*Area (thousand hectares)*	*Av. Annual growth rate of area (%)*	*Production (million kgs)*	*Av. Annual growth rate of Production (%)*	*Yield (kgs/ hectare)*	*Share of Iran's tea to global production (%)*
1985	30	–	45	–	1500	2.85
1989	32	1.66	46	0.74	1438	1.84
1990	32	0	44	–1.49	1375	1.90
1993	33	1.04	45	0.75	1364	1.92
1996	34	1.01	50	3.70	1471	1.97
1999	35	1.07	60	6.66	1714	2.02
2000	35	0	53	–3.88	1514	2.01
2003	36	0.95	47	–3.77	1305	1.98
2004	35.5	–1.40	47.5	1.06	1338	1.87
2005	36.2	1.97	48	1.05	1326	1.81
2006	36.5	0.82	48.5	1.04	1329	1.78

Source: Tea Statistics, Various Issues, Tea Board, Kolkata, India.

Area under tea cultivation increased from 30 thousand hectares to 36.5thousand hectares during 1985 to 2006 showing an increase of 21.6 per cent while production improved from 45 million kgs to 48.5 million kgs accounting for 7.78 per cent during the period. Thus, increase in area was three times more than production. The lower growth of production was mainly attributed to decline in yield rate that reduced from 1500 kgs per hectare to 1329 kgs per hectare constituting a fall of 4.4 per cent over the years. Share of Iran in global tea production was 2.85 per cent in 1985. It, however, declined to 1.84 per cent in 1989 and further increased to 2.02 per cent in 1999. It was 1.55 per cent in 2002 and 1.78 per cent in 2006.

Import Pattern of Tea

Taking into account the indigenous production and the average annual imports to the tune of 26 million kgs, the total consumption in this country is about 70 million kgs.Tea imports for consumption were about 68 million kgs in 2006. India exports about 18 million kgs to Iran representing 26 per cent of the total imports. The largest supplier is Sri Lanka constituting 50 per cent.

Table 11.2: Import Pattern of Tea in Iran during 1951-2006

(in thousand kgs)

Year			*Imports from*		
	India	*Sri Lanka*	*Indonesia*	*Other countries*	*Total*
1951	875	6142	2391	77	9485
1961	2156	16368	9	4	18537
1971	2607	15897	10	1373	19877
1981	1300	800	15	1400	3515
1991	1400	900	20	1500	3820
1997	1300	4300	5200	12700	23500
1999	7100	9000	11800	14400	42300
2001	16800	13300	8500	24100	62700
2003	17200	13800	9500	24700	64900
2004	17500	14300	9600	24800	66200
2005	17900	14500	9750	25000	67150
2006	18100	15000	9800	25540	68440
Average	8687 (23.11)	10360 (27.61)	5550 (14.79)	12940 (34.49)	35517 (100.00)

Source : Tea Statistics, Tea Board, Various Issues, Kolkata.

The data presented in the table above brought out the fact that, on an average, quantum of imports stood at 35 million kgs.Of this Sri Lanka constitutes 27.61 per cent followed by India (23.11 per cent) and Indonesia (14.79 per cent). Other Countries represents for more than one third of total imports (34.49 per cent). Most interestingly, imports from India, Sri Lanka, Indonesia and other countries, started increasing from 2001 onwards. Imports from India were 20.69 times, while it was 1.68 times for Sri Lanka, 4.10 for Indonesia and 3.31 times for other countries). Total imports from all countries were 68.44 million kgs in 2006 as against 9.49 million kgs in 1951 showing 7.21 times.Tea imports for consumption in Iran exhibited an increasing trend. It increased by 721 per cent during the period between 1951 and 2006. Sri Lanka was the major supplier of tea between the three pints of time 1951, 1961 and 1971, but India became the major supplier in 1981 and 1991. In 1997 and 1999, Indonesia was major supplier followed by Sri Lanka. During the year 2001-07, India became the major supplier followed by Sri Lanka/Indonesia. On an average, Sri Lanka accounted for 27.61 per cent of total imports (35.51 million kgs) while India constituted 23.11 per cent and Indonesia 14.79 per cent. Other countries represented 34.49 per cent.

Exports of Tea and Value Added Tea from India to Iran

Exports of tea from India to Iran increased from 2 million kgs in 1964-65 to 1 million kgs in 1984-85. On an average, India exports 13.5 million kgs annually to Iran. India was, however, able to increase her exports to 20 million kgs in 1983-84. These exports were, however, reduced by 1 million kgs in the next year and again increased by another 1 million kgs in 1985-86. Exports of tea from India to Iran were negligible at 2.5 million kgs during 2006-07.

Although India's packet tea in consumer packs could make a good entry in the initial stages, tempo could not be sustained in recent years. India's exports of packet teas in 1970 were 1 lakh kgs but from 1971 onwards exports declined sharply and in 1979 these rose to 2 lakh kgs. Exports of packet tea again declined to 0.59 lakh kgs in 1980-81 and again increased to 2.6 lakh kgs in 1981-82. There were no exports of packet tea during 1982-83 and 1983-84. India started exporting tea to the tune of 22 lakh kgs in 1984-85 and 8.3 lakh kgs in 1985-86. Packet tea exports were 19 lakh kgs in 1999. It, however, reduced to 4 lakh kgs in 2006. As regards exports of tea bag, it was 1.23 lakh kgs in 2000 and only 2 lakh kgs in 2006.

The most significant aspect is that Persians consumed those varieties of tea that represent the world's best "Tippy Teas". Although Iran produces teas, not only the quantity is inadequate but also the quality does not meet the standards preferred by the consumers. In fact, the Government of Iran may strengthen special measures to ensure the consumption of local tea. Under the regulations, there exists a ratio between local tea and imported tea. Importers who purchased local tea during the ten months of the current Iranian year may release any foreign tea they import by next May by buying only 700 gms of local tea per kg of foreign tea. The reason for the above regulations is to bring down the price of tea by offering more tea on the market.

Problems of Tea Exporters from Iran in 2000s

Some major Indian tea exporters to Iran who had contracted with the State Tea Organization of Iran to supply 13.550 million kgs of bulk and packet teas valued at around Rs.93 crores sometimes in August 2005 faced serious problem due to Iran's inability to open L/Cs for the full quantity. The officials of the Kolkata Tea Traders Association informed that as per the terms of contract, the tea was shipped during September to December 2005. However, during December some of the exporters were asked to offer their contracts and line of credit (L/Cs) for part quantities. In March 2005, a few exporters with relatively smaller quantities got their L/Cs and were able to complete the shipment. At present, around 10 million kgstea valued at Rs.95 crores were awaiting shipment for the past seven to eight months, it was reported. The exporters are facing serious problems in holding such huge stocks due to high warehouse charges and high interest costs.

Feasibility Study by ITC, UNCTAD, GATT etc..

The feasibility study conducted by International Trade Committee, United Nation Conference on Trade (UNCTAD), General Agreement of Trade and Tariff (GATT) revealed that the Iranian consumer is guided mostly by the appearance of the raw tea. Bulk of tea consumed in Iran is sold loose, mainly because the consumer thinks he knows how his tea should look and insists on seeing it before he buys. Perhaps there could be one of the reasons for tapering our exports of packet tea. The same story appears to be applicable to tea bags. Exports of tea bags started increasing. It was 2 thousand kgs valued at Rs.0.47 lakh (in 1974) that enhanced to 108 thousand kgs valued at Rs.47.0 lakh (in 1981-82). There was no export of tea bags from 1982-83 onwards. On an average, India exported 160 thousand kgs of tea bags to Iran.

Tea Imports for Consumption and Exports from India to Iran

During the year 1999 total tea imports for consumption in Iran was 38.5 million kgs that increased to 46.9 million kgs in 2000. It, however, declined to 40.2 million kgs in 2001. The quantum increased to 45.6 million kgs in 2007. The details of imports for consumption and exports from India are depicted in Table 11.3.

Table 11.3: Tea Imports for Consumption and Exports from India during 1999 to 2006

(in thousand Kgs)

Year	*Imports for Consumption*	*Increase (+)/ decrease (-)*	*Exports from India*	*Increase (+) / decrease (-)*
1999	38500	–	4061	–
2000	46900	(+) 8400	3437	(-) 624
2001	40200	(-) 6700	2829	(-) 608
2003	41800	(+) 1600	3150	(+) 321
2004	42600	(+) 800	3395	(+) 245
2005	43700	(+) 1100	3495	(+) 100
2006	44900	(+) 1200	3550	(+) 55
2007	45600	(+) 700	3645	(+) 95
Average	43025	–	3465	–

* Provisional.

Source : Tea Statistics, Various Issues, Tea Board, Kolkata, India.

It revealed from the data that average imports for tea consumption in Iran were 43.02 million kgs , while exports from India were 34.65 million kgs. Thus there is a dearth of 8.37 million kgs, for which Iran has to resort for procuring tea from other countries. Exports of tea from India ranged from 2.83 million kgs to 4.06 million kgs during 1999 to 2007. In 2000 it was 3.44 million kgs, which reduced to 3.15 million kgs in 2003. It further enhanced to 3.40 million kgs in 2004. The exports started increasing from 2005 onwards.

Exports of Green Tea

Data available with the Tea Board, Kolkata, revealed that India exports green tea also to Iran. On an average, exports of green tea were in the order of 8 thousand kgs per year. It was 5 thousand kgs in 1979-80 and 3 thousand kgs in 1980-81. There were no exports of green tea from 1981-82 onwards. Exports of green tea stood at 10 thousand kgs in 2006.

Taxes & Duties and Additional Taxes

Apart from the marketing regulations started earlier, the import duty and commercial benefits tax levied on tea is as under:

(Rials per kg gross)

Description of tea	*Customs*	*Commercial Profit Tax*
Black Tea	31 (20 per cent)	3
Green Tea	31 (20 per cent)	33
Others	31 (20 per cent)	23

(Packet tea is subject to customs charges including the weight of paper wrapping or containers)

The extracts, essence etc,	45 per cent	500

(Imports at present prohibited)

Additional Taxes

Charity Tax	:	1 ½ percent of import duty + CBT
Municipal Tax	:	6 per cent import duty + CBT
Health Tax	:	5 Rials per metric ton
Porterage Tax	:	720 Rials per metric ton
Registration of order fees	:	1 per cent of the amount of order, effected on the basis of seller's offer.

Importers must apply to the exchange control authorities for all allocation of currency, when this is received Iranian Custom Authorities will issue the relevant import licence on the arrival of goods at an Iranian Port.

Conclusions

Tea imports for consumption into Iran had been appreciably increasing. India may now take the opportunity of exporting more teas to Iran so that Sri Lanka's export to Iran may be reduced. Apart from this, there is vast scope for India to export value added teas to Iran. Government may strengthen further possibility of evolving a scheme so that India's value-added items may again be exported to Iran. For this, a favourable climate is required to be created in order to have better understanding between the two countries in relation to various issues. In conclusion, although there are some problems, the export of tea to Iran may be increased and all endeavour may be made in this direction.

12

Singapore—A Potential Market for Indian Tea Exports

Introduction

The Republic of Singapore, which is a city of state, consists of an island territory and several offshore islands. It is flanked by Malaysia in the north, Philippines to the northeast and Indonesia in the southwest. The capital is Singapore city. Singapore is the second largest port in the world after Rotterdrum in terms of tonnage of cargo handled. The country had an area of 238 sq. miles (23800 hectare) with an estimated population of 3.8 million in 2006. The national language is Malay but Tamil, Chinese, and English are official languages. The projected Gross Domestic Product was 52452 million Singapore Dollars in 2006. Singapore enjoys the second highest per capita income in Far East after Japan. The annual growth rate of Gross Domestic Product in real terms varied from 7.8 per cent to 10.2 per cent between 2003 and 2006. The per capita Gross Domestic Product was 22,324 in Singapore Dollars (S).

Singapore is the centre for export-import of Malaysia and other South Asian countries. It handles most of the Malaysia's external trade and is the main centre of the rubber and tin markets. Manufacturing has become an increasingly significant sector of the economy. The industries are petroleum refining, shipping and repairing textiles and electric. Even though Singapore has not petroleum reserves of its own, oil plays a vital role in the economy. Singapore has the largest refining complex in the world. Agriculture constitutes nearly 3 per cent of the national income and the major products are fruits and vegetables.

Singapore's Trade with India

The major commodities exported from India to Singapore are cotton piece and goods jute manufactures, spices, coffee, tea, tobacco (un-manufactured), breading staff for animals etc. while the major commodities imported to India from Singapore are iron, copper, plastic materials, etc. The growth of trade between Singapore and India is given in the following table:

Table 12.1: Balance of Trade between India and Singapore During 1971-72 to 2006-07

(in million Rupees)

Year	*Exports from India*	*Imports to India*	*Balance of trade with India*
1971-72	29.89	175.16	- 145.27
1976-77	116.18	511.32	- 395.14
1981-82	1845.20	925.06	+929.14
1986-87	5435.05	1525.05	+3910.00
1991-92	6592.83	2095.25	+4497.58
1996-97	10452.50	2694.30	+7758.20
2001-02	15632.60	3235.05	+9397.55
2006-07	11580.65	3860.50	+7720.15

Source: Director General of Intelligence and Statistics, Govt. of India.

Imports for Consumption

Prior to 1980, the figures for tea imports were not separately available for Singapore. These were the combined figure for both Malaya and Singapore. Malaya is a tea producing and exporting country. At the same time, she is importing tea for the country. The imports to Malaya may be considered as imports to Singapore, since there are many tea-growing regions in Singapore and Malaya. Malaya has, on an average, 3 thousand hectares under tea with a production of less than 6 million kgs annually. Area and production has been stagnant over the last two decades because of which her exports of tea almost stopped since 1973. Prior to 1973, Malaya exported, on an average a million kgs. a year to Singapore, UK and the

Table 12.2: Tea Imports for Consumption and Exports in Singapore during 1971 to 2006

(in thousand Kgs)

Year	Total tea imports for consumption	Exports from									Total Exports from all countries
		India	Bangladesh	Sri Lanka	Argentina	Taiwan	Kenya	China	Papua & New Guinea	Indonesia	
1971	1861	2	Negl	439	Nil	1882	Negl	Negl	Negl	820	3,143
1972	2079	7	-	450	-	791	-	-	-	1,468	2,716
1973	1216	9	-	857	-	56	-	-	-	2,453	3,375
1974	1497	84	812	594	-	177	-	-	-	2,085	3,752
1975	1203	124	839	500	86	255	-	-	-	1,880	4,686
1976	2182	230	686	881	21	339	-	-	-	1,231	3,181
1977	3106	260	321	877	278	661	568	-	-	1,228	3,933
1978	3333	300	228	595	278	54	472	-	32	2,815	4,823
1979	3000	539	274	1197	846	64	486	-	42	5,737	9,058
1980	3500	1200	334	1633	721	270	717	-	365	9,776	15,048
1981	4000	1164	536	1531	614	81	619	-	1408	9,046	14,826
1982	4000	1450	438	1538	300	120	760		778	6,630	11,047
1986	6005	1695	800	1635	200	184	840	850	850	7540	20,599
1991	7850	2067	1010	1740	350	194	940	920	806	8430	24,307
1996	8135	2267	1250	1925	420	140	825	750	700	8750	25,162
2001	8540	2750	1670	2050	520	120	900	650	640	9260	27,708
2006	8960	3125	2050	2270	640	140	750	640	750	9560	28,885

Source: *Tea Statistics*, Various Issues, Tea Board, India, Kolkata.

Netherlands. From 1973 onwards, the import requirements of Singapore been mostly met by Indonesia due to its proximity and facility for transport. Singapore, on an average, imports around 3 million kgs in a year. Next to Indonesia, Taiwan, Sri Lanka and India are the other suppliers. In recent years, Bangladesh, Argentina, Kenya, China, Papua and New Guinea entered into Singapore tea market and they are contributing a sizeable amount of total import requirements of Singapore. Tea imports for consumption into Singapore are given in Table 12.2.

Exports of Tea from India

Exports of tea from India to Singapore showed an increasing trend during the last few decades. It increased from 32 thousand kgs in 1973-74 to 2700 thousand kgs in 2006-07. In value terms, exports in 1973-74 were Rs. 383 thousand, which increased to Rs. 185625 thousand in 2006-07. Exports of tea from India to Singapore averaged 2700 thousand kgs during the last three years. Details of exports of tea from India to Singapore are given in Table 12.3.

Table 12.3: Exports of Tea from India to Singapore during 1973-74 to 2006-07

Year	*Quantity (thousand kgs)*	*Value (thousand Rs.)*	*Unit value (Rs./Kg)*
1973-74	32	383	11.96
1978-79	550	8500	15.46
1981-82	1273	21498	16.89
1983-84	1270	26225	20.65
1988-89	1895	46901	24.75
1993-94	2005	61532	30.50
1998-99	2400	109560	50.65
2001-02	430	4311	110.26
2004-05	2650	160325	60.50
2005-06	2750	177595	64.58
2006-07	2700	185625	68.75

Source : *Tea Statistics*, Various Issues, Tea Board, India, Kolkata.

Exports of Packet Tea from India

Singapore started purchasing some quantities of *packet teas* from India in recent years. In 1973-74, as much as of 18 thousand kgs of packet tea at Rs. 201 thousand were exported to Singapore. The export *of packet* tea to Singapore was not increased over the years. It was 53 thousand kgs valued at Rs.8990 thousand in 2005-06. It was 49 thousand kgs in 2001-02. The following table shows the details.

Table 12.4: Exports of Packet Tea from India to Singapore during 1973-74 to 2005-06

Year	*Quantity (thousand kgs)*	*Value (thousand Rs.)*	*Unit Value (Rs/kg)*
1973-74	18	201	11.17
1981-82	18	357	19.83
1999-00	5	704	140.80
2000-01	46	7571	164.59
2001-02	49	4311	87.97
2005-06	53	8990	169.62

Source : *Tea Statistics,* Various Issues, Tea Board, India, Kolkata.

Singapore also purchased small quantities of *tea bags* from India. In 1973-74, small quantities of 4 thousand kgs of tea bags valued at Rs.1.25 lakh were exported to Singapore. The exports were, however, on the lower side at one thousand kgs. valued at Rs. 3.57 lakh in 1981-82. *Instant tea* was not exported to Singapore. During the year 2005-06, the exports were less than one thousand kgs.

Taxes and Duties on Tea in Singapore

There is neither any import duty on tea nor any internal taxes. Import license, however, is required.

Problems and Prospects

With the stagnation of tea production in Malaya, the requirements of Singapore are mostly met by Indonesia. In recent years exports of teas in consumer packs from Singapore has increased. This is because Singapore is a tourist spot and many foreigners visit this country every year. However, efforts been taken to strengthen to find a place for Indian teas in this market. The Director of Tea Promotion (Kolkata) conducted a few years back export potentials of tea in the markets like Poland, Indonesia and Singapore. It was sated in the survey report that systematic attempt had to be further strengthened to promote Indian tea in the market. There is a good prospect of packet teas for consumption as well as exports from Singapore for which promotional work has to be further initiated.

13

Nigeria: A Market for Indian Tea

Attempt has been made in this chapter to assess the export prospects of Indian tea in Nigeria. Accordingly the following aspects like: *(i)* geographical location of Nigeria, *(ii)* its economy, *(iii)* pattern of trade between Nigeria and India, *(iv)* tea imports for consumption into Nigeria, *(v)* exports of tea from India to Nigeria, *(vi)* exports of packet tea, tea bags and instant tea from India to Nigeria and *(vii)* taxes and duties of tea imports have been discussed. To start with let us have a glimpse on the Nigerian economy as a whole giving emphasis on area, population, density of population, gross domestic product, per capita income etc..

Nigerian Economy

The Republic of Nigeria lies in West Africa. It is bounded by river Niger on the north; Gulf Guinea on the south; Cameroon on the east and Benin on the west. Lagos was its capital. It is now shifted to ABUTA north of river Niger. The major harbours are Lagos, Port d Apapa. Nigeria has a land area of 359,669 square miles (927,768 sq.km), which is almost 4 times of the U.K. The population of the country is estimated about approximately 150 million in 2006. The population is growing at an average annual rate between 2.5 and 3 per cent. Population density is 415 per square mile, although this figure was much higher in urban areas. Urban population is now growing at 4.7 per cent annually and accounts for 20 per cent of the total. Real annual growth rate of Gross Domestic Product (GDP) was 10.8 per cent in 2006 and 9.8 per cent in 2005. The per capita income is 856 in US Dollars. Unit of currency is Naria.

Agriculture is the main stay of the economy. It constitutes more than 60 per cent of all exports. The main crops are coca, palm oil kernels, groundnuts, cotton and rubber. Nigeria produces oil and within a few years, she has become the largest oil producer in Africa. The soaring oil export revenue enabled the economy to achieve a growth rate of around 7 per cent over the past decade. The eighth National Development Plan (NDP), however, assumes a real average annual growth of 8.2 per cent per annum of Gross Domestic Product over the five-year period.

Nigeria's Trade with India during 1968-69 to 2005-06

Transport equipment, machinery other than electric, cotton yarn and thread, manufacturers of metal etc. are some of the items of exports from India to Nigeria, while imports into India from Nigeria are mainly crude materials, natural gums, resins, laces, non-ferrous metal waste and alloys, etc. The Table provides the position of trade with India during the last decade.

Table 13.1: Balance of Trade between India and Nigeria during 1968-69 to 2005-06

(in million Rs.)

Year	*Exports from India*	*Imports to India*	*Balance of trade with India*
1968-69	30.8	1.2	(+) 29.6
1970-71	86.20	Neg	(+) 86.2
1975-76	374.24	110.02	(+) 264.22
1980-81	530.07	75.16	(+) 454.91
1985-86	720.05	150.16	(+) 569.19
1990-91	845.60	260.40	(+) 585.19
2000-01	945.60	455.60	(+) 295.00
2004-05	950.25	640.20	(+) 310.05
2005-06	1060.20	690.40	(+) 369.80

Source : Director General of Intelligence and Statistics, Govt. of India.

It is interesting to note that exports from India were always higher than imports to India in all the years. As a result balance of trade was favourable. Balance of trade in value terms was highest at Rs. 569.19 million in 1985-86 while it was lowest at Rs. 29.6 million in 1968-69.

Tea Economy of Nigeria—Imports for Tea Consumption

Nigeria is a small but growing market for tea. In 1967 tea imports for consumption recorded at 393 thousand kgs, which enhanced to 490 thousand kgs in 1975 and 1600 thousand kgs in 1980. It further boosted to 2000 thousand kgs in 1985 and 2259 thousand kgs in 1990. It was 2600 thousand kgs in 2000, 2900 thousand kgs in 2005 and 3015 thousand kgs in 2006.

Table 13.2: Tea Imports for Consumption in Nigeria during 1967 to 2006

(in thousand Kgs)

Year	*Tea imports for consumption*	*Percentage increase (+) or decrease (–)*	*Exports* Kenya	Argentina	Brazil	UK
1967	393	–	–	–	–	–
1970	490	+ 24.68	–	9	109	167
1975	800	+ 63.25	576	6	994	484
1980	1600	+ 100.00	645	20	990	500
1985	2000	+ 25.00	700	40	1025	600
1990	2256	+ 12.50	900	100	1250	900
2000	2600	+ 15.55	1200	320	1460	1200
2005	2900	+ 11.54	1410	420	1550	1300
2006	3015	+ 3.96	1500	650	1740	1400

Source : Tea Statistics, Various Issues, Tea Board, India, Kolkata.

Kenya, Brazil and Argentina are the main suppliers of tea to Nigeria. On an average, Kenya supplies 1300 thousand kgs annually followed by Argentina (440 thousand kgs) and Brazil (15 thousand kgs). The United Kingdom also supplies tea to Nigeria by way of re-exports. She supplies 1300 thousand kgs a year. Zaire and China also supply substantial quantities of tea to Nigeria.

Export of Tea and Tea Bag

Export of Indian Tea to Nigeria was negligible in 1979-80 at 21 thousand kgs only, which was increased to 139 thousand kgs (i.e. by 7 times) during 1980-81. The export was further enhanced in 1990-91 to the level of 560 thousand kgs, which appreciated to 750 thousand kgs in 2000-01 and 850 th .kgs in 2005-06. Unit price improved from Rs. 45.33 per kg to Rs. 48.95 per kg. There was fall in unit price in 1980-81 (Rs. 24.57 per kg) and 1990-91 (Rs. 30.00 per kg). Table 13.3 brings out the details.

Table 13.3: Exports of Tea from India during 1979-80 to 2005-06

(Qty. in thousand kgs, Value in thousand. Rs and Unit Value in Rs/kg)

Year	*Quantity*	*Absolute inc./dec.*	*Value*	*Absolute inc./dec.*	*Unit*	*Absolute inc./dec.*
1979-80	21	–	952	–	45.33	–
1980-81	139	+118	2415	+1463	24.57	-20.66
1990-91	560	+421	16800	+14385	30.00	-5.43
2000-01	750	+190	30938	+14138	47.95	+17.95
2005-06	850	+100	41607	+10669	48.95	+1.00

Source : Tea Statistics, Various Issues, Tea Board, India, Kolkata.

Nigeria did not import *packet tea* from India. However, India exported 16 thousand kgs of tea bag, valued at Rs. 818 thousand with a unit value of Rs. 51.13 per kg to Nigeria in 1979-80. In 1980-81, exports of tea bag increased to 25 thousand kgs worth Rs. 1406 thousand. It however declined to 17 thousand kgs in 1981-82, 10 thousand kgs in 1991-92 and 5 thousand kgs in 2000-01. The export figure was very negligible. The exports of *tea bag* from India to Nigeria are depicted in Table 13.4.

Table 13.4: Exports of Tea Bags from India to Nigeria during 1979-80 to 2005-06

(Qty. in thousand kgs, Value in thousand. Rs and Unit Value in Rs/kg)

Year	*Quantity*	*Absolute inc./dec.*	*Value*	*Absolute inc./dec.*	*Unit*	*Absolute inc./dec.*
1979-80	16	–	818	–	51.13	–
1980-81	25	+9	1406	+588	56.24	+5.11
1981-82	17	-8	924	-482	54.35	-1.89
1991-92	10	-7	605	-319	60.5	+6.15
2000-01	05	-5	378	-227	75.7	+520
2005-06	Neg.	Neg.	–	–	–	–

Source : Tea Statistics, Various Issues, Tea Board, India, Kolkata.

Taxes and Duties on Tea Imports in Nigeria

Tea can be imported into Nigeria freely, after obtaining a form of domiciliation or an import license depending upon the country of origin. Import of tea is subject to various fiscal Imports viz., custom duty, fiscal duty, import tax on turn over, complementary tax and phytosanitary inspection. It therefore seems that even tea imports are freely allowed, such imports are very high in tariff rates.

Conclusion

Keeping the geographical location of country in mind and considering Syria, Uganda, Tanzania, Malawi, Mozambique and Zaire are the tea producing and exporting countries in Africa, there requires great deal of effort on the part of India to find a foothold in this market. At present transport facilities in some of the African regions appear not to be much satisfactory. However, opening of the Central African Highway from Mombassa to Lagos has eventually facilitated transport. It may not be out of the context to point out that the multinationals is already having a Tea Packing Factory in Zaire, which is one of the major suppliers of tea to Nigeria. Shipping facilities for India to Nigeria require further improvements. The publicity of Indian tea is required to be further strengthening, in a higher way in this oil rich market.

14

Sri Lankan Tea Industry: Competitor to Indian Tea Industry in World Market

Sri Lanka Tea: An Overview

A young interesting Scotsman named James Taylor *undertook the first commercial planting of tea in Sri Lanka*. As everybody may be aware, 150 years ago, it was not Sri Lanka tea—it was Sri Lanka Coffee. In addition, young Mr Taylor thought he would try an experiment; he did the first commercial planting of tea. It was very successful. Some year later came along blight, which knocked of the coffee. Luckily, thanks to Mr. Taylor, tea had already worked, so they quickly uprooted the coffee bushes and planted tea. All that is left today is Mr. Taylor's Bungalow. It helped a lot because it is one of the great instances. Mr. Churchill compares the story of Sri Lanka tea and the plantation industry with Waterloo. Then, they had first explored—it is a very small item bought for 4000 pounds at the time. However, it was a start and the people in London liked it.

The Industry got impetus with the *formation of the Kalampur Tea Trade Association (KTTA)*. In all the tea-growing districts, there is a KTTA. Today it is the apex body for marketing tea. The other organisations like the Planters Association of Ceylon, which is the equivalent to UPASI, is an affiliated association of the CTTA. Other affiliated associations are the Private Factory Owners Association, the Tea Exporters Association and the Tea Small Holdings Development Authority. Therefore, there is one apex body for tea working very close to the Tea Board.

One of the things that the happened first is that the Ceylon started *to get an identity. Very soon, the trade felt that there was a need to have a special body to look at promotion and therefore, the Ceylon Tea Propaganda Board was formed* with the sole purpose of promoting Ceylon tea. It was run by the private sector and with small beginning, it started growing. Around the world, the name Ceylon started replacing China as the source of tea. One of the important things that Ceylon Tea Propaganda Board did was to ensure quality standards and perhaps for the first time, they set up a panel to monitor quality. All the participants in the trade monitored it, because they felt the exporting low quality teas was self-defeating. So the shipping of tea below certain standard was prohibited. Then not content with the Ceylon Tea, they encouraged and set up a thing *called the International Tea Marketing Board stationed in the UK, which was then the head of tea trade, including India and what is now Indonesia and started promoting not only Ceylon Tea, but tea as a beverage.* So these have always gone hand in hand.

Power cuts and water cuts are some of the hardships Sri Lanka is likely to face. Though this is not entirely new to the tea industry there, it has to encounter this. Authorities keep fingers crossed as the weather conditions not presenting any rosy picture. Unless there is turn of events for good, the Government is not left with any other option but to curb water and power supply. In such situation, the country is in the brink of yet another drought notwithstanding the fact that some of the desert areas in the Middle East are experiencing sharp showers. The natural disasters of unprecedented dimensions that affected some part of the globe in a uncomparable manner in few years back (i.e. 1992) was no doubt history today. However, all hopes were pinned on stability, and for more stable and balanced weather conditions to emerge. The current situations do not seem to indicate so.

In the marketing scene, *the CIS is in the forefront. It has once again emerged as a strong buyer of Sri Lankan teas.* The rate at which their buying orders are expanding only confirm the even under very difficult conditions their addiction to tea has not suffered in anyway. It is said that the three main items of purchase in any Russian homemaker's shopping list are salt, soap and tea. Despite the break up of the Soviet Union, it is very unlikely the other beverages are now being pursued in these areas in a more forceful manner than ever before. This will overshadow the identity of tea. The tea drinking habit was established in the former Union of Soviet Socialist Republics long before. Some of the Middle East countries began to show a preference to this beverage. Former Russia had also been a supplier of teas to some of the satellite countries. Poland, Mangolia had for a long time obtained bulk of their supplies of tea from Russia.

Reciprocal Trading Arrangements

To penetrate the Russian market and to ensure the tea is freely available, perhaps a different approach will have to be adopted based on *reciprocal trading arrangements or counter trade arrangements*. Sri Lanka is happy that its shippers are not making use of these facilities and traders in Singapore and Hong Kong and elsewhere mostly finance the current trade in tea. This mode of operations could change as the Soviet Republics have the potential to become wealthy countries soon. From a control economy, they have not been liberalized. Sri Lanka has already secured large export orders to the CIS and will definitely utilize to its full advantage the offerings of outside financials to service the Russian market. After all Russian need the tea a decent cup of tea and if it could be made available price Sri Lanka tea could make a lasting impression.

Privatisation of Sri Lankan Tea

Sri Lankan tea industry was privatized. Outlining the pitfalls of state ownership, a paper prepared by Sri Lankan government indicated that the industry was *thrown open to the private sector because the island state continued to be the top exporter of tea.* Stressing the role of private enterprise in increasing productivity, the paper laid the foundation of an Indo-Sri Lanka joint tea export effort. Much of the credit for the new initiative went to the late Ranjan Wijeratne, who held the key portfolios of plantation development and defence before his death. Wijeratne had successfully lobbied in government for privatization of the industry. A confidential report prepared by the Union commerce ministry said Sri Lanka wants India to take the initiative in matters related to supply management, common minimum export price, and joint response to global tenders among others.

Indo-Sri Lankan Economic Commission

The deliberations of the *Indo Sri Lankan Economic Commission favoured a joint initiative,* and took the clue from the recommendations of the meetings. The commerce ministry had also backed the idea. India is estimated to produce 900 million kgs of tea in 2007 against 340 million kgs produced by Sri Lanka, which depends heavily on tea exports for its dollar earnings. Tea accounts for about 38 per cent of the country's foreign exchange earnings. India, on the other hand, exported a little under 200 kgs in 2006 yielding its niche of the top tea to exporting nation to Sri Lanka. India would be hard put to regain its number one position in tea exports, with the island nation set to post a 15 per cent output growth over 2000 levels. In 1971, the Sri Lankan government nationalized all the tea gardens with a cultivated area exceeding 20 hectares. The idea was to keep tea mostly in the state sector so the subsidized inputs could be provided to push exports. The move was backed at the time, but periodic anlaysis revealed that the productivity of small gardens was substantially higher than those under the state. A comparative study of tea gardens under two state sector outfits—Janata Exports Development Board and Sri Lankan State Plantation Corporation (SLSPC), which together own 56 per cent of the area under tea—and privately held gardens showed that the latter recorded better productivity. Aside from this, establishment and subsidy costs made state sector tea production far more expensive. Even compared with South Indian teas, production cost and unit value realization for Sri Lankan tea was much below the average, the study revealed. Studying these factors, the Plantation Restructuring Unit offered the government's estates on long-term contracts to private bidders and management consultants. Twenty-two independent "Regional Management Enterprises", each with 15 to 25 estates were set up. Out of 499 plantations were regrouped from the former 552 corporation owned estates. The regional boards of SLSPC and JEDB were also amalgamated after reclassification. The remaining 53 estates were not viable enough to the prospective private sector and they were left out to JEDB a DIPR Feature) By: P. Teperkrovi Kiso.

Indo-Sri Lanka Relationship

The relationship between the Indian and Sri Lankan tea industries has been deceptive. On the one hand, they are eager to complement each other's role in the global tea trade. On the other, each endeavours to compete with the other to gain a better share in the world arena. In other words, if the marketing circumstances suit, the Indian and Sri Lankan tea industries would like to earn for themselves the highest possible share by competing with each other. If the market dips or the crop is less conducive for open competetion, they consider joint ventures so that they could share between themselves the overall realization. India's admission of facing severe competetion from Sri Lanka has been made clear on many occasions. This was more so on the South Indian front. In the mid-eighties when the exports from the South were tracing a downward curve, the major reason attributed was the inefficiency of the South Indian Tea industry to overcome the competetions posed by Sri Lanka. India was seriously concerned at the fall of exports from the South. Thus, United Planters' Association of South India (UPASI) in Coonoor organized South Indian Tea Convention sometimes in 1990s when it demonstrated to the large number of importers who had assembled there, the supremacy of South Indian tea over the Sri Lankan tea. This convention openly canvassed for South Indian tea against the Sri Lankan counterpart by attempting to explode myths like; Sri Lankan tea is substitutable to South Indian teas, Sri Lanka is more reliable than South India in honouring supply orders, South Indian tea is costlier etc. The trick worked and the exports rose impressively over the years. What, however, should be simultaneously considered is the Sri Lanka has also been doing very well? Unmindful of its ethnic problems and the concomitant economic bottlenecks, the island has not only been producing a sizeable volume, but has been steadily increasing its share in the global market. In 2005, its exports surpassed those of India by 91 million kgs and emerged, for the last one and a half decade as the largest explorer of tea in the world. Although 2001 was a record year for India on the production front a crop of 854 million kgs., events were not very good on the export front. The exports fell to 182 million kgs—the lowest in the eighties and nineties except for 1982 and they were lower than Sri Lankan exports. On the other hand, it was an exceptionally good year for Sri Lanka. Its production rose to a record level of 310 million kgs in 2002 and as much as 285 million kgs in 2001 were exported, surpassing the Indian performance.

It is in this context that the *consideration for Indo Sri Lankan cooperation in tea marketing has once again surfaced.* Shri Ranjan Wijeratne, the then Sri Lankan Minister for Defence and Plantations, had expressed a keen desire to argue such cooperation. The perception was to moot it at the SAARC level. Shri Wijeratne made it clear that India and Sri Lanka should jointly extend a pressure on the world market as they account for an export of over 400 million kgs. This idea was almost on the lines of OPERC or coffee. While all these considerations are still alive, there are indications thatf both these countries are wanting to create an Asian dominance by subsequently bring into the fold Bangladesh. This combination would distance Kenya and other East African countries.

Emphasis on Valued Added Exports

The emphasis on value added exports were given so that the bulk exports could supplement the earning of higher returns. Talks of such cooperation between the two countries had figured a couple of times in the past, but the most significant of them were held in Colombo in September 1988. They were the most significant because; they had the official support of the Governments. Led by Mr. M.R. Sivaraman, the then Joint Secretary in Commerce Ministry, the Indian delegation included Tea Board Chairman and representatives of tea industry from North and South. It was decided that the both the countries should consider rejoining the International Tea Promotion Association and also help in setting up of an international tea producers' community on the lines of pepper, rather than striving for an international tea agreement on the coffee pattern.

As for the specific terms of the cooperation between the two countries, it was broadly agreed that:

(a) Some bilateral understanding should be reached on undercutting of prices in response to global tenders and granting of export incentives;

(b) The modalities and other aspects relating to the setting up of a joint packaging venture would be examined on priority;

(c) Importing of each country's teas by the other to be allowed;

(d) Collaborative research to be undertaken on the health aspects of tea drinking;

(e) Reciprocal study relating to terms of plantations and security could be arranged; and

(f) There should be periodic exchange of data on production, prices, exports and taxes.

However, immediately thereafter, things were looking bright for India and the exports from South India also began to see up. As a result, Indian did not press much for the formalization of the proposals. Nevertheless, there is now regular exchange of information. Study teams are also on. Even in few years back, a delegation from Sri Lanka was in India. As for imports, India has taken up a different stand now—there should be no imports, be they from Sri Lanka or otherwise! The most sensitive aspect of agreement on prices, packaging and joint marketing has been crystallized into some shape. Apart from changes in the marketing scenario, the development on the political front has also had their impact on the slow start of the agreement. The overall Indo-Sri Lanka relationship in the context of dealing with Tamils, curtailing of militancy, IPKF operations, accommodation of Sri Lankan refugees etc. all have lent some impact. The assassination of Mr. Rajiv Gandhi and thereafter matter also had some influence in decisions affecting the tea cooperation between the two countries.

Neverthless, India is concerned on the growth of Sri Lankan exports. The island has chalked out a five-year plan, which targets a production of 350 million kgs by 2010. This would mean an export of around 310 million kgs with eyes clearly to Indian on two fronts. One is to wrest the global market from India to the extent possible and the other is to export to

India itself some CTC teas to bridge the gap here! In fact, Sri Lanka's tea production enhanced from 310 million kgs to 320 million kgs during 2002-05. Similarly, the export records a rise from 285 million kgs to 291 million kgs during the same period. Besides, Sri Lanka enjoys a lower cost of production, which helps the country to beat India's price. It is against this backdrop the India is alive to the initiation on joint ventures with Sri Lanka. Although not many gains have so far been achieved, the issue is very much alive.

Cautions to Sri Lankan Tea—Major areas of Concern

The following factors require re-look for accelerating the growth of Sri Lankan teas:

- ✓ The private sector management companies, which took over the management of tea estates in Sri Lanka, had suffered a setback to the tune of Rs. 3.5 billion in 1994. They asked for more subsidies and loans from the Government and pointed out that the erstwhile state owned corporations had lost almost Rs. 5 billion every year.
- ✓ Mr. Maxwell Fernado, tea consultant of Forbes and Walker, one of the management companies, however, said, "we have cut down costs to some extent and reduced the losses by Rs. 1.5 billion".
- ✓ "The main problem is the low prices about which we cannot do much. We can do something about the second problem, which is the low productivity. Our productivity is well below what is prevailing in India or East Africa", he said.
- ✓ Most of the experts advocated the induction of foreign capital to revamp and restructure tea estates. Nevertheless, the Government did not give the green signal until 1998.
- ✓ Only the management companies were allowed to obtain foreign expertise to make improvement in productivity and technology. Some companies have obtained Indian experts to introduce CTC tea, which has a promising market in West Asia.
- ✓ Sri Lanka's Orthodox teas go mostly to West Asia, but

they are least preferred in Europe, USA or the Far East. There is increased emphasis on producing CTC tea that is expected to double to million kilos by the end of 2007. By the next year-end, the island hopes to increase the proportion of CTC production to 20 per cent. However, the demand of conventional teas is not moving upward. Rather the existing market in Russia and CIS is falling.

- ✓ Iran is also reportedly not buying teas directly. In addition, with the emergence of China and Vietnam as major players in the global tea arena, the possibility of further loosing the market is very much there.
- ✓ The Tea Board in Sri Lanka has expressed concern looking at the current market trend as well as the future.
- ✓ Jordon unlike before is buying a major share in bulk form. It was twenty (20) per cent of country's total exports and only 16 per cent had been in packets. Other Middle East buyers worth reckoning are the United Arab Emeritus (UAE), United Arab Republic (UAR) and Libya. These countries have increased purchases comparing to previous year.
- ✓ Iran, a major buyer of Sri Lanka teas has not been active enough to qualify for a place within the first 12 major buyers.
- ✓ Libya remains as the largest buyer of packeted tea.
- ✓ Report further shows that Australia continues to be the major buyer of tea bags and accounts for 25 per cent of the country's total exports.
- ✓ Green tea is comparatively a new kind of Sri Lanka's export. Japan has emerged as a potential buyer with an initial purchase of about 10 per cent of the total exports. Jordan and Pakistan are also showing much interest in Green tea.

Main Importers of Sri Lankan Tea

The major importers of Sri Lankan Value Added Tea are Jorand, U.A.E, UK, UAR, Libya, Syria, Saudi Arabia, Australia and Japan. Jordan is the main importer of Sri Lankan Tea (11516 thousand Kgs). In fact, Jordan has emerged as the largest importer of Sri Lanka Tea, followed by USA and the UK. The largest importer of tea in value added form is Jordan with a quantity of approx 11.52 million kgs followed by U.A.E. (6.38 million kgs) and Libya (2.16 million kgs). The details are brought in Table 14.1 below:

Table 14.1: Major Importers of Sri Lanka's Tea in 2006

(Thousand kgs)

Country	*Bulk Tea*	*Packeted Tea*	*Tea Bag*	*Instant Teas*	*Other Tea*	*Total*
Jordan	8133	2067	58	–	1258 (B)	11516
U.A.E.	3857	2467	42	–	23 (B) 719 (C)	6389
U.K.	2816	2	36	Neg	7 (B)	2861
U.A.R.	2118	–	150	–	–	2268
Libya	–	2164	–	–	–	2164
C.I.S.	365	1635	75	–	2 (B)	2077
Syria	1667	98	16	–	9 (B)	1790
Saudi Arabia	24	1535	143	–	6 (B)	1708
Pakistan	1528	–	–	–	16 (A)	1544
Australia	590	49	552	–	39 (B) 177 (C)*	1230
Japan	1001	–	5	–	13 (A)	1019
0.70	–	–	14	–	752 (B)* 20651 (C)	836
U.S.A	880	7	7	–	* 324 (A) 1879 (B)	918

Note : * only in Kgs, (A) Green Tea, (B) Tea Imported and Re-exported, (C) Black Tea not Elsewhere Specified

Source : Weekly Auction Report – Forbes and Walker Limited.

World Production of Tea during 1994-2006

World tea Production in 1994 was 1337 million kgs, which increased to 3091 million kgs in 2001 and 3127 million kgs in 2006. Country wise, India constituted 844 million kgs followed by China (705 million kgs.), Sri Lanka (316 million kgs), Kenya (292 million kgs), Indonesia (166 million kgs) and Turkey (142 million kgs). Other countries accounted for 400 million kgs in 2006. Country wise Indonesia's production was more than double between 1994 and 2006. Production was stagnant in the case of Bangladesh, Vietnam, Tanzania, Malawi, and

Argentina over the years. The details are exhibited in Table 14.2.

Table 14.2: Country-wise World Production of Tea during 1994-2006

(in million kgs)

Country / year	*1994*	*2001*	*2002*	*2005*	*2006*	*Diff. (+) or (–)*
India	744	854	826	840	844	(+) 4
Sri Lanka	223	296	310	315	316	(+) 1
Indonesia	77	161	166	167	166	(–) 1
Bangladesh	52	57	53	54	55	(+) 1
China	NA	702	715	715	705	(–) 10
Kenya	185	295	287	288	292	(+) 4
Vietnam	NA	80	84	84	80	(–) 4
Tanzania	NA	25	28	28	26	(–) 2
Malawi	32	37	39	39	38	(–) 1
Turkey	NA	143	145	144	142	(–) 2
Argentina	NA	59	62	61	63	(+) 2
Others*	24	382	384	388	400	(+) 12
Total	1337	3091	3099	3123	3127	(+) 4

* Others include Taiwan, Japan, USSR. CIS, Iran, Uganda, Mozambique, Zaire, Mauritius, Rwanda, Burundi, Cameroon, Brazil, Peru, Ecquador, Zimbabwe, Myanmar, Thailand, Malaysia, South Africa, Australia, Nepal and Euthopia.

Source: Tea Statistics, Various Issues, Tea Board, Kolkata, India.

Reframing the State-Owned Plantation Management Industry

The restructuring of Sri Lanka tea Plantation Sector took place in the year 1992. During the year, the death centenary of James Taylor's, the pioneered Sri Lanka's tea industry was observed. Earlier, Sri Lanka celebrated the 125th anniversary of establishing tea on the island. The year 1992 was marked as the turning point for its plantation industry towards a dynamic future, commencing with the privatization of the State owned plantation management. Twenty-two private sector management contractors were finally selected to manage the twenty-two regional management enterprises after a labourious process of qualification. The deal discussed some of the burning issues which are as follows:

Table 14.3: Crop and Average Price of Sri Lankan Tea Industry during 1980 to 2006

Particular/ Year :	*1980*	*1985*	*1988*	*1989*	*1990*	*1991*	*1992*	*1993*	*2003*	*2005*	*2006*
Crop (Million kgs) :	191.4	214.1	227.0	206.9	234.1	241.6	178.8	231.8	312	315.4	321.6
Sale {Averages price per Kg (Sri Lanka Rs) }	18.33	39.01	42.77	55.47	71.62	58.73	62.24	69.24	72.35	74.5	74.5

Source : Tea Statistics, Tea Board, India, Kolkata, Various Issues.

Mismatch between Price and Cost of Production: The cost of production (COP) of tea in Sri Lanka is rapidly increasing. It went up to Sri Lankan Rs.80 per kg. The price realization is nowhere near this exorbitant COP. The main reason for this high cost of production is the ever increasing cost of labour which contributes anywhere from 65 per cent to 75 per cent. Even after the contracts were awarded, an exorbitant wage increase came about making a further dent in the already high cost of production. The wage increase was announced without any dialogue for discussion with the management contractors. Some of the contractors, disillusioned by the government policy, even threatened to give up the management of these properties.

Corelation between Wage Increase and Productivity: The management contractors believe that the wage increases should be related to productivity and suggested that they should be allowed to reduce the number of days worked. Their excess labour should be shifted to estates where labour is short. However, the Ceylon Workers Congress (CWC) is not agreeable to these suggestions. The CWC which repeatedly wrested wage hikes from the government by threatening strikes, demands its workers be given 300 days of work each year or be paid instead. This, of course, is unaffordable. Although the crop recorded in 2006 was 321.6 million kgs against 315 million kgs of 2005, the plantation section in Sri Lanka continues to be sick. Serious thought was again given to reframe the existing arrangement with the management consultants.

Area under Tea Cultivation by Revenue District and Elevation

Registered tea areas in Sri Lanka are classified according to revenue districts. During 2006, Kandy district accounted for 31.26 per cent followed by Nuwwara Eliya (17.96 per cent), Bandulla (15.42 per cent) and Ratnapura (9.85 per cent). The share of Karunegala, Colombo and Hambantota jointly represented less than 0.45 per cent. Details are shown below:

Table 14.4: Area under Tea Cultivation in Sri Lanka during 2006

Particulars	*Estates (in ha.)*	*Small Holdings (in ha.)*	*Total (in ha)*	*Percentage to total*
Kandy	42,226	17,000	59,226	31.26
Nuwara Eliya	31,046	3,000	34,046	17.96
Badulla	25,277	3,950	29,227	15.42
Ratnapura	12,773	5,886	18,659	9.85
Matara	7,388	6,577	13,965	7.37
Kegalle	5,260	3,999	9,259	4.89
Galle	6,298	8,563	14,861	7.84
Matale	5,041	888	5,929	3.13
Kalutara	2,586	964	3,550	1.87
Karunegala	244	101	345	0.18
Colombo	201	108	309	0.16
Hambantota	5	134	139	0.07
Total	138,345	51,170	189,515	100.00

Source: The Assam Review and Tea News, Various issues, India, Kolkata.

Distribution of Tea Lands: Further, tea lands are distributed according to various elevations. It reveals from the table that tea estates with an elevation of between 610 and 1220 mm accounted for 37.53 per cent followed by estates at high elevation above 1220 mm (32.98 per cent) and estates at low elevation below 610 mm (29.49 per cent). Table 14.5 gives the details:

Table 14.5: Distribution of Tea Lands in Sri Lanka according to Elevation during 2006

Elevation/Year	*2006*	*2005*	*Percentage of total in 2006*
High (above 1220 m)	62,504	62,181	32.98
Medium (610to 1220 m)	71,125	71,500	37.53
Low (below 610 m)	55,866	55,219	29.49
Total	189,515	188,900	100.00

Source: The Assam Review and *Tea News,* Various issues, India, Kolkata.

Classification of Estates: At present, there are altogether 15872 small holdings. Estates below 4.047 hectares constitute 27.02

per cent of total area. Estates above 4.047 to 20.235 hectares covers 11.18 per cent while the estates between 20.235 ha and 40.470 ha constitute 3.64 per cent. Big estates with a holding of above 202.350 ha account for 42.33 per cent of total area owned. The estates with the size groups of 40.470 to 202.350 ha. represent 15.83 per cent. The distribution of tea estates according to size of the holding is given below.

Table 14.6: Classification of Estates by Size of Holdings in Sri Lanka during 2006

Particulars	*No. of holdings*	*Area covered (in hectare)*	*percentage to total*
Small holdings (below 4.047 ha)	154,204	51,225	27.02
Estates from 4.047-20.235 ha	2,782	21,187	11.18
Estates above 20.235- 40.470 ha	273	6,906	3.64
Estates above 40.470-202.350 ha	337	30,001	15.83
Estates over 202.350 ha	276	80,196	42.33
Total :	157,872	189,515	100.00

Source: The Assam Review and Tea News, Various issues, India, Kolkata.

High, Medium and Low Grown Tea in Sri Lanka

The total crop in 2006 was 321.6 million kgs. The significant feature is the contribution made by Low Growns tea (147.3 mkgs in 2006) towards the total crop. The figure of not only confirms its position as a category leader but this figure had not been attained previously by any other sector. In 2003, it was once again the Low Growns tipperd the scale to secure the position as the forerunner by subscribing 141.6 mkgs towards the 312.8 mkgs thereby relegating High Growns to second place. Production from High Growns has been leading the way from the time tea came to be grown in Sri Lanka as a commercial crop. Its share was 40 per cent in 1960. It however declined to 38.2 per cent in 1970, 37.9 per cent in 1980 and 32.6 in 1990. The share rose to 34.5 per cent in 2003. However, it reduced to 33.0 per cent in 2006.

Contribution from High Growns teas had been maintained

at around 40.0 per cent for a considerable length of time until the tide began to turn in favour of Low Grown teas from 1985. On the production front, High Growns have shown a marked decline since 1970 and the lowest figure for the past four and a half decades of 72.6 mkgs was recorded in 1980. The pride of place enjoyed by liquoring teas reversed for the first time in 1990 and since then Low Growns have enjoyed the top berth during the past five years, a further production improvement was recorded for Low Growns. Today, teas manufactured in factories situated below 2000 ft contribute as much as 45.8 per cent of Sri Lanka's total intakes and the position of liquoring teas has eroded gradually. In 1990, contribution from High Growns was only in the region of 32.6 per cent of the total and Medium Growns just 22.2 per cent. The part played by Low Growns in achieving this marked improvement in crop needs to be further enumerated and the potential available for future expansion seems well established. This is the only sector that has shown a steady potential for growth and small beginning in 1960. Low Growns have come a long way to provide noi only 45.8 per cent of total crop but also realizing the best possible prices, which for last year is 20.5 per cent higher to Low Grown.

Table 14.7: Scenario in Production Pattern in Sri Lanka Tea during 1960 to 2006

(in million kgs.)

Year	*High Grown*	*Per cent to total*	*Medium Grown*	*Per cent to total*	*Low Grown*	*Per cent to total*	*Total*
1960	79.7	40.3	69.3	35.2	48.2	24.5	197.2
1970	81.3	38.2	72.3	34.0	59.0	27.8	212.6
1980	72.6	37.9	55.6	29.1	63.2	33.0	191.4
1990	76.1	32.6	51.9	22.3	105.0	45.1	233.0
2003	107.5	34.5	62.7	20.1	141.6	45.4	312.8
2006	106.1	33.0	68.2	21.2	147.3	45.8	321.6

Source: Forbes & Walker Ltd.

The above set of figures clearly identifies the areas that enjoy the highest potential for growth. In the case of High Growns, production levels have only improved by 33 per cent since 1960. In the case of Medium Growns, the position is somewhat serious and only a negative growth is indicated. In this instance, it is important to take into account that quite a sizeable extent of land has come under cultivation of tea due to implementation of various development projects.

On the other hand, it is most revealing that the production from *Low Grown areas has increased over the years.* It is most significant to know that the exceptionally high growth rate was recorded between 1980 and 2006 was the result of various factors that emerged in the entire marketing structure during the period. If this trend continued over next decade, one could expect a substantial increase in Sri Lanka's tea industry. This will facilitate their hopes on this sector for future growth.

Considering the past trend, this year's (2006) Western season exhibited high *quality teas in Sri Lanka*. Useful range of good leaf, and coloury teas from these areas adequately satisfied by the buyers. Teas from Western areas undoubtedly had a success for inclusion in top quality blends. Encouraging enquiry from traditional buyers assured buoyancy in so far the prices are concerned, which are somewhat unmatched earlier. A distinct feature of this season was the inquiry was not restricted to standard grades alone but also for a range of fancy exquisite character which fetched record prices in the current season.

The declining of leafy grade, which is manifesting more clearly as years pass by, is owing to the extensive use of Rotorvanes. Inventive methods used to manufacture *this variety of tea has paid rich dividend and the consumers too got variety of ways to sip this favourite beverage.* In buying patterns, buyers for Syria were active and they were able to secure the requirements at slightly lower levels to last. Buyers to the CIS have been actively participating in all catalogues. This development is closely watched by India with concern that she may lose her dominant role as a major supplier of tea to CIS. During the past decade, Sri Lanka has successfully increased its share of the Russian market by about 300 per cent. This is not a mean achievement.

Tea Manufacturend and Exports

The Sri Lanka Government has manufacturing standards through factory modernization programmes. Tea bags are the growth segment of the international tea market. CTC tea is preferred for tea bags due to its quick brewing quality, colour and small particles. CTC production increased from 6 million kgs to 85 million kgs (or 26 per cent of total production) by 2006. CTC production targets are shown below:

Table 14.8: CTC Tea Manufacture in Sri Lanka—Targets during 1990 to 2005

(in million kgs)

	JEDB	*SLSPC*	*Total*
1990	2.0	4.0	6.0
1993	6.4	13.6	20.0
1995	10.0	20.0	30.0
2000	36.0	19.0	55.0
2003	22.0	48.0	70.0
2005	29.0	56.0	85.0

Source: The Assam Review and *Tea News,* Various issues, India, Kolkata.

Only 1.5 million kgs of Green and Oolong tea per annum is produced currently. It is planned to increase the production of Green and Oolong teas, which command a premium, to 5 million kgs by 2010. Sri Lanka produces 5.5 million kgs of Instant tea at present. This is another area of growth. Investors are being encouraged to establish additional factories to compliment the single existing factory.

Exports: The main thrust of Sri Lanka's export strategy is to switch over from *bulk tea exports to value added exports.* It is proposed to step up exports of tea packets and tea bags as follows :

Table 14.9: Export Targets for Value Added Tea Products during 1970 to 2005

(in million kgs)

Particulars/ Year	*1970*	*1975*	*1980*	*1985*	*1990*	*1995*	*2000*	*2002*	*2005*
Packet Tea	7.72	17.03	31.13	56.03	75.93	93.87	74.91	84.25	92.95
Instant Tea	0.10	0.25	0.20	0.40	0.36	0.71	1.21	1.45	1.75
Tea Bag	-	-	0.28	2.12	4.78	7.54	12.13	13.54	14.45
Total	7.82	17.28	31.67	58.55	81.07	102.12	88.25	99.24	109.15

Source: Tea Statistics, Various issues, Tea Board, India, Kolkata.

Direction of Exports: More than 60 per cent of Sri Lankan teas are marketed in the Middle East, West Asia and North America. While safeguarding Sri Lanka's share in these markets, a sustained effort was made to regain its share in the developed countries. Steps are underway to penetrate the newly emerging free markets of erstwhile USSR and Eastern Europe.

Promotion is receiving due attention. As in the past, the LION logo was the main focal point for the promotion of Sri Lanka teas. The main guidelines for the use of the logo were as follows:

1. The Lion logo is franchised for use in packs per bag conforming to the stipulated quality standards for tea and packing.
2. An only pack per bag containing 100 percent Sri Lanka tea is eligible to use the logo.
3. The franchise of the logo is on the payment of a fee.

Incentives & Taxes: The present incentives and subsidies available for the tea industry are given below:

	Incentive Schemes	
	Private Sector	*Rate*
1	Replanting	Rs. 60,000 (High & Mid Grown Areas) per hectare Rs. 50,000 (Low Grown Areas) per hectare.
2	New Planting	Rs. 45,000 per hectare
3	Infilling	Rs. 10 per plant
4	Credit for fertilizer	Supply of fertilizer through factories. Interest on credit will be borne by the Tea Board.
5	Factory Modernisation and construction of new factories	80 per cent of the cost of approved items of machinery.
6	Conversion to CTC Manufacture	2 per 3rd the cost of CTC Machinery
	Export Promotion	
1	Tea Bagging Machines	The Tea Board will meet 95 per cent of the interest on loans obtained from the purchase of new Tea Bagging Machines.
2	Export Development & Investment Support Scheme (EDISS)	Grants for exports of value added teas.
3	Import Duty Rebate Scheme for Packing materials.	Rebate of 20 per cent of the difference of FOB price and cost of tea for Tea

		Bag Exports.
4	Export Duty	Bulk Tea – Re. 1 per kg.
		Packeted Tea – cts. 50 per kg.
		Tea Bags – cts. 50 per kg.
		Instant Tea – Rs.6 per kg.
		Green Tea – Re.1 per kg.
		Tea Board Cess – Rs.2 per kg.
5	Import of Tea Bagging Machinery	Free of Duty
6	Brand Promotion	Interest free loans
	Taxes	
1	Export Duty	NIL
2	Ad Valorem Sales Tax	NIL
3	Cess (with effect from 2nd April 1979)	
	(i) Medical Aid not payable on instant tea	0.35 cents per kg
	(ii) Tea Board Cell	250.00 cents per kg
	Total (i + ii)	253.35 cents per kg

Source: Tea Statistics, Various Issues, Tea Board of India.

Note: All incentives referred to above are subject to revision.

Important Strategies for Listing the Companies In the Colombo Stock Market

Srategic proposals were submitted to the government who accepted the same in principle. Some of the important strategies are enumerated below:

- ✓ Those then configurations of the estates, grouped under the 22 Plantation Companies, were reviewed, to determine, as to whether these estates should be regrouped into a larger number of smaller groups or whether the grouping into the present 22 groups would be reconfirmed after such review.
- ✓ Once the grouping of the estates was agreed upon, the groups were converted into separate Public Companies under the conversion of Public Corporations into Public Companies Act No.23 of '87, such groups were parts of the respective corporations.
- ✓ Prior to conversion into public companies, appropriate arrangements was made to ensure that the freehold estate lands would continue to be owned by the Government, without being vested in the public companies proposed to be formed. An appropriate strategy was worked out to achieve this.

- ✓ Consideration was given to the desirability to transferring to liabilities, if any, to the public companies which were formed or whether, such liabilities was excluded from being transferred to such companies. An appropriate strategy was worked out, if so, to achieve this.
- ✓ Accordingly, if the liabilities were so excluded, with the incorporation of the companies, in accordance with the provisions of the Conversion Act No.23 of '87, the Buildings, Plant and Machinery, Vehicles, Stocks and other Moveable Assets of the groups identified were vested with the respective companies. Therefore, the companies had an asset base of Buildings, Plant and Machinery, Vehicles, Stocks and other Moveable Assets at the point of incorporation of such companies under the Companies Act.
- ✓ The share capital of these companies was determined based on the net Assets Value and or the Present Value of the reckoned future earning potentials. According to the provisions of the Conversion Act No.23 of '87, at the point of incorporation, such entire share capital of each company was allotted in the name of the Secretary Treasury.
- ✓ The Estate Lands pertaining to the respective companies were made available to the relevant companies based on a 30-year lease. Either the lease rental was payable to the Government by the companies, quarterly or annually, or the net Present Value of such 30 year Leasehold right was capitalised in the Balance Sheet of the respective companies and further shares allotted to the Secretary, Treasury for the corresponding capitalized values.
- ✓ If the leasehold values were so capitalized, then the proposed companies would have further enhanced their respective share capital.
- ✓ The Working Capital requirement of each of the respective proposed companies was evaluated, including provisions for any immediate improvement for refurbishment costs. Arrangements for such

Working Capital funds would no doubt be a prerequisite for the operational viability of each of the proposed companies. It was preferable to raise such funds on a zero based basis, i.e. by way of share capital.

Of the Share Capital determined in respect of each of the proposed companies, Share Capital disposed off in the following proportions:

1 Government (To be retained by Secretary Treasury) 20 per cent

2 Corporate Investor (Mangers of the Public Companies) 40 per cent

3 Employees of the respective Pub. . Companies 10 per cent

4 Public 30 per cent

Total 100 per cent

✓ If need be, consideration was given to reduce the Corporate Investor's Share portfolio and to increase the share portfolio offered to the public. Twenty per cent of the shareholding in each of the companies is proposed to be retained by the Government and may be considered even to be reduced to 10 per cent, if deemed adequate. Because of the proposed shareholding structure, i.e. the Government holding 20 per cent and the Corporate Investor, who is to manage holding 40 per cent the Government and such corporate investor control holding of 60 per cent of the Share Capital of each of the proposed companies.

✓ An appropriate Shareholders' Agreement was entered into between the Government and such Corporate Investor, to ensure that the objectives required by the Government were adhered to and or achieved, with adequate protection to any interests of the Government, if any. The Government agreed to dispose of its 20 per cent shareholding, progressively or otherwise after a transitional period to ensure the stabilization of the restructuring process.

✓ On the other hand, the Articles of Association of these proposed companies defined appropriately such Government Shareholding as a Golden Shareholding.

- ✓ The voting rights of such Golden Shareholding was appropriately defined, such as with veto power, to be exercised in national interest, under certain pre- defined circumstances, affording the Government a certain degree of precautionary safety, to act in the protection of national interest in a given eventuality. If such safety considerations were not necessary, then the feature need not be considered or could be considered as operative for a reckoned transitional period only, as a precautionary measure.
- ✓ The present Estate Management Companies or those who propose to manage the relevant public companies were required to subscribe to such minimum shareholding of the respective companies. This ensured that the Management Companies would have a commitment, financial stake and bear a risk.
- ✓ The management of the proposed companies should not be entrusted to any party, if they were unable to make such financial investment.
- ✓ The employees of the respective companies were given 10 per cent of the shareholdings free, in conformity with Government policy practised in relation to the popularization programme of the Government.
- ✓ The balance shareholdings of each of the proposed companies are to be sold to the public at the Colombo Stock Exchange, ensuring the widest possible spread of such shareholdings.
- ✓ This involved the investing public in the shareholdings of the companies, affording the public an opportunity to have a stake in the plantation sector, thereby defusing any socio political stresses and strains, arising from a feeling of having been left out.
- ✓ The corporate investors did not buy further shares, if they so wish to, in such public share offer and or in the subsequent secondary share market.
- ✓ Consideration was given for arranging underwriting agreements for such public share offers, so that the underwriter progressively sold at the secondary share market.

- ✓ The configuration of the Board of Directors of the companies was also defined in the Articles of Association, to give proportionate representation, i.e. say 1 Directorate to every 10 per cent of the shareholding. Government could consider, if necessary, to have 2 nominees for its 10 per cent, if its shareholding is determined at 10 per cent.
- ✓ The Working Capital requirement, which was funded, would also be raised by way of share capital through a Rights Issue. Consideration was given to providing for such Rights issue, at the point of distribution sale of the original shares.
- ✓ An aspect was considered as to whether the employees were called upon to subscribe for such Rights Issue or whether the Employees Trust Fund Board on their behalf subscribed for their Rights. The proceeds of such Rights Issue were a cash injection into the companies, providing the essentially pre-requisite working capital and any improvement per refurbishments costs, to achieve viability of operations of the companies.
- ✓ A major factor of financial consequence to the Government was the practice of payment of compensation and gratuities to the employees at the point of conversion into such public companies. Such payment was made in Government Bonds and was spread over say 5 to 8 years.
- ✓ The sale of Government shareholdings, particularly with the capitalization of the Leasehold rights, afforded the Government a certain cash inflow. The momentary values involved were reckoned taking into account, the present liabilities of the plantation sector.

The foregoing strategies made the companies listed at the Colombo Stock Exchange. In addition, hence those companies were required to publish Annual Reports and Accounts maintaining transparent ness and accountability to the investing public, thereby affording a satisfactory public review and scrutiny, with checks and balances in the free market system.

Review the Performance of Each Company

The best mechanism in an open competitive market is to review the performance of each of the respective companies. However, it was a Herculean, an unenviable and an ineffective task, to monitor the performance with the best of Evaluation or Monitoring Committees.

- ✓ The Government Nominee Directors on the companies, was no doubt be still required, if deemed necessary, to submit Performance Report, to 'such an Evaluation or Monitoring Committee, for review and appraisal, but without infringement on such companies' strategies and priority of open competetion.
- ✓ The management of the respective companies was no doubt concerned of their respective share price at the Colombo Stock Exchange. They were motivated towards achieving higher price indicators and requisite dividend policy. In the long term, more important of such performance monitoring would be the strategies and directions towards research and development, particularly into the plantation machinery manufacturing and processing sectors, with electronic and computer applications.
- ✓ Plantation sector machinery manufacture was an indigenous mechanical engineering industry, now overtaken by foreign manufacturers supplying to Sri Lanka; whereas Sri Lanka exported such machinery in the past.

Overseas Marketing Strategies: Thursts and Efforts

Quality buyers commenced operating in Colombo on a limited scale, reported Forbes & Walker Limited. Today these buyers have a variety of teas to choose from the thick coloury teas from the Bogo and Maskeliya areas to light bright teas. Speciality teas, which were in limited supply sometime ago, are now available sufficiently. Demand for these teas is well maintained and some of the better sorts are fetching very attractive prices, the Report further indicated.

Most important thrust and effort need be directed towards well coordinated overseas marketing strategies, primarily safeguarding the national interests, with the anticipation of growth, resulting from improvement in productivity and further directed towards processing of retail consumer packs, with improvement in quality. An additional feature of those strategic proposals was that the Colombo stock Exchange grew with the entry of such a large number of public companies representing the plantation sector, the base of the country's economy, a traditional export sector. This also enhanced the market capitalization and the share transactions volume of the Colombo Stock Exchange, giving the Colombo capital market, further impetus and thrust. In the context of the foregoing, it would be relevant to consider whether or not, the present grouping of the Estates into 22 groups, was broken down into a larger number of smaller viable groups, to improve greater participation by the private sector in the management of the plantation sector and thereby creating more competetion. The above strategic proposals were implemented and the existing corporate structures of the 22 Plantation Companies were examined to evolve a strategy to dismantle the same. It considered the requisite strategies. To achieve the objectives of those strategic proposals of corporate structures already existing, were not been examined and reviewed. However, until and unless objective and labour policys are evolved, the Sri Lankan tea industry will not be out of the woods, especially as tea prices are unlikely to show an upward trend in the near future.

Sri Lanka's Tea Imports

On an average, tea export figures indicate that Iran stands as the largest buyer of Sri Lankan tea. Jordan is once again holding the second position with the import of 33.5 million kgs. These two countries, it is observed, in a combination, import a little over 25 per cent of Sri Lanka's total tea exports. Available figures further state, the country has been able to make its presence felt by the United Arab Emirates. The quantum of export has increased from about 4 million kgs during 1992 to 26 million kgs in 2006. Export to Pakistan has improved marginally. Market in Germany has been better. Future prospect in Syria is also considered bright. It is however note worthy to mention here that the Egyptian market is continuing to shrink. Export to Iran has dwindled, recording a drop in the purchase of the country by 66 per cent. Although Sri Lanka has exported additional quantities to certain sectors in the Middle East, and the overall position is not much appreciable. Of course, there has been modest improvement in the shipment of tea to the more affluent markets in the world. Future of Sri Lanka's tea industry largely depends on her ability to obtain a greater foothold in these countries the have the ability to pay freely for the right type of tea says Forbes & Walker Limited. (See Table 14.10)

Table 14.10: Major Importers of Sri Lanka Tea during 2001-05 (in million kgs)

Country	*2005*	*2004*	*2003*	*2002*	*2001*
Jordan	30	32	25	32	33
Syria	25	20	16	12	12
UAE	26	18	6	13	13
UK	20	16	12	15	14
Egypt	18	15	20	25	26
CIS	15	30	5	6	7
Saudi Arabia	14	10	12	15	14
Pakistan	14	9	5	9	9
Libya	8	9	6	13	12
Japan	7	5	6	6	6
Germany	6	7	5	5	4
Iran	5	9	26	34	32

Source: The Assam Review and Tea News, Various issues, India, Kolkata.

Steps to Boost Sri Lanka's Tea Industry

It is interesting to note the in Sri Lanka's tea industry; private sector management entered into the Government owned plantations. All commodity taxes and duties were abolished, licenses and permits covering the tea sector dismantled. Only cess with effect from 2nd April, 1997 was levied on: *(i)* medical aid not payable on instant tea @ 0.35 cents per kg, and *(ii)* Tea Board Cess @ 250 cents per kg. Thus, cess worked out was 250.35 cents per kg. Sri Lanka took further steps to permit the tea producers sell up to 50 per cent of their produce outside the auction floor. Prior to the promulgation of this relaxation, it was mandatory the all tea producers market 90 per cent of their produce through the Colombo Tea auctions. The Sri Lanka Tea Board opened an office in Moscow to facilitate tea trade between the two countries and provide support services to the Russian importers of Sri Lanka tea. Subsequently Russia emerged as the largest buyer of Sri Lanka tea. Sri Lankan tea exports such as bulk tea, packet tea, tea bags, instant tea and green teas are given in Table 14.11.

Table 14.11: Sri Lanka Tea Exports during 2001-05

(in million kgs)

Description/ Year	*2005*	*2004*	*2003*	*2002*	*2001*
Bulk	185	183	182	183	180
Packet	82.5	83	82	83	84
Bag	14.5	14	14	13	12
Instant Tea	2.0	2.5	2	1	2
Green Tea	1.5	1.5	1	1	1
Other Tea	4.5	4	5	6	5
Total	290	288	286	287	285

Source: Tea Statistics, Various issues, India, Kolkata.

Production, Imports, Sales and Exports of Value Added Teas

Tea production in Sri Lanka registered 352 million kgs in 2005. In 2001, it was 296 million kgs and thereafter the position started improving. It was 320 million kgs in 2003 and 335 million kgs in 2004. Report indicates the High Growns teas have improved their contributions from 31 per cent in 2003 to 33 percent in 2005. Medium Growns have virtually maintained her position at around 21 per cent but Low Growns have come down to 41 per cent in 2005 from 45 per cent in 1993. The splendid performance witnessed during the first half of the year could not be maintained and the crop intake began to decline subsequently. The crop fell far short of expectation for the last two quarters of the year, which prevented a better record being established. Details are brought out in table below.

Table 14.12: Sri Lanka Tea Production, Imports and Sales during 2001-05

(in million kgs)

Parameters/ Year	*2005*	*2004*	*2003*	*2002*	*2001*
Production	352	335	320	310	296
Imports	18	15.5	14	12	9
Sales	320	312	305	298	291

Source: Tea Statistics, Various issues, Tea Board India, Kolkata.

In Sri Lanka, there are number of export companies. Top ten exporters name with quantity is given in Table 14.13.

Table 14.13: Sri Lanka Tea Top Ten Exporters 2005

Sr. No.	*Company*	*(in m. kgs)*
1	Akbar Brothers Group	30
2	Unilever Group	28
3	Ms Hebtulabhoy Group	20
4	Stassen Group	16
5	Qualitea Ceylon Pvt. Ltd.	14
6	Jafferjee Bros.	15
7	Van Rees Ceylon Ltd.	15
8	Maharaja Group	15
9	MJF Group	8
10	Standard Trading Co. Ltd.	9

Source: Tea Statistics, Various issues, Tea Board India, Kolkata.

The Planters' Association of Sri Lanka and Colombo Tea Auction—Some Observations

The main impediment in managing these enterprises was increase in cost of production compared to the price realization. Consequently, all companies have heavy borrowings. The interest costs are mounting and creating further difficulties. The current statistics from Sri Lanka show that the wage segment of the cost of production is between 65 per cent and 75 per cent. Even a price escalation in the short term, may not solve the problem as the cost of production, largely due to wages, is very high.

The Planters Association of Sri Lanka suggested that the Colombo tea auctions would be held in US Dollars with the following observations:

- ✓ All plantation companies secure their working capital requirements from local financial institutions in Sri Lanka rupees at interest rates as high as 23 per cent or more.
- ✓ If they are permitted access to offshore funds, they could borrow in US Dollars at interest rates of around 7 per cent for their working capital requirements.
- ✓ In the near future, long term funding for capital development will also need to be obtained and in all probability will have to be secured direct from overseas financial agencies in US Dollars.
- ✓ Such borrowings in US Dollars – whether for working capital or development expenditure – will expose the plantation companies to exchange risks.
- ✓ The only manner in which such exchange risks can be eliminated would be if the plantation companies derived their sales revenue in US Dollars.
- ✓ Hence, the proposal the all bids at the Colombo Tea Auctions and payment for tea purchases should be made in US Dollars.
- ✓ As the current liberalized exchange control regulations in Sri Lanka enable local tea exporters to retain their export proceeds in foreign exchange and also borrow off shore in foreign currency, there should be no difficulty in bidding and paying for tea purchases at the Colombo Auctions in US Dollars.
- ✓ While the major proportion of tea exports from Sri Lanka is invoiced in US Dollars, shipments are also effected in other units such as pounds, sterling and ACU currencies. In such cases, the tea exporters concerned could insulate themselves against exchange risks, if any, by entering into appropriate forward exchange contracts with local banks.
- ✓ Approximately, 10 per cent of the teas sold at the Colombo Auctions are destined for the local market and the buyers of such teas may not have access to

foreign exchange earnings. Such local buyers should be permitted to purchase US Dollars from local banks against Bankers' Sale Notice. In fact the bankers' payment orders in US dollars may be made direct in favour of the broker concerned.

- ✓ The plantation companies should be permitted to retain only 90 per cent of the net sale proceeds in US Dollars while the balance 10 per cent (representing the component for local tea sales) should be surrendered to the Central Bank for conversion into Sri Lanka rupee at the prevailing rate of exchange.
- ✓ Plantation companies are presently permitted to sell upto 10 per cent of their production outside the auction and within this limit, 3 per cent could be disposed of at the factory door. It is recommended that the buyer in US Dollars for the sales through ex factory, should continue to be effected in Sri Lanka rupees as at the present, while any teas disposed of by private or direct sales against the appropriate certification by the Tea Board, should pay for payment.
- ✓ When auction bids are expressed in US Dollars, any deteriorating trend in prices becomes very transparent, and at the same time will eliminate the sense of complacency among producers, exporters and other concerned, which have often been deluded by an apparently favourable movement in Sri Lanka rupee prices.
- ✓ The above proposals will provide a much-needed fillip towards improving the viability of the presently ailing plantation companies without any detriment to the national exchequer, as it does not involve any subsidies, grants or similar financial assistance.
- ✓ In Kenya, the system of tea auction bids in US Dollars was introduced almost overnight by a Presidential edict in October 1992 and shortly thereafter Malawi adopted this system. It is understood that tea auctions in dollars are now well established in Kenya as well as Malawi, and are a great success with benefits accruing to all concerned—producers, exporters and brokers.

Strong Incentive to Producers—Bidding in US Dollars

The introduction of bidding in US Dollars in October 1992 has also proved a further strong incentive to producers offering tea in the Mombasa Auctions and additional quantities not only from Kenya but also from Uganda, Burundi, Rwanda, Tanzania and Zaire have now been attracted to Mombasa. This allows payment for teas sold in US Dollars within ten working days from the date of sale and obviates any devaluation in local rates and rapid payment in a stable currency. However, the 'dollar auction proposal' has not had universal acceptance in Sri Lanka and the exporters, in particular, have voiced anxiety. The Central Bank of Sri Lanka studied the proposal. All things being equal, the Sri Lankan tea situation was quite bleak. On the one hand, the banks tightened up on credit and on the other profits were virtually non-existent due to high cost of production and sluggish export prices. Therefore, if Sri Lanka tea industry is to get out of the woods, then the goal posts will have to be firmly fixed. Indonesia has also been following the dollar system of auctions. The system may have validity for India as well, of course requiring small modifications due to substantial domestic demand.

Colombo a Hive of Activity

The restoration of stability from the commencement of 1990s brought about a complete change in the attitudes and aspirations of all concerned. So far, the tea industry is concerned; there was a firm determination to utilize to its maximum all facilities made available towards the improvement of the industry. Weather was favourable and conditions were ideal for growth after the fields had been rested the previous year due to forced work stoppages. All fields had recovered fully and with favourable weather, fertilizerto applications went down at the right time resulting in a surge in crop. Marketing of produce was undisrupted and prices obtained were most attractive, which facilitated the producers to keep the tea fields in pro per agricultural conditions. Confidence was once again restored and orders channeled to Colombo improved. Colombo became a hive of activity and auction prices rose. Maximum efficiency was restored at the Port of Colombo and exports affected, with the least amount of delay. All sectors associated with the tea industry and trade did a grand job to achieve the result of 2006.

Positive Aspects of Tea: Area covered under tea cultivation has various positivects. These are as follows:

- ✓ Helps maintain fluid balance required by the human body.
- ✓ Contains beneficial minerals including fluoride and potassium with low sodium.
- ✓ Has zero calorie content.

Colombo Tea Market

According to Colombo Tea Market sources, all eyes were focused on the Gulf area and the main concern was to ascertain whether the escalating ground situation in the Gulf and the economic blockade of Iraq and Kuwait effectively prevented Ceylon's tea exports from reaching Iraq. The reports said that an appeal was made to the U N Security Council with regard to the special problems, which Sri Lanka faced, if it abided with the mandatory resolution and embargoes on tea exports. The same sources pointed out those shipping routes to the countries. Other trading sources not only in the gulf areas but also in the Red Sea and the Mediteranean Ports remained open with forward bookings currently accepted. The only draw back in this connection, however, was the extra freight the shippers were called upon to pay in view of the price escalation of all petroleum products. Sri Lankan Government circles hoped that the country's resolution presented to United Nations could have been viewed on humanitarian grounds. Sri Lanka permitted to keep its main sources of revenue coming in without any disruption—"as this means our very existence", as some authoritative sources in Colombo put it. Meanwhile, according to reports circulated by Forbes & Walker Limited, the uncertainty that prevailed in the world political arena could have contributed to the low prices at the Colombo auctions in 2000s. It was however significant to note that Egypt Trade Center recommenced operating in Colombo after a long absence.

Before the sudden Gulf Crisis struck the world, the Sri Lankan Tea Industry was filled with hope for the future. The market behaved most buoyantly. Other important factors for pushing up optimism were most aptly summed up by Forbes & Walker thus, "the weather had been exceptionally favourable so far—this year and normal patterns of rainfall had prevailed so as to facilitate the proper agricultural practices to be carried out. There had been neither prolonged droughts nor excess rainfall. Preplanned fertilizer programmes have been adhered to and pruned fields have recovered fast." What was significant was that a new trend emerged not only on the production front but also in the marketing of various categories of tea. Now the question asked is what the immediate future holds out. The overall position, according to Forbes & Walker is that a crop of 127.0 million kgs have already been harvested for the first six months, it is very likely that the final reckoning, a crop of about 290 million kgs could result. Another very significant factor in Sri Lankan Tea Crop was enhancement of both production and exports. Of this increase, the biggest segment was concerned to packeted tea compared to bulk tea exports. A tea bag export was virtually double. The FOB unit value of all teas exported up to April 2005 registered a much-increased percentage.

Low Domestic Consumption

Faced with very low consumption of tea in Sri Lanka and its main competitor India having to divert more and more tea to the domestic market, it was thought initially that Sri Lanka tea would secure bigger orders. In the context of the world demand growing by about 30 million kgs each year and Indian on the other hand needing an equal quantity of extra tea every year to keep the domestic market adequately fed it was the hope in Sri Lankan tea circles that Russia would turn more and more towards it. This hope could not yet adequately materialize though Russia was reportedly looking for extra requirements of about 80 million kgs. This problem was solved itself in the context of the Gulf Crisis, increased Russian preferences for CTC and the uncertainty of Indian production because of the formidable constraints. In the context of the world requiring an additional quantity of 130 million kgs the world markets are buoyant but which country will ultimately benefit remained a prizes question. All major tea producing countries in the world recorded surpluses for this year, according to reports reaching Colombo and is comfortably placed when compared to last year with a total harvest of about 70 million kgs extra so far during the first six months of the year. It is hoped that the Sri Lankan Tea Industry that the country will further grow speedily.

International Arena—Merit of Tea before Buying Decision

In the international arena, there is marked trend to analyze the merits of tea before buying decision is made. A system has been evolved to identify between several types of tea. The country from where the tea originates, and the elevation at which the beverage grows, the manufacturing process and last but not the least, quality is keenly looked into now a day. So far, the Island Nation is concerned; teas are broadly classified into high, medium and low grown depending on the elevation of the factory. As per manufacturing process, the beverage is also classified into two: Orthodox and CTC. Similar classification exists in case of export too. Bulk form contains major portion of export and other forms of instant tea and biotea are gaining added importance. This trend is more visible in the countries, which export tea, and Sri Lanka has realized its importance. It is acutely felt in the tea trade and Industry in Sri Lanka that, in the marketing arena it could play an increased vital role by offering the consumers a wide choice rather than sell tea in international markets in its basic form thus leaving the job of value addition to other countries. By denying the due importance to value added exports, Sri Lanka has realized that, it would permanently lose a growing potential marketing segment. It is increasingly felt in Sri Lanka that it is essential to break away from tradition and explore new markets for specialty teas. Obviously, here lie the long-term interests of Sri Lanka. Predictably, there could be some problems at the initial level but better planning and strategy could overcome so that Colombo gets a firm footing in the international tea market in the years to come. Thus, the report on tea scene of Sri Lanka underscores the increased awareness in the country's tea trade and industry about value addition.

Health Hazards—Tea Factory Cough and Tea Makers' Asthma

Health hazards—Health hazards associated with prolonged exposure to tea dust was first reported more than 100 years ago. Reference to 'tea factory cough' and 'tea maker's asthma' was made in Sri Lanka over 70 years ago. Coughing up of blood was a common symptom among those exposed to tea dust for a long time. A study on ventilatory function of tea factory workers in Sri Lanka revealed a higher prevalence of chronic bronchitis, asthma and other chronic respiratory symptoms such as cough, phlegm and difficulty in breathing. Although not much attention was paid to these problems in the past, occupational safety is now receiving more attention world over. It is imperative, therefore, to address such problems to safeguard the well being of workers.

Airborne Particles: Airborne particles are produced during drying and grading of tea. Finer particles are produced in CTC and Orthodox rotorvane manufacture compared to pure Orthodox manufacture. Fluid Bed Dryer (FBD) also produces more airborne particles compared to Endless Chain Pressure (ECP) dryer. Leaving the 'dust fan' on while grading also aggravates the problem. During rolling, roll breaking and fermenting, particles do not get airborne, as they are wet. However, the particles generated during drying could settle down in the plenum chamber of the ring trough. When the workers loosen the leaf on the trough with the ring fan on, they might get exposed to these particles. However, switching the fan on and leaving the door of the trough open for a short time while the leaves are on the trough could blow off these particles.

Airborne particles are also generated during blending of tea. Studies have shown the prevalence of chronic bronchitis and asthma among tea blending workers. Diameter of airborne particles generated during tea manufacture range from sub micron to millimeter size. Particles with a diameter of 0.65–3.50 mm are the most hazardous to health. Most particles smaller than 0.65 mm are brought out again with exhaled air while particles larger than 3.50 mm are deposited in that, south or upper bronchi. Particles with a diameter range of 0.65 to 3.5 mm are retained in the inner respiratory system (bronchi and alveoli of the lungs). There they will either be slowly absorbed into the blood stream or destroyed by phagocytes. However, the process is slow and the tissues are inflamed for a long period resulting in respiratory difficulties and diseases.

Installation of Dust Collectors or Use of Masks: Installation of dust collectors or use of masks could prevent the inhalation of these particles. There are more than 10 types of dust collectors used in industries to separate the dust from air depending on the size of particles, concentration, type of material etc. Single cyclones are effectively used to separate particles larger than 10 mm. Multiple cyclones are used to separate particles larger than 5 mm. Viscous coated air filter, dry fibre filter and cloth bags are effective in filtering particles of sizes 0.3 to 5.0 mm. However, the simplest and cost effective method of preventing inhalation of fine particles (less than 3.5 mm) is the use of masks made with three materials.

Sri Lanka Tea Board

As part of this socialistic move, the Sri Lanka Tea Board was formed. The Sri Lanka Tea Board at the time encompassed all the existing organizations in tea; it was intended to be a sole body. Under the Tea Board came what was the former Tea Promotion Board, which is now a Tea Promotion Division. Over the 80s, unfortunately, the nationalized part of the industry went into decay: genes came down, quality came down and everybody was to blame except the people there itself—they blamed the system, they blamed the weather. It was also a period of opportunity, in the sense that the State sector started declining and the private sector took off. Most of the private sector is operating on the low grown areas and a very interesting phenomenon was observed during the 1980s. There was stagnant production where Sri Lanka's total tea output was around 220 million kgs. But the word stagnant led to a boom in the small holding area. It also led to a boom in marketing because these private factory owners were very receptive to market conditions. It explored many innovations – it is said the when the going gets tough, the tough gets going and in retrospect the privatization. It helped to jog the Sri Lanka tea industry to reach new heights.

New Levels of Marketing

Many new levels were done in marketing during the time. The growth of value-added exports boomed. The State sector came down and down at the early 1990s. The government was actually pumping in Rs.400 million per month just to keep the State Corporations running. However, the private sectors were making money. Finally in 1992, the Government handed over the management of most of the State plantations to the private sector.

Tea Industry Beats the Cola: The trade realized that they had to be together because under the State there was a mistaken notion that the competitor was the plantation next door. However, the trade's realization is not so and the competitors are out there in the mighty world, particularly in the Colas. The Colas at the time had a massive boom and gradually taking over the tea markets. So the industry came up with innovative products, which required with skillful marketing. The industry couldn't match the Colas. However, the industry had some advantages because small is beautiful and in a sense that the industry beats the Colas in many instances. Tea came into zone and just after the privatization of management, under the auspices of the Colombo Tea Traders Association (CTTA). All the sectors got together and said that there is no point of privatization of management unless one knows which way one is going. So there were survéys and interviews were done, Unions were talked to. And suddenly an import book came out. It was intended to publish in 1993 but actually brought out at the start of 1994. The title of the book was "Towards the Year 2000". The book itself served as a guideline to promoting tea. It also indicated the way the industry was going. The industry promoted Ceylon Tea and ultimately the chain breaks. To it had to be a win-win situation, thus the industry had to take the tea small holders, the factory owners, unions, Government and all State Holders into being.

Lessons from Other Industries: One such industry particularly is the French Vine industry. The tea industry has a lot to learn on how the industry can improve its marketing. But now they have a nice word for it, they call bench marking. The tea industry feels that the French industry has a lot to offer. French

Vine Industry had a legal letter from the French Government threatening to sue the Sri Lanka Tea Board for the use of the word 'Champagne.' The sense it was the French, so the tea industry changed its slogan from "Nuwara Eliya—the champagne of Ceylon tea", to an acceptable slogan which is, "Nuwara Eliya: Ceylon Tea or Champagne: French Vine". It is mentioned that the tea industry has to take everyone with them and the industry in Sri Lanka is huge, it employs over a million people directly and indirectly and many more dependants.

Strengths of Sri Lankan Tea

One looks at one's strengths. It is important always to play to one's strengths. If one looks at the Sri Lankan Cricket Team, one had certain strengths and one always plays to them. Some people complain that Murali bowls too long, but he does it, because it is his strength. He may not be fair on other bowlers to give a chance to bowl, but like the cricket team, the tea industry also has to play to its strengths. One has to cover up one's weaknesses and play to one's strengths. What is strength of the Industry? One will have to analyze.

The first strength is that the Sri Lanka is relatively a small country, but it has unique agro climatic zones, each is producing a different type of tea. The industry decided a long time ago—let's promote teas. There is no Ceylon tea—it is a generic term for a wide variety of teas and what are these teas? Firstly, Ceylon has the 'Kandy' of the medium teas having elevation between 600 metres to 1200 metres producing strong brewed. Along the western side of the country, Ceylon has a unique tea—it used to be called Western. However, it is not catchy term for marketing purposes, so the industry circle is named it after one of the towns there 'Dimbula'. It has 'Nuwara Eliya' that is right at the top of the country produces unique teas as the Darjeeling in India. 'Udapussellawa', which is next to Nuwara Eliya, but has its teas of its own. Then 'Uva' makes good quality, especially during the South West monsoon. Finally, there is the vast extent of tea in the lower elevations, which one calls low growns—but some people think lower refers to quality— so one has marketed it as 'Ruhuna'—again after ancient capital area, this is known as six fine Ceylon teas, which suit all tastes and one of the big things is variety. Sri Lanka had option, as did Kenya many years ago, as to which direction should go in. As you know, Kenya set out to be the lowest cost producer, succeeded, and made teas for the mass market. In Sri Lanka it was decided that the industry couldn't do that.

The second strength is that the country has unique products. Some of which are familiar with everybody—various grades. It is not catering to the mass markets; it is catering to the individual customer—giving the consumer a range of whatever teas he or she wants. Officially, there were 24 grades of black tea. This is the part from green tea, instant tea and the concentrates. So a committee of marketing experts was constituted. The Committee was to oversee 24 grades and see whether there is need to reduce some and may give up some, they did a lot of work and came up with interesting answer, increasing the numbers to 30. It may sound odd, but actually what they are doing is they are catering to each market. The more segmentation is done, the more is the value addition. The more unique is the range of products the more the industry succeeds. Contrary to what one might feel, Sri Lanka does not have any mass to market products. All the brands, all teas are unique catering to niche markets. There are a few brands, which are quite popular—but look carefully; those brands are all niche brands. For example, it is intended and aimed at Australian and New Zealand markets. The Albaza or Soan brand and Algazin are aimed at the Middle East. A special tea for a special type of water, a special type of consumer similarly we have been into the infra going into the ICS and a range of other specialties for special people.

Third strength is Colombo Hub: The CTTA made hub in Colombo and by its Rules, ensured that all the packinghouses come in Colombo (in the north of Colombo exact). All the warehouses come in the same area. The area is called Colombo the Hub—one of the biggest strengths. Everything happened in the Colombo, and it is the largest auction of its kind in the world. By doing so, the industry has been able to increase the demand because industry concentrated all the demand in one place. How does the industry do that, by concentrating all the supply in one place? If there is no supply, there is no demand. In addition, the industry dependent on demand and all the demands have been focused in one spot i.e Colombo. Thus, it is the largest auctions of its kind in the world. A few statistics are given such as some 600 sellers, 150 buyers, 8 brokers and the amount of samples (1,000,000 samples sent out per week) and the amount of lots (8000–12000 different lots) per week. It is a lot of work, but it is well rewarding. It is also probably the largest packing operations of its kind in the world.

All the packers are doing their jobs with 350 and odd tea bagging machines. Colombo town has the largest number of tea bagging machines in the world. It also makes Sri Lanka—the Third largest tea bagging supplier or tea bag supplier and largest in the Asian–Pacific region. It is also the hub port in the Indian Ocean, in fact they call us from the far to east, stop at about ports, Hong Kong, Singapore, Colombo and from Colombo it is non-stop to the Western world. This has been a great advantage because the industry has fixed its selling opportunities. It can actually plan and plan very well. As a matter of interest there have been occasions where the industry has received an order for tea bags on Monday, bought the tea on Tuesday, after the next been on the shelf. Of course, it is possible because infrastructure has been built up. There is a possible eight weeks between bush and cup. From the time it is plucked to the time it is drunk can be as low as eight weeks and therefore, if one wants fresh tea come to the industry because it is packed where it is grown and some of our packers themselves use the same slogan—"Tea from the factory to your cup... etc."

Role of the Industry—Past, Present and Future

Over the years, there is a lot of confusion on the industry itself, what role it has played, what role it is playing and what role it can play? Therefore, the trade has to take an initiative to do a TV programme, which should be in all three languages: Tamil, Singalese and English. It will be a series; it will be aimed at all the players and even the non-players. It is a very important decision because the industry has to take everyone with them. The humble plucker who plucks the tea should know what happens to it eventually. What potential there is smallholder who tends his little plot, should know what becomes to his tea? Even the Government people should know what happens to their tea after it leaves the country. So the industry is having a series of programmes, which will help to take the whole nation.

In fact, the commodity trap has been broken. When a country produces a commodity its standards are fixed and it (country) is at the mercy of the world market, just to watch the standard available about the commodity of the country. Prices go down, sometimes even if there are short supply the prices, still go down. So the industry has emphasized the individuality of each tea and in the sense beaten the commodity trap. It is lot of effort, every auction, there are 12,000 lots of tea and there is lot of tasting to do. It is done because of the part of value enhancement of the whole industry. One thought is what industries can one piggyback on, what industries can one tie up with and the obvious answer was the tourist industry. 400,000 and odd tourists come to Sri Lanka every year and if each of them take back a range of fine Ceylon teas and introduce them to their friends etc., even if they don't take back the samples, but the industry convince some of the beverage to drink Ceylon tea, that's another convert.

What is the future? Is it sufficient to look the industry has done well in the past, pat the industry on the back and all relax with a cup of tea? Nevertheless, it is not so, it is hard world, other beverages are already in the sale. Other beverages are all grasping for the share of throat and some are very innovative. As one knows ten years ago, hardly anybody used bottle water, now bottle water has taken off and this puts even tea under some threat. Therefore, the industry has to be innovative all the time and looking as to what the industry can do to be one-step ahead. So what are the measures that the industry is doing?

Conclusion

Quality has to be vermouth because the industry does not have a low cost of, one might envy some of the plantations with their sale average but some of them have actually run on losses because their costs are high. Therefore, the industry has to keep on emphasizing the quality aspect. The industry is looking of ways and means of doing, it, may be competetion among the plantations for the best quality product. The industry has started a dialogue with the research people. Some of the companies are waiting for high yield at the detriment of quality. Immediately the prices come right down and are visible. Thus, the industry has to emphasize quality, which is difficult. It is easy to measure yields but price is different it is not tangible; one can see the only once.

Quality is of paramount importance. Why, because the customer is of paramount importance and it is highly customer focused. People want to try out new products. In the old days they drank tea, now they want to know what type of tea they are drinking. An let us take the United States of America, which till recently used to drink some of the world's worst teas purely because they mix it up with peach and other flavours and hit the tea flavour or the tea non flavour. The specialty market in US is growing. It is enormous, there are catalogues, which are offering a whole range of teas, and one ought to get all one's teas on to this catalogue. There are mail order companies offering a range of teas—one wants to get ones teas on those catalogues. One sees this as a part of the specialty market. It is not exclusive because specialty teas or specialty herbs, herbal teas, etc. Nevertheless, the main thing is to increase demand and get there on those catalogues, get there on the shelves, get there to the consumer. One has also embarked on what may be called the completeness initiative. One has been looking on one's self and seeing how one can reduce transaction costs. It is mentioned that it is possible to go from bush to cup in 8 weeks. However, one is asking oneself is one content with that? Can't one do better? Cause transaction costs make a huge burden on the final price. The consumer is not going to increase the price he pays to the seller because producer's costs are high. He is not even concerned about producer costs. All he wants is value for money, which has to come and meet costs. So looking at ways and means of reducing transaction costs, one must concentrate on the plantations, mechanical pruning, holing—one is trying to make the export industry more efficient and trying to get on line with technology to the customs where one does not have to send a messenger to pass his documents, but only has to press the button.

Let us also look at the whole auction system; it has been a great success. It has been very transparent. It has encouraged buyers all over the world to come to auction center, because nothing is more transparent than auction. New buyers will come on the scene or normally vary about dealing in the places they don't know anything about. But if the whole system is transparent, they have no problem. In auction there is no under the table, over the table etc. the teas as they go to the highest bidder. So now, for example, tea company has both plantation interests as well as export interest, company puts its tea in the auction and buy it back and it has been experienced the very often some buyers pay higher price and the industry or company does not get it. Looking at the auction, the transparency, and the competetion, one has signed up with a partner. The partner is working on automating auction. If all goes well, this time, next year one should have a auction where one does not shout.

The above chapter, thus, dealt with the major developments, which took place over a period of fifty years in Sri Lankan Tea industry. While deliberating such aspects various issues have emerged. Efforts have been made to document the legendary perseverance at perfecting the art of tea manufacture since 1857 by John Tailor, the Father of Srilankan Tea. He was instrumental in transferring state owned plantations to private sector, nationalization of foreign companies and setting up of 22 independent 'Regional Management Enterprises', each with 15 to 25 states. Major recommendations of South Indian Tea Convention held in 1990s emphasizing the cooperation between India and Sri Lanka on marketing, value added exports and follow up measures were incorporated in this chapter. The conventions cautioned the industry in this regard. The industry was thrown open to private sector. Major buyers/importers of Sri Lankan tea, apparent consumption per head, estimated world production and Sri Lankan share, mis-matched between price realization and cost of production along with strategies been spelt out. Sri Lanka Dairy takes into account hardship like power cut, water cut, etc. Besides, expansions of credit, production/ import/sales/exports have been propagated. Various suggestions by planters associations of Sri Lanka for development of the tea industry were inserted. A comprehensive note on the 'Reformist Zeal' indicating distribution of tea area by district/elevation/holding was made. Further attempt have been made to include export of value added products during 1970 to 2005, incentives, changing scenario in production pattern during 1960 to 2000, and restoration of stability. In the process, attempts are made to cover strength and future of Sri Lankan Tea industry. The strength includes formation of Tea Association/Tea Propagation Board, Sri Lanka Tea Board, enactment of Tea Control Export Act, implementation of new levels of marketing, exports of value added products, introduction of Colombo Hub, existence of tea bagging machine and tea bag supply, etc. The future of the industry suggests further ensuring quality and customer focus, more transparency in auction system and propagation of tea as tourist industry.

15

Medical Efficacy of Pu'er Tea of China

Introduction

The name Pu'er Tea was a specialized term used to describe a kind of tea *characterized by its processing technology, commodity variety and quality all that evolved under certain circumstances: political, economical, production, consumption, communication and transportation*. Thus, the so-called Pu'er Tea was a kind of post-fermented tea, produced in the Xishuangbana and the Simao localities of Yunnan Province. This was again transported to markets in Pu'er Town, the then political and economic center of (Xizhuangbana) Simao. It is recorded in the *"Dianhai Wuheng Annals" (vol 11) the "Pu'er Tea enjoys fame all over the world, this being the reason why Yunnan produce it to generate income... thus of people cultivate tea on the mountains, buyers collect the tea and transport it to other places for sale. Huge profits are reaped when business is good"*. Since the early periods of the Qing Dynasty, Pu'er Tea has been sold plentifully all over China. It could contest with other kinds of tea such as Mengding, Wuyi, Liuan and Longjing and was sold in distant lands such as Thailand, Laos, the South Pacific countries, Hong Kong, and Macao. In 1729 the Pu'er Tea trade was concentrated in Pu'er Town, where during 1911 to 1919 after the founding of the Chinese Republic, 30 to 40 companies were still dealing in tea business. At the time green tea was sun dried to yield a heart shaped product called *"Tight Tea" or "Ball Tea". Pu'er "Square Tea Cakes" and "QuizBing Tea Cake"* (so named from its disc shape and the fact they were packaged in one cylinder), the last being the Pu'er Tea Cakes of today. Towards the end of the Qing Dynasty "Tuo Cha Tea" was be made in Xiaguan (bowl shaped, the Pu'er Tuo Cha of today). These belonged to natural Post fermented tea. After the liberation, artificial Post fermentation replaced the previous natural Post fermentation (done mainly by sprinkling water).

Exports of Pu'er Tea

China Pu'er Tea was originally produced in the Xishuangbana area Pu'er and Xiaguan localities and concomitant with the popularization of the large leaf varieties. Guangdong and Guangxi Provinces also commenced to cultivate this kind of tea. Other provinces like Hunan, Sichuan and Guizhou also produced this kind of tea utilizing small and medium sized leaf varieties. Pu'er Tea is available in Yunna, Sichuan, and Xizang (Tibet) and Guangdong Province. It is sold to Hon Kong, Macao, Japan, Singapore, Malaysia and Western European counties. Pu'er Tea is the primary tea variety on the Hong Kong market. According to the Hong Kong 27 April, 1987 cumulative No.2016 issue of the *"Economic Guide"* journal, a total of 11,480 thousand kgs of tea was sold in Hong Kong. Out of which, over 4,000 thousand Kgs.was Pu'er Tea, Qolong Tea running second with 1,000 thousand kgs, while Scented Tea and White Tea together accounted for only about 500 thousand kgs. At present, the sale of Pu'er Tea on the Hong Kong market is about 6,000 thousand kgs. Hong Kong's recent reselling of tea to Taiwan and Japan involves mainly Pu'er Tea also. Japan's yearly consumption of Pu'er Tea increased from 100 to 2,000 thousand kgs. *Ever since the Yunnan Tuo Cha (a variety of Pu'er Tea) won in 1986 and 1987 twice the white marble World gold cup, its production has been increased 5 to 6 times, but still not enough to meet the demand.* In retrospect, of all the special varieties of tea exported by China over recent 20 years, the volume of Pu'er Tea showed the greatest increase.

Table 15.1: Export of Tea Brand of China during 1965 to 2005

(Qty: in million kgs)

Year / Tea Brand	*1965*	*1975*	*1983*	*1988*	*1992*	*2001*	*2005*
Pu'er Tea	23.57	36.0	51.5	78.4	62	79.0	86.90
Oolong Tea	57.8	47.3	43.1	48.3	93.0	114.7	126.3
Scented Tea	19.3	20.3	30.2	31.3	35.0	44.5	48.9
White Tea	5.2	11.2	6.3	-	Negl	79.	8.7
Libdio Tea	14.0	23.8	13.9	-	-	-	-
Louging Tea	2.2	1.4	1.0	7.0	-	3.9	4.2
Total Tea	122.0	140.0	146.0	165.0	190.0	250.0	275.0

NB –1965 to 1985 figures for Oolong tea, Scented tea and Whito tea represent export by Fujian Province.

Source: International Tea Committee.

Analysis of data in the above table shows that the export volume of total special teas for the year 2005 increased by 2.25 times compared to 1965. The increase of Pu'er Tea was 3.70 times, Qolong Tea 2.19 times, Scented Tea 2.53 times, White Tea 1.53 times. Thus, the export volume of Pu'er Tea not only was higher than that the averages figure for other teas, but also its increase was greater than other kinds of special teas. Guangdong Province has put great efforts into the development of Pu'er Tea production and can compare with Yunnan Province in export volume and product quality. Moreover, Guangdong has exceeded Yunnan on the Japan market. About 23 million kgs of Pu'er Tea was imported by Japan, of which 18 million kgs were produced in Guangdong comprising 78 per cent Yunnan Province the contributed 1.70 million kgs (7.4 per cent); the remaining 22 per cent consisted of products from Sichuan Province, Hunan Province and competitive products from Vietnam and other foreign countries.

Pu'er Tea—With Miraculous Functions

The pue'r Tea has many health giving properties that are discussed below:

The Nutritive and Health Functions: In modern times, people largely have three attitudes towards goods: namely, commodities should provide *novelty, beauty and health*. Of these requirements, health is the major one that is also the basic factor for any commodity to excel on the market. *"High mountains shrouded with clouds and mist yield famous tea"* is an old saying. Such places in Yunnan are cold mountains and plateaus in unparalleled geographical surroundings with picturesque mountains and ravines. Moderate climate, non-frost winters and springs, abundant rainfall, winding clouds and mist, and fertile soil are also prevalent. They are the cradle of the world's tea culture and sometimes referred to as the homeland of tea. According to an ancient *Dai document* of the Xishuangbana Dai Nationality Autonomous District, tea cultivation in Yunnan Province existed as early as 1700 years ago. In the primeval forests of Mount Dahei Menghai County, a giant wild growing tea tree was discovered and given the name *"King of all tea trees in the world"*. The excellent natural conditions of Yunnan allowed the large leaf tea grown there to become one for the best tea varieties of the world. This together with the unique processing technology adopted which permits full oxidation of the polyphones and caffeine, substances beneficial to the human body, yielded a product of unique flavour and quality.

Pharmacological and Health Giving Properties: In ancient times many books such as *"Diannan Record"* and *"Supplements to the Compendium of Materia Medica"* recorded the pharmacological and health giving properties of Pu'er Tea. In the chapter on trees of "Supplement to the Compendium of Materia Medica" volume 6, which was edited by Prof. Zhao Xuemin during the reign of Emperor Qian Long of the Qing Dynasty was stated: *"Pu'er Tea is a panacea for all illness. For example, when ginger tea is given in tympany and colds, healing occurs immediately after sweating; in oral ulcers and sore throat, or fever and pain, one need only to hold 0.05 ounce of the tea in the south overnight to achieve cure..."*. These are early description of the medical efficacy of Pu'er Tea. Sorting out the clinical evidence provided by China's medical profession, it can be seen the Pu'er Tea has shown significant effect in reducing *cholesterol level*. It can be taken for long periods of time without any side effects, and also has *bacteria static effects*, being able to prevent and cure *dysentery and enteritis*. Since 1978, Dr. Emile Karoubi, Head of the Clinical Instruction Department of the

Saint Antolne Medical College, Paris, has subjected the Pu'er Tea (Tuo Cha) of Yunnan to tests, focusing on the *weight reducing and anti steroid actions of Pu'er Tea in human beings. The* study demonstrated that 40 per cent of the people who took part in the test showed weight reduction, and the results were especially notable in those over the age of 50. The anti steroid efficiency attained 67 per cent, and the effect on the tricaboxylic glycosides of the human body more marked, with 30 per cent of the under test exhibiting reduction of cholesterol. When the results of the tests were published in France, it made an impact not only on France but also some other European countries. Consequently, the little known Tuo Cha suddenly loomed to prominence in Western Europe.

Clinical Trials by NRIHM: Clinical trials conducted by the National Research Institute for Health and Medicine (NRIHM) in France since the eighties have demonstrated that Pu'er Tea (Tuo Cha) can lower the blood fat level. The patients' with very high blood fat level, 20 per cent showed a reduction of 22 per cent within two months. Professor Lu Tong of the Laboratory of Nutrition, Orson, also performed similar tests and concluded, "This kind of tea apparently contains one or more constituents which can influence the metabolism of lipoids". The *book "Pu'er Tea – the Tea with Miraculous Function"* written by Nu Setsuo and Soyama Ichiro created a Pu'er Tea fad in Japan. The Kunming Medical College under took the clinical trials. It analysed that "when 55 high blood to fat cases were treated with Pu'er Tea and the results compared with those obtained by treating 31 cases with the well recognized anti lipermia drug Clofibrate, that therapeutic effect of Pu'er Tea was better than the of Clofibrate in regards to the lowering of blood fat levels. Similar efficacies were seen in reducing blood cholesterol levels.

Helping the Digestion, Appetizing, etc.: Some of our researchers in China doing in vitro experiments with sections of excised rat intestine, have found that pu'er Tea possesses functions such as helping digestion, appetizing, relieving over stuffiness and weight reducing functions. On the "Tea and Health International Symposium" held in Shizuoka, Japan, on 26 to 29 August 1991, the participants evinced great interest in the paper *"Tea benzene in Genuine Black Tea and the Antioxidant*

Activity Induced by it" presented by Chinese and Japanese scholars. Thus has created a sensation. Compatriots in Hong Kong and Macao believed the Pu'er Tea can generate body fluid and relieve thirst. It invigorates the digestive functions, alleviates drunkenness, increases appetite and relieves overstuff ness. It is bacteiostatic and weight reducing. It values a marvelous item for maintaining health and a health -handy beverage that one must take every day. They think the Green *Tea is cold in nature, Black Tea hot in nature, whereas Pu'er Tea is neither cold nor hot, easy to afford and worth one's money, and so is a popular drink given the name "Baoli Tea"*. Pu'er Tea is moderate and mild in nature, can strengthen the body's defense mechanisms, and is suited to the digestive system of the people in Hong Kong. This may be the main reason why the Hong Kong people prefer to drink Pu'er Tea. Since so many people like to take it, others are influenced to follow suit. Recently, the chairperson of the Hong Kong and Kowloon Tea Business Association gave five reasons why the Hong Kong people like to drink Pu'er Tea. There are *strong flavour, better reusability, moderate nature, health giving properties and affordability*. Pu'er Tea imported by Japan is often further processed into exquisite small packages, which after given attractive names like *Royal Concubine Tea, Beauty Tea, Health Tea, Seclusion Tea and Longevity Tea* are put on the market with good sales value. Pu'er Tea has been entitled "The Unimaginable Precious Tea".

Pu'er Tea full of Vitality today

Sale of Tuo Cha in Drug Stores or Departmental Stores: At present, quite a few West European countries put Tuo Cha on sale in drug stores or in the cosmetics showcases of department stores. Some set them up in home as curios. In France there exists even the saying: *"Do you want a beautiful body? Well, you should drink Tuo Cha"*. From ancient recordings of the pharmacological action of Pu'er Tea to research utilizing improved physical and chemical means, reliable results have been coming not only from empirical prescriptions and clinical observations, but also from in depth studies using bio-chemistry, biophysics, molecular biology and genetics as well as in vivo experiments on animals. In recent years Ina Kazuo and Liu Qinjin, using biological and physical methods have conducted studies on the profound changes occurring in the characteristic aromatic constituents and flavour producing substances during manufacture. These studies have great significance in studying the development of the characteristic flavour and pharmacological action of Pu'er Tea. Further, research to elucidate the overall effect of Pu'er Tea on the immune competence of the human body is of great significance. The head, Itamo Keishiro, of the Japanese Oriental and Western Produce Co said: "*The marvelous thing about Yunnan Pu'er Tea is that despite its thousands odd year's history, it is still full of vitality today. As long as you regularly drink it, you will enjoy innumerable health preserving effects. For the benefit of more people in the world, it should be popularized*".

Production, Yield and Exports

Area, Production, Yield and Exports of China Tea during 1989 to 2005 are shown in Table 15.2.

Table 15.2: Area, Production, Yield and Exports Tea in China during 1989 to 2005

(Area in thousand ha, Production and Exports in million kgs, Yield in Kgs per ha)

Year	*Area*	*Absolute inc./dec. (ha)*	*Production*	*Absolute inc./ dec. (kg)*	*Yield*	*Absolute inc./dec. (kgs)*	*Export*	*Percentage of export to production*
1989	1065	-	535	-	502	-	204	38.31
1990	1061	- 4	540	+ 4	509	+ 7	195	36.11
1991	1061	0	542	+ 2	511	+ 2	184	33.94
1999	1130	+ 69	675	+ 133	598	+ 87	200	29.62
2000	1090	- 40	683	+ 8	627	+ 29	227	33.24
2001	1141	+ 51	702	+ 19	615	- 12	250	35.62
2002	1134	- 7	745	+ 43	657	+ 42	252	33.82
2003	1207	+ 73	768	+ 23	635	- 22	260	33.85
2004	1262	+ 55	835	+ 67	662	+ 27	280	33.53
2005	1310	- 48	870	+ 35	665	+ 3	285	32.76

Source: Tea Statistics, Tea Board, Kolkata, India.

In 1989 China's total field area was 1065 thousand hectares (ha), which was reduced to 1061 thousand ha in 1991. Tea area was reduced because of tea fields falling into disuse or even being abandoned. The situation improved from 2000 onwards. Area under tea in 2000 was 1090 thousand ha which enhanced to 1310 thousand ha in 2005. Production enhanced from 683 million kgs to 870 million kgs during the same period. Increase in production was mainly attributed to increase in area and partial improvement in yield from 627 kgs per ha to 665 kgs per ha. The area increased by 23 per cent and production by 63 per cent during 1989 to 2005. In 2006, output was estimated around 895 million kgs a rise of over 25 million kgs the figure for the previous year. However, it is likely that the final output figure will be higher than this.

Destination-wise Export of China Tea

Following the accepted international practices approved by the Ministry of Commerce of the People's Republic of China and Shanghai Municipal People's Government, the tea auction center in China, known as the Shanghai International Tea Commodity Auction Center (SITAC), was established in the form of a limited liability company. It was registered capital RMB 20 million (USD 2.5 million). Its major business is although tea auction, spot and forward contracts of domestic and foreign commodities are dealt in. The members may make the dealings either or their own accounts or on a commission basis through the open competitive prices in the Center. Current objective of the SITAC is to shape itself into a legal international tea and other commodities auction market. It further aims at transforming the internal market system to meet the requirements of GATT.

China exports tea to 16 countries. During 1972, she exported 50.15 million kgs, which enhanced to 284.57 million kgs in 2005. This shows an increase of 440 per cent i.e. an average annual growth rate of 13.32 per cent. Out of 50.15 million kgs, black tea constitutes 40 per cent while green and other tea 60 per cent in 1972. The trend was totally reversed in 2005. Black tea accounted for 16 per cent and green and other tea 84 per cent. Among the 16 countries, share of USA to total tea production ranged from 7.7 million kgs to 12.74 million kgs during the period under review. The China's export of tea was highest at 15.44 million kgs in 1991 and lowest at 7.2 million kgs in 2000. China exports to USSR/CIS in 1974 to

Table 15.3: Exports from China by destination during 1972 to 2005

(Qty. in thousand .kgs)

Destination	*1972*	*1973*	*1974*	*1981*	*1991*	*1997*	*1998*	*1999*	*2000*	*2001*	*2005*
United Kingdom	-	-	7454	8366	5835	8032	6742	4806	3721	4743	4824
Germany Fed. Republic	-	-	2593	3617	1894	4224	3491	2405	1963	2668	2695
German Dem. Republic	-	-	-	-	-	-	-	-	-	-	-
Netherlands	-	-	2827	2059	1217	2324	1869	571	550	462	472
USSR/CIS	-	-	1110	50	21560	7080	7406	5814	2077	7265	8421
Poland	-	-	3643	1620	326	2710	3020	2808	2935	4481	4710
USA	-	-	7709	7318	15442	12747	12111	7875	7214	7300	8310
Iraq	-	-	1445	400	to	5138	9816	1999	-	-	-
Pakistan	-	-	3943	4536	1488	1996	1290	135	1772	3873	3970
Yen Arab Republic	-	-	1573	315	2451	847	664	256	-	-	-
Yen Dem. Republic	-	-	1035	159	-	—	-	—	-	-	-
ARE	-	-	2000	-	311	8	128	22	-	-	-
Libya	-	-	1100	-	3150	1000	550	-	-	-	-
Sudan	-	—	4676	2916	28	57	-	-	-	-	-
Tunisia	-	-	2057	2500	5500	3334	4217	1700	2000	1097	1192
New Zealand	-	-	2041	1561	1891	356	422	53	96	71	75
Other Countries	-	-	7002	9041	137226	37291	17785	5150	7121	8987	10017
Total Black	20881	29053	52210	44458	74829	87144	69591	33594	29449	40947	44631
Green and Other Tea	29873	34510	54620	47510	110043	115320	147843	166014	198212	208731	239935
Total All Tea	50153	63564	106830	91968	184872	202464	217434	199608	227661	249678	284566

Source: International Tea Committee, Various Issues , Dash (-) indicates nil.

the extent of 1.10 million kgs, which was hiked to 8.42 million kgs in 2005. Exports of tea from China to Netherland started declining from 1981 except 1997 and 1998. During 1999 to 2005, export was less than a million kgs. The countries like New Zealand, Tunisia, Sudan, etc are buying China tea from 1974 onwards.

Government's Efforts or Incentives

In an effort to stem the time in late 2005, the Ministry of Finance announced a reduction of 10 per cent in the agricultural special products tax on the raw materials, which went into the making of border tea. This favourable treatment was extended only to those 16 designated tea factories, which procured, and processed the tea. The Ministry of Finance and the Bureau of Taxation announced further that the value added tax was not levied on those units designated by the state to sell border tea to minority nationalities. The anomaly of tight state control over the production, sales and price of border tea were open to market forces. Those were resolved by counter productive use of administrative edicts or the completion of the opening of all sectors of the tea industry.

Fall and Rise of China's Tea Industry

There were factors responsible for decline of the Chinese tea industry in the late 19 th Century. Those were backward technology, ignorance of marketing and consumption trends, poor extension services, exploitation of small farmers by the rural proprietors and urban merchants. In addition, the burden of excessive charges and taxes levied by governments contributed to the rapid fall of tea industry in China. Besides, the British took advantage of this situation and established large-scale plantations and latest processing equipments in India and Sri Lanka for production of black. Borrowing Chinese tea production techniques, Japan devoted to the production of green tea. China had practically lost its predominance in the international tea trade by the beginning of twenty thousand century. What is more significant to note that just in a span of fifty years since then China's tea production had fallen to a fraction of what it had once been. Nevertheless, China was unprepared to accept this disgraceful situation for long. Rather it started the struggle for reviving the tea industry with vigorous effort. Between 1949 and 2004 the total tea area increased by 8 times i.e 11,70,000 ha. Output increased from 410 million kgs to 725 million kgs i.e. more than 20 times over the same period. Export increase accounted for 4 times from 101 million kgs in 1950 to 270 million kgs in 2004.

Modeled along Soviet lines, China was a planned economy between 1950 and 1980s. During the period, prices and standards for the wide range of teas produced in the country were specified. These were supervised by state agencies like the Ministry of Commerce and the All China Supply and Marketing Cooperative and their local branches. Nevertheless, this was not easy task for the bureaucracy. The situation has considerably changed with the leaning towards liberalization of the economy. Tea marketing has been partially deregulated. In addition, the country intends to be at the top of the list of tea traders in the world market. China possesses the largest tea growing area in the world. Total area in 2004 equaled 23 per cent of the world's tea growing area. The country is also the world's greatest producer and exporter of green tea. In 2004, it produced 66 per cent of world output and contributed 72 per cent of world trade in the commodity. China has greater expertise in green tea. These besides China have the greatest range of tea in different grades and varieties. The country cultivates tea in a wide range of climate and topographical environments – from the moist of temperate Yunnan province to the more severe climates in the north.

China Tea Captures American Market

Chinese tea was virtually unknown in America two decades ago and attributed to just one percent share of the market. It has successfully captured the American market in recent years. During that period Sri Lanka teas have been their favorite and responsible for a market share of 24 per cent with Indonesia coming a close second securing 16 per cent share of the market. Nevertheless, over the past 20 years the entire tea import scenario of the country has changed. During this period, America imported a fair quantity from non-producing countries such as the UK, Hongkong, Netherlands and Canada. Their reliance on this market has been greatly reduced now. However, about 5 per cent is still obtained from Germany in the form of decaffeinated tea. China has taken the top berth with 24 per cent market share. America's imports have increased from 88 million kgs in 1974 to 211 million kgs in 2004, which has mostly benefited other producers. China commands a market share of about a quarter of America's total imports and enjoy dollar earning of 18 per cent of the total expenditure on the import of tea. China's exports to America are not only confined to Black Tea but the country enjoys a significant market for Green Tea, Oolong Tea and Jasmine Tea. It has been noted that China and Vietnam have emerged as major players in the global tea arena. Cost of production in these two countries is much low comparing that of India and Sri Lanka. Production cost of tea is also low in Kenya. In essence, world's two major tea producers India and Sri Lanka are likely to face steep competetion in near future.

China Produces An Extensive Range of Tea

China, unlike other major tea producing countries such as India, Sri Lanka or Kenya, produces an extensive range of teas. The shape of the leaf, initial method of manufacturing (the ring or fixation) and extent of processing (crude, refined or reprocessed) may classify tea in China. The time of plucking (spring, summer or autumn), the region of production, scale of production (state farm, agricultural collective or smallholder), final market (domestic or foreign), counter trade or cash and color, aroma and taste are some of the aspects for classification of tea. The connoisseur has, therefore, ample scope to judge varieties and quality. Crude green consumed by peasant households is quite a different beverage to the refined gunpowder green tea exported to Morocco or the re processed jasmine scented tea, which uses green tea as its base.

Crude and Refined Processing: The division of processing into two distinct stages of crude and refined processing is a function of China's backward transport system and the miniature scale of the industry. Apart from the state farms run by the government, tea gardens in the country are small, dispersed and subject to vastly different levels of management expertise. Individual tea farmers in their homes, or in factories, which are very small, carry out crude processing by international standards. Unrefined or crude teas are subject to refining before being exported. Some domestically consumed tea is also refined. Tea refiners are usually large state to run factories in provincial cities and towns. In recent years smaller factories, many of them contracted to individuals and using old and inferior equipment and backward technology, have mushroomed in tea producing areas, outbidding the estate sector for raw material. The object of refining is to improve the product's external appearance, grade it, eliminate foreign bodies and raise its purity. The tea is also dried to lower its moisture content, increase its aroma and thus prepare it for storage and transportation. Final blending quality adjustment and unification of standards thus takes place.

Standards of Tea: Two standards of tea are now ready for the market. The first is called *"trade standard"*. Large state refineries at major ports of export, such as Shangai or Canton (Guangzhou), are authorized to designate export code numbers to their teas and to stipulate variety and grade. If, on the other hand, the tea is processed, packed, inspected and exported directly by a local factory, its water and dust content must be 0.5 per cent below the criteria set for the above refineries. The second standard is called *"processing standard"* in which water content must be one per cent below the standard set for export quality and where the dust content is subject to inspection at the port of export after blending is completed.

In relation to method of manufacture, teas pass through the initial process of the ring – *including Wulong (Oolong), black (Chinese red) and white tea*—in increasing intensity of the ring so the processed leaf for white tea bears least resemblance to the freshly—plucked buds and tips. Other teas pass through an initial stage of fixation to prevent fermentation, including *green, yellow and dark green (Chinese black)*, in increasing degree of oxidation so the dark green tea least resembles the fresh leaf. Chinese teas may also be grouped into six major categories such as *(i) green, (ii) black, (iii) yellow, (iv) white, (v) dark green and (vi) gray*. The Chinese names their teas according to the color, the liquid whereas in English the color is given to the dried leaf. Hence, the Chinese word for what the English-speaking world is called black tea is red.

Green and Black Tea Processing

Green and black tea is familiar to most tea consumers. In China, they make up the bulk of national output. In 2006, green tea comprised 60 per cent of China's output of 725 million kgs, *black tea* 25 per cent, *gray* 5.6 per cent, *compressed* (essentially dark green) 3.9 per cent, with unspecified *"Other"* teas making up the total. In 2005, *green tea* made up 65 per cent of total production of 720 million kgs, a significant increase due to the higher prices it could fetch on the domestic market. By volume, China exports more black tea, than green, but because it is generally of a low grade, black tea brings less revenue than green. For example, in 2005 just over 50 per cent of China's tea exports of 260 million kgs were black with green making up 38 per cent. However, black tea comprised only 40 per cent of tea export earnings.

Green Tea with Three Stages in Processing: Green tea, the most popular hot beverage in China, passes through three stages in processing: *fixation either by steam (preferred by the Japanese), or roasted (favored by the Chinese)*. Implements used for fixation include copper bowls, troughs or rollers. The next processing stage *is kneading and twisting followed by drying*—in copper works, by *curing or sun drying*.

Roasted and Cured Green: The most common green tea in China is called *chaoqing* (roasted green) and is differentiated from *hongging* (cured green) by two factors. *First, in the kneading and twisting stage*—the process is lighter for the latter because most of this tea is sold on the domestic market, it must be able to withstand water of a high temperature and retain its original shape. Additionally, in the kneading and rolling stage, hongging green is sifted and twisted a second time. *Second, in the drying stage*, hongging green passes through a two-stage-curing-process of high temperature curing as well as low temperature drying. Hongqing is the base green for jasmine and other scented teas.

Division of Choosing Green Tea: Chaoquing green is in turn divided into two principal types according to the shape of the leaf i.e oval, known as *mei*, and pearl *shape known as gunpowder*. There are also needles shape and flat leaf chaoqing greens. The famous Longjing (dragon well) green tea from

Hangzhou is a well known example of a flat leaf. Complications arise from the fact that the *Mei* has traditionally been dried in a work and its shape is commonly called chaoqing or long chaoqing. Thus, it is confused with the generic term.

Black Tea with Four Stages in Processing: Black (Chinese red) passes through the four stages*: ring, kneading and twisting, fermentation and drying*. Black tea is divided into three principal *varieties: (i) small leaf black, (ii) gongfu (gongou)* or traditional Chinese black and *(iii) broken black (CTC)*, the tea most widely consumed in the West. Small leaf black is a traditional tea produced in very small quantities in Fujian province in South East China. The leaves are plucked relatively late in spring. After fermentation, the leaf is work fired at 200 degrees centigrade to halt fermentation by destroying the active enzymes and to increase its aroma. It is then rolled a second time for 8 to 10 minutes and smoked cured. The finished product caries a faint pine aroma that mark of identification. The most famous of all gongfu tea is produced in Qimen county, Anhui province. One bud and two or three leaves are plucked to produce this tea. After refining the tea, it is divided into *(a) graded tea, (b) ungraded tea* and *(c) leftovers*.

China began producing broken black in the 50's for the Eastern European market. Most broken black is produced on state farms in the Southern province of Guangdong, Guanxi, Guizhou and Jiangxi. Because a large leaf bush is more suitable for the processing of this variety, production has been concentrated in the Southeastern province of Yunnan in recent years. Since 1964, production has increased rapidly to the point where, today, 80 per cent of China's black tea exports are of broken black. However, only one-third is processed from the large leaf bush. Sales are directed almost entirely toward the international market as very little of this is consumed domestically.

Four Categories of Tea

Yellow Tea: The remaining four categories of *yellow, white, gray and dark green*, because of their unfamiliarity to Western consumers, merit more detailed discussion. Yellow and white teas are traditional products, which command a specialized, and shrinking market. Very little is produced and even then output is intermittent. In fact Chinese statistics group both under the category of "other teas". In 2006, Huoshan country in Anhui province, with an output of 1.5 million kgs was the highest producer of yellow tea in the country. Yellow tea in the cup is characterized by its color, clear and pleasant fragrance and rich flavor. Processing is similar to that for green tea except that after three processing stages a process of covering is added to impart extra color to the tea.

White Tea: White tea is especially product from Fujian province in east China and a small amount is also produced in Taiwan. It was discovered in 1885 in Fujian's Fuding County. Production is miniscule and in 1976 only 500 thousand Kgs were produced, equal to four per cent of tea output in the province. It's production increased to 1.5 million kgs in 2006. Most of the tea is exported to Chinese communities in Hong Kong and Macau. In 2006, China exported 800 thousand Kgs of tea. Tea passes through *two stages of the ring and drying. The rings are of two kinds— complete the ring or partial the ring.*

Dark Green Tea: Dark green tea (Chinese black) goes through four processing stages : *(i) fixation, (ii) kneading and twisting, (iii) stacking and moistening, and (iv) drying*. The stacking and moistening, performed in order to promote fermentation, is carried out in three ways: when the *semi-finished product is wet, when it is dry, or to the finished product as repeated fermentation*. This tea is normally reprocessed into compressed tea, which is consumed in large quantities by China's minority nationalities, the Tibetans, Mongolians, and Uighurs of Xinjiang in particular.

Gray/ Wulong Green Tea: Gray or Wulong (black dragon) tea is the most difficult of all teas to process. It is a semi - fermented tea combining the rich and sweet flavour of black and the freshness and fragrance of green. Wulong tea is an acquired taste, but one well worth acquiring. Its production is confined to the Southeastern coastal province of Fujian and Guangdong and the island of Taiwan. Processing skills are jealously guarded and it is difficult to inspect a factory producing Wulong. There are five processing stages (i) the ring, (ii) semi fermentation (according to the degree of which and the area grown the tea is known as north Fujian gray,

South Fujian gray, Guangdong gray or Taiwan gray), (iii) roasting, (iv) kneading & twisting and (v) drying.

Consumption of Wulong, Scented and Compressed Tea

The consumption *of Wulong tea* is highest in the three producing provinces of Fujian, Guangdong and Taiwan. It also finds appeal in Hong Kong and Macau. In recent years, *Chinese Wulong has found niche in Japan* where it commands good prices. This is a good example of how new markets can be sought out and consumers, who have traditionally favoured steamed green, can be attracted to a different product if quality is consistently high.

Two others types of tea do not belong to separate categories, but, because they are made with different base teas, belong to one of the six categories above. The first is *scented tea and the second compressed*. Both are teas, which are reprocessed from either crude or refined tea. Fragrances have been added to tea in China since the Song dynasty (960 AD). In the late 19th century, production of scented tea was centered in Fujian province. Processing of the tea is now concentrated in two large factories in Suzhou (Jiankgsu province) and Fuzhou (Fujian province). In the processing of scented tea, fragrant flowers are added to the semi finished tea base. The resultant tea retains the characteristics of the base tea whether it be cured green (*hongqing*) with jasmine flowers (*jasmine tea*), gray tea with osmanthus (*osmanthus tea)* or black tea with roses (*rose tea)*.

Production of Scented and Compressed Tea : The main difficulty in producing scented tea is to synchronize the flowering of the jasmines or roses with the plucking of the leaf. Good quality scented tea contains no flowers, only the fragrance resulting from the pressing of flowers between layers of tea. The northern cities of Baijing and Tianjin, Shandong province and Guangdong and Fujian province in the South of China are the leading domestic consumers. When tea is served in Chinese restaurants in the West it is most likely to be *jasmine tea,* and not always of a very good quality. Compressed tea in the form of bricks or cakes is so made for the convenience of shipment to outlying areas. This depends on the base tea used, it comes under the category of black tea (millet brick) or dark green tea, (*Sichuan fu brick, Hubei green brick, Slchuan gold tip and west Sichuan brick), which are all steamed, or Anhuafu brick and Sichuan fangbao tea,* which are roasted, and scented brick. If the tea base is green and it is then steam compressed and piled up to ferment, it comes under the category, dark green, and not green tea.

Instant Tea, Tea Bags, Tea Cola, Tea Orange, Lemon Tea, etc.: Finally there are instant teas, most of which are made from black tea and some from green tea. China first produced experimental batches of instant tea in 1972. She in 1974 has sold the tea at the Canton Trade Fair. Instant tea in tea bags now commands a growing share of the tea market. Soft drinks, such as tea cola made with green tea, are now available in limited supplies in China. Canned lemon tea manufactured in Hong King is sold in joint venture hotels. While it appeals to younger Chinese, traditional tea drinkers of an older generation find it to sweet.

Tea Processing Machinery in China

It has been reported that by the mid 1980s there were over 4,00,000 pieces of tea machinery installed in Chinese tea factories. Most of the China's tea processing machinery is produced in Zhejiang province in East China. In 1978 she produced as many as 39,100 pieces of machinery for the tea processing industry. This increased to 63,300 units in 1990. However, a Sino Japanese joint venture was set up in Hangzhou in 1990 to produce tea plantation machinery. The aim is to harvest 330 thousand hectares of tea fields by the year 2015. One million US $ was invested to produce bush trimmers and pluckers. The venture attained the set output target of 10,000 units by 1995, increasing to 70,000 units in 2015. Since 1974, a total of 1,550 items of tea machinery have been imported into China, the opening of this joint venture was partly as an import replacement exercise. The machine harvesting will reduce the cost of plucking by 50 per cent.

Area, Production and Exports of Tea—World and China

World area under tea was 2450 thousand ha in 1992 whereas China owns an area of 1084 thousand ha constituting 44.24 per cent of total. In 2004, world area increased to 2775 thousand ha compared to 1262 thousand hectares of China tea accounting for 45.50 per cent. Thus, the growth rates of area under tea of world and china increased by 13.22 per cent and 16.42 per cent respectively. Table below shows the details:

Table 15.4: China's Share of World Area, Production and Export during 1992 to 2004

Year	*Area (thousand ha)*			*Production (million kgs)*			*Exports (million kgs)*		
	World	*China*	*percent Share*	*World*	*China*	*percent Share*	*World*	*China*	*percent Share*
1992	2450	1084	44.24	2438	560	22.96	1017	175	17.26
1993	2533	1171	46.22	2553	600	23.50	1156	201	17.43
1994	2448	1134	46.32	2523	588	23.32	1036	180	17.34
2001	2638	1141	43.25	3035	702	23.12	1391	250	17.94
2002	2646	1134	42.86	3055	745	24.40	1440	252	17.51
2003	2713	1207	44.49	3174	768	24.20	1401	260	18.56
2004	2775	1262	45.48	3306	835	25.26	1540	280	18.19

Source: Tea Statistics, Tea Board, India, Various Issues.

China occupies an important role in world tea economy. In 2004, she covers a little less than 50 per cent of total world area, one fourth of world production and one fifth of world exports. Year wise China' s share of area to world area ranged from 42.86 per cent to 46.32 per cent, production from 22.96 to 25.26 per cent and export from 17.26 to 18.56 per cent.

Future of China's Tea Industry

The tea industry in China must continue to attract domestic consumers against increasing competetion from imported drinks such as coffee and Coca Cola, which have become very fashionable in recent years despite their high prices. In 1988 a new teahouse was opened in Hangzhou. It was elaborately decorated in the traditional style of the Song dynasty (960-1127 AD), and situated in a street specializing in restaurants and designated a *tourist* attraction up the city government. It failed to attract customers and closed its door within six months—a warning sign that the local consumers cannot be taken for granted even in a city where the citizens are as addicted to green as Hangzhou.

Untapped Potential in the International Market: On the international market there is untapped potential for China's great variety of exotic teas. Over the past few years there has been a lot of writing in the Chinese press on the subject but apparently little action to match the rhetoric. Penetration of the Western market will require levels of skill, determination and flair which to date have been noticeably absent from Chinese marketing techniques.

Marketing of Green Tea: With clever marketing green tea could become a trendy drink in the high-income countries of the West. It has an appealing appearance and a refreshing taste. Chinese writers on the subject argue that the tea suffers from the disadvantage of the size of the leaf, which swells and returns to its original shape when hot water is added. They believe that a way must be found to process it into the desiccated size and shape of dried black tea.

Presence of Green Tea in West: The fact that the Chinese green tea has not yet established a strong presence in the West is due more to poor promotion by the Chinese to the product itself. If, for example, a decent grade of green tea was placed in Chinese hotel rooms for foreign tourists, satisfied consumers might take their discovery back home and create a strong demand for a satisfying and safe drink in this age of obsession for health foodstuffs. In this respect, China has gone backwards over the last decade. In 1977, the Longjing (green) tea supplied to guests of the Hanzhou Hotel was excellent quality. Prof. Keith Forster, Contemporary China Center Research Scholar of Pacific Studies, Australian National University, and his wife drank green tea regularly during their stay in the hotel for three years. The hotel people supplied with good quality tea. Sadly, the same cannot be said now days for the tea in the hotel. This issue was raised and various people connected with the tea industry in Hangzhou but no positive response was forthcoming.

Difference in Opinion on the Development of China Tea: Regular reading of the Chinese press confirms the view each department holds its own view of how the industry should develop. For example, ideas differ as to whether China should increase its export of black teas or concentrate on green tea. This has resulted in the constant switching of production from one variety to another, especially during the past decade. In 1984, a rise in the international price of black tea induced Chinese producers to process this tea. In 1985 Wulong tea attracted producers and green during 1987-88 tea became the rage. At present, the emphasis is on reducing production of green tea and switching over to black.

Price Reforms The economic and politically sensitive question as to how far China should go in price reform and allow the market to determine prices has obvious and pressing relevance for the tea industry. The state fixed export price is well below the domestic market price, resulting in shortages of supplies for export. Even the favourable exchange rate granted to exporters does not compensate for the losses incurred in placing the commodity on the international market. At present, China has back away from the limited deregulation of marketing and price instituted in 1984 and return to mandatory procurements and state fixed prices. This calls for various commentators to establish domestic auctions that are unlikely to be heeded in the present political climate.

Conclusion

China produced 25 per cent of the world's tea output which was second only to India's 26 per cent. One problem for China is theatonly 25 per cent of the world's tea output is green tea of which China produced 71 per cent, Japan 15 per cent and Indonesia 7 per cent. Vietnam is the significant producer. China supplied 15 per cent of the world's tea trade, second only to Sri Lanka's 18 per cent. Almost 33 per cent of China's exports were black tea and the rest being green Oolong compressed and specialist teas. Chinese authorities believe the green tea market has limited growth potential and the future lies in the black tea market. However China's black teas are generally of poor quality and fetch low prices. Authorities must decide whether to concentrate on volumes, which seem to have been their strategy to date or to switch their emphasis to quality and price where the non black tea varieties perform significantly better. With alarm bells now ringing in the industry as tea area declines, prices fall, output follows a roller coaster ride and young consumer shift away from tea it is time for the Chinese government to introduce a coherent and viable package of reforms to sustain the industry into the next century. One final point is that in 1994, the Sri Lankan authorities suggested the leading tea producing countries including Sri Lanka, Indonesia and Kenya, to establish a producers association along the lines OPEC in order to stabilize tea prices which have fallen to 1984 levels. A Chinese newspaper reported the proposal without comment. To give itself any influence at all such an association would have to enforce production constraints on member countries. In the past China has shown little interest in joining international producer cartels. Interestingly, China did attend the first meeting of tea producing countries but if the major threat to the international price of black tea is the over supply of low quality teas, as recent reports presented to the Food and Agricultural Organization suggest, then the responsibility was vested with China. The question is whether China is now ready to address this issue.

It is worthwhile to state here that the China must have some stated and agreed strategy to take State's tea industry to the 21st century. If the growth rates of the past, 50 years are to be maintained it is essential that feasible plan be to be mapped out and put into place. Only in this way will China have hoper of overtaking India and resume its position as the world's number one producer of tea to a product.

16

Export Prospects of Indian Tea in Bangladesh

Introduction

Tea estates in Bangladesh are concentrated in Sylhet district. Their originating history is alike as that of North East India. However, the sad reality is parting out of 150 tea estates from the mainstream of Cacher and North Tripura in August 1947. Otherwise, these areas are agro-climatologically similar. An advisory subcenter of Tocklai was located in Srimangal (Sylhet), but with the dawn of independence of India, Tocklai lost part of its jurisdiction and ultimately Tea Research Institute of Bangladesh was born. Tea Industry in Bangladesh possibly did not receive due attention so far. As a result, productivity of tea is very poor, average being 900 kgs or so per hectare. The productivity in 95 well-managed tea estates is around 1500 kgs per hectare that is indicative of future scope of development. Research on important areas, like water technology and quality manufacture appeared to receive less attention. Trading of Bangladesh tea was earlier confined to domestic consumption only i.e. transporting to West Pakistan. However, from 1972 the situation changed and now roughly 30 million kgs is exported annually out of the total production of 56 million kgs. Since exportable surplus is too small a quantity, limited export was made to the traditional sectors only like Pakistan, Iraq and Iran. Other than traditional countries, 2 million kgs was sold to London auction annually from Bangladesh. Launching of promotional propaganda for export of such small quantity might be a fashion and costlier too. Possibly this situation made them to approach for support from India. Again, with the increase of their domestic consumption, exportable surplus has to be further enhanced subject to condition that productivity be raised, having no scope for extension plantations.

Tea Economy of Bangladesh

Bangladesh produced on an average a crop of 55.5 million kgs. In 2006, the crop production was 55.80 million kgs, which is the highest and is in line with projected for the season. Good growing conditions and improved husbandry contributed to this. Total export for the year 2006 is fixed at 15 million kgs in the tea policy. This is expected to earn approximately taka (TK) 1780 crore. There is high hope that this would be achieved for nearly 5 million kgs more tea, which was bought by exporters. The increased crop posed little difficulty in marketing for the auctions. The entire quantity was handled virtually in most efficient manner. The average prices were also higher than the previous season, which was TK 65.45 per kg as against Tk. 62.30 per kg last season. The highlight of the market was the consistent support given by Iran for all clean leaf grades and emerged to be the largest buyer.

Area under tea cultivation in Bangladesh has shown a moderate increase. However, production exhibited a sharp rise. Average annual growth rates of area and production are very 0.35 per cent and 20.35 per cent respectively. Details of area, production and yield of tea during 1989 to 2005 are brought out in table below.

Table 16.1: Area, Production and Yield of Bangladesh Tea during 1989 to 2006

(Area in th. ha., Production in m.kgs. and yields in kg/ ha.)

Year	*Area*	*Absolute inc./dec.*	*Production*	*Absolute inc./dec.*	*Yield*	*Absolute inc./dec.*	*Bangladesh tea as percentage to global production*
1989	47.4	–	39.0	–	824	–	1.56
1999	48.6	1.2	46.3	7.3	954	130	1.56
2000	49.2	1.8	52.6	6.3	1070	116	1.76

2001	49.3	0.1	57.3	4.7	1163	93	1.85
2002	49.5	0.3	52.7	0.4	1085	-79	1.71
2003	49.7	0.2	53.5	0.8	1088	3	1.76
2004	49.9	0.2	54.0	0.5	1098	10	1.77
2005	50.1	0.2	55.7	0.7	1117	19	1.79
2006	50.1	0	55.8	0.3	1118	01	1.79

Source: Tea Statistics, Various Issues, Tea Board, India, Kolkata.

The increase in production is mainly due to rise in yield rate from 824 kgs per hectare to 1118 kgs per hectare (35.6 per cent). In terms of global production, Bangladesh only constitutes less than 2 per cent of total world production.

Exports of Bangladesh Tea in 2004 by Destination

Pakistan was the top most buyer of Bangladesh tea followed by Poland, Russia, Sudan, Jordan, Afganistan etc.. Pakistan accounted for 38 per cent of total export, while it was 26 per cent for Poland, 15 per cent for Russia, 5.60 percent for Sudan, 4.55 per cent for Jordan and 4.44 per cent for Afghanistan. Internal market purchased a considerable quantity reflecting a reduced percent in off take from the auctions. There has been a strong emphasis for brand promotions, which are indicative of the present trend. It is note worthy that there has been a steady increase in export of packet teas although the quantity is still small to sophisticated markets like the Gulf. The export of Bangladesh tea in 2004 is presented below.

Table 16.2: Export of Bangladesh Tea in 2004

Sr. No.	*Name of Country*	*Quantity (in thousand Kgs)*	*Percentage to total*
1	Pakistan	5380	37.83
2	Poland	3699	25.98
3	Russia	2187	15.34
4	Sudan	797	5.60
5	Jordan	648	4.55
6	Afganistan	639	4.42
7	UK	264	1.85
8	Germany	133	0.93
9	Iran	121	0.85
10	Japan	126	0.81
11	Oman	108	0.76

12	ARE	92	0.64
13	Kenya	45	0.31
14	Kuwait	20	0.14
	Total :	14250	100.00

Source : National Brokers Ltd., Chittagong.

Bangladesh and World— Quantity and Value of Tea Exports

Quantum of exports and export earnings of Bangladesh tea during the period from 1989 to 2006 are depicted below:

Table 16.3: Exports, Value of Exports of Bangladesh Tea during 1989 to 2006

Year	*Exports (million kgs)*	*Absolute increase/ decrease*	*Value of exports (million US dollars)*	*Absolute increase/ decrease*	*Percentage of Bangladesh tea to world exports*
1989	23.43	–	38.80	0	2.08
1999	15.18	–18.25	20.50	18.30	1.20
2000	18.10	2.92	23.14	2.64	1.36
2001	12.92	–5.18	16.03	7.11	0.93
2002	13.65	0.73	17.05	1.02	0.95
2003	13.85	1.02	17.30	0.25	1.15
2004	14.05	0.20	17.58	0.28	1.25
2005	14.25	0.20	17.80	0.22	1.35
2006	14.30	0.05	17.85	0.05	1.06
Av.	15.74	0.44	20.99	3.14	1.05

As stated earlier, Bangladesh exports of tea to Pakistan, Poland, USSR, Sudan, Jordan, Afghnistan, UK, etc. Total quantity exported to various countries in 1950 stood at 25.97 million kgs, which increased to 30.89 million kgs in 1961, further increased to 31.88 million kgs in 1971, and again declined to 29.1 million kgs in 1981. It was 25.38 million kgs in 1991 and 12.92 million kgs in 2001. It started increasing from 2002 onwards. The export figure reached to 14.30 million kgs in 2006. The details of quantity exports from Bangladesh to various countries during 1951 to 2005 are presented below.

Year-wise, exports of tea from Bangladesh showed that Ireland received tea upto 1981, whereas Netherland all the

Table 16.4: Exports of Tea from Bangladesh during 1951 to 2006

(Qty in million kgs.)

Destination/Year	*1951*	*1961*	*1971*	*1981*	*1991*	*2001*	*2002*	*2003*	*2004*	*2005*	*2006*
United Kindom	5.76	4.38	5.39	4.19	0.02	1.02	1.02	1.05	1.05	1.00	1.00
West Germany	1.13	0.57	0.61	1.28	0.44	0.07	0.09	1.00	0.95	0.98	0.98
Ireland	0.28	0.04	0.03	0.03	–	–	–	–	–	–	–
Netherlands	1.73	0.22	0.37	0.09	0.32	-	0.10	-	0.10	0.10	0.10
Poland	0.06	0.05	0.07	–	1.17	0.40	0.44	0.48	0.51	0.55	0.55
USSR/US	0.39	4.49	2.15	2.27	2.00	1.87	1.25	1.32	1.00	1.75	1.75
Canada	1.50	2.80	1.92	0.93	–	–	–	0.25	0.20	–	1.00
USA	0.87	0.60	0.05	0.02	–	–	–	–	–	–	–
Afghnistan	0.34	0.23	0.48	1.18	0.20	4.35	3.65	3.60	3.50	3.50	3.50
Malaysia & Singapore	0.32	0.23	0.07	0.54	–	–	–	–	–	–	–
Pakistan	7.79	10.84	14.52	15.25	5.33	2.73	1.80	1.85	2.00	2.00	2.00
ARE	4.32	6.15	5.90	2.79	3.62	–	3.00	3.10	2.54	2.50	2.50
Australia	0.15	–	0.01	–	–	–	–	–	–	–	–
Others	1.33	0.29	0.31	0.53	12.28	2.48	2.30	2.22	2.20	2.37	2.39
Total	25.97	30.89	31.88	29.1	25.38	12.92	13.65	13.85	14.05	14.25	14.30

years except 2001 and 2003. Bangladesh exports tea to Poland in all the years except 1981. Teas dispatched to Canada were upto 1981. Exports of tea from Bangladesh continued for all the years in respect of United Kingdom, USSR and Pakistan and West Germany.

Bangladesh Tea—Marketing

Bangladesh tea sold in Chittagong auction stood at 47.78 million kgs in 2006 compared to 50.72 million kgs in 2005. Thus, there was a fall of 2.94 million kgs representing a decline of 5.77 per cent. Average price increased from US dollar 1.03 per kg in 2002 to US dollar 1.17 per kg. It is hoped that average price in Chittagong auction will further increase.

Table 16.5: Quantity Sold and Average Price of Bangladesh Tea

(Qty. in thousand kg, price in US £)

	January to December				*% of increase (+) or decrease (-) in 2006 over 2005*	
	2006		*2005*			
Auction Centre	*Qty.*	*Price*	*Qty.*	*Price*	*Qty.*	*Price*
Kolkata	133874	1.46	105806	1.42	26.53	2.82
Guwahati	138664	1.27	131424	1.26	5.51	0.79
Siliguri	87090	1.17	73293	1.15	18.82	1.74
Amritsar	190	0.61	507	0.50	(-) 62.52	22.00
North India	359828	1.32	311030	1.29	15.69	2.33
Cochin	50633	0.98	58196	0.97	(-) 13.00	1.03
Coonoor	40586	0.74	60665	0.76	(-) 33.10	(-) 2.63
Coimbatore	22331	0.82	26658	0.83	(-) 16.23	(-) 1.20
Tea Serve	4403	0.66	–	–	–	–
South India	117953	0.86	145519	0.86	(-) 18.94	0
All India	477771	1.20	456549	1.15	4.65	4.35
Colombo	273234	1.54	280024	1.55	(-) 2.42	(-) 0.65
Chittagong	47782	1.17	50722	1.03	(-) 5.77	13.59
Jakarta	33775	0.95	37432	1.01	(-) 9.77	(-) 5.94
Mombasa	285843	1.54	270635	1.49	5.62	3.36
Limbe	15900	0.93	17241	0.91	(-) 7.78	4.40

Report of National Broker's Limited Regarding Bangladesh Tea

According to a report by National Brokers Limited, Chittagong, the tea industry in Bangladesh is currently in a very jolly mood due to its satisfactory position in terms of both production and price realization. On the one hand, favourable weather, timely inputs and improved agricultural prices contributed to a very satisfactory production, on the other, a stable market attracted brisk activity from exporters and helped to achieve a higher price level. Poland, Russia, Jordan, Sudan and Pakistan accounted for increased buying by the export sector. The domestic demand remained high throughout for dust, well-made fannings and smaller brokens. The report further mentioned that projects initiated by the Government with British and EC grants contributed to increasing tea production in the country over the past few years. These aided projects been helpful for both intensive and extensive cultivation of tea.

Inspite of great hardships, Bangladesh was able to produce more crops with better quality. It produced the crop of 56 million kgs in 2006. In 2001, the largest crop achieved was 57.3 million kgs mark. Quality was generally superior particularly early season teas. Liquor quality showed a marked improvement about colour and brightness conforming well to market requirements. Export performance was quite satisfactory and export target in 2006 was fixed at 14 million kgs. Of the major buyers operated in Chittagong, Pakistan was most noticeable and absorbed the bulk of the Fannings and small Brokens. Their activity greatly helped in bringing about some stability to an otherwise erratic market. Poland was a very important buyer and accounted for more than 6 million kgs.UK imported a significant quantity, highest in recent years mostly by way of direct sales and London auctions. On the debit side, Iran, which was the largest buyer, bought a nominal weight whilst Egypt was totally absent for a few years.

Duties and Taxes on Tea

There is no export duty on tea in Bangladesh. Cess is levied at the rate 1 per cent ad valorem auction price. Vat is imposed at the rate of 15 per cent of auction price of tea for internal consumption.

Conclusion

The developments in the USSR and Eastern Europe brought about some elements of uncertainities on the price levels particularly in Chittagong where their presence may have been a strong element in the market and contributed much towards a healthy tone. Furthermore, following the war, Iraq was no longer remaining a significant force in the market place and this affected the world prices adversely. However, there is room for optimism as Iran has emerged as the largest buyer of Bangladesh Tea that is likely to operate in greater strength. Of the other export buyers, Pakistan would lift a sizeable quantity. Egypt and Poland should also step up their buying from Bangladesh, UK Continent, Unified Germany and China will lend usual support. Indian restrictions on the USSR's buying may increase their activities in other major centers including Chittagong. This may also result in additional Indian buying from Chittagong for re-export.

The stable condition of the country will have a favourable influence on the internal consumption of tea. In view of the availability of plainer types of tea in the world market in excess of requirement, one would like to put all *the emphasis on the quality of the* product. All efforts must maintain consistency in standard throughout. One strongly feels for Chittagong auctions well-made clean *liquoring. Brokens* would fetch a premium over Fannings. Thus, there is a need to *maximize this grade*. However, large grades should not be more than 5 per cent. Dust per centage may be reduced to a bare minimum preferably fewer than 15 per cent. CTC teas with grainy appearance and good clean cups will continue to attract interest from the export and internal markets. Poor liquoring teas will be neglected. Estates producing Orthodox teas should consider seriously switching over to CTC manufacture.

Discussions with the foreign delegation concentrated on *(i)* India's cooperation in Bangladesh tea, and *(ii) R and D aspects*, since Bangladesh tea industry is very dependent on India for tea machineries. Machinery manufacturers here were called on to express their views for possible future export of tea *machineries like CTC rollers, breakers, dryers* and so on to Bangladesh. The other interest of Bangladesh, which was visibly critical for both, was import of tea by India for re-exporting purpose. With the recent development of *permitting import of tea by govt.* of India for re-export purpose, the proposal opened up with new vigour in growth Traders of both the countries examined the pros and cons of such trade and development of brands. It was thought whether Indian exporters of tea engaged themselves in exporting tea directly from Dheka after participating in auctions there to minimize cost and hasten export trade. Bangladesh, it appeared, was more hopeful to export her *tea to India after the recent liberalization of tea import and export policy* here. The visit was a coincidence, a gesture well responded by India, so tea should stimulate all concerned!

The then Brigadier Abdul Amed Chaudhury, Chairman, Bangladesh Tea Board headed a seven-member trade delegation from Bangladesh. The team visited India from 19 to 25 August 1991 at the invitation of Indian Govt.. Beside officials from Bangladesh Tea Board; the team included well-known tea traders from Ispani and Finlay. The purpose of visit was diverse like reviewing and strengthening of old ties between the two countries in tea trade and India's cooperation in research and development. Indian side was also equally enthusiastic under the stewardship of Mr. P.K. Bora, the then Chairman, Tea Board of India. Discussions were held on various subjects of mutual interests.

17

Marketing Strategy of Indian Tea in Middle East Countries

The UPASI had sent a delegation of planter from South India to some Middle East countries in 1992 to study the markets and design the appropriate strategies for exploring export possibilities to such countries. The objectives and major findings of the delegation are summarized below:

Objectives and Major Highlights of the Market Study of Tea

The major objectives of the study are as follows:

- To promote Exports of South Indian Teas both bulk and value added at competitive prices in view of the uncertainties surroundings the future buying plans of the former Soviet Union.
- To study the current Tea import situation and policies in Middle East.
- To know the product profile (Tea) in each country to match our resources and positioning the same.
- To ascertain the pricing aspect of competitor's vis-à-vis their make for suitable offer.
- To appraise the importers in Middle East/West Asia about the changing ground realities in the Indian Tea Market, and
- Its consequent effect on the price, quality and quantities of Teas available from South India for exports.

Highlights

The major highlights of the delegation's visit to Middle East/ West is given below:-

- First Producer Delegation to meet the Trade in Middle East.
- Indian Teas enjoy premium image all over Middle East.
- Trade wants intensive Marketing and Publicity for Indian Teas, Sri Lanka is doing its best.
- Active participation of Indian Teas required in all Trade Fairs in Middle East.
- Offers made by some of us seem to be falling in line with their expectation.
- Trade wants consistent supply at competitive prices.
- Gunny bags as alternative packages seem to be acceptable in Egypt.
- Many more food stuff companies interested in Tea at Dubai for re-exports, Vigorous follow up needed by our members.
- Most of the CTC dust offered by the Delegates to private Traders seems to be acceptable on both quality and price.

The Delegation undertook the visit to Middle East/West Asia as part of United Planters' Association of Southern India's Marketing Plan with a view to explore possibilities of increasing Tea exports from South India. This was the first producer delegation to these countries and the visit facilitated to become closer and ensured direct contacts with the overseas buyers. The delegation met various importers in the respective countries with the help of Mr. K.S. Chaturvedi, the then Director of Tea Promotion (Middle East), Tea Board of India based in Dubai and the Indian High Commissions in the respective countries.

If the Planters do direct exports, Overseas Buyers would start realizing that they: *(i)* are getting a better service, *(ii)* assured of larger/fresh quantities of tea, and *(iii)* assured quantity shipments. Thus, teas can be tailor made to their requirements.

Major highlights in respect of the various countries in Middle East are given below:

(1) Saudi Arabia

- The Kingdom of Saudi Arabia has an estimated population of 35 million including 8 million foreigners. It is well known that the strength of Saudi economy rests on oil revenue. The per capita income is more than Rs. 1 lakh.
- Saudi Arabia is predominantly an Orthodox whole leaf market with CTC Teas having barely a 15 per cent share of the total tea (excluding tea bags) sold in the Kingdom. India's share during the last five year ending 2005 in the total market is just over 10 per cent. Saudi Arabia is overwhelmingly packet Tea/Tea Bag oriented market with little or no scope for bulk teas as such, except for the odd Defence Tender.
- Sri Lankan Rabea Brand Packet Tea dominates Saudi Arabian Market. The prevalent price level for imports from Sri Lanka in packets varied from USD 1.90 to 2.00 per kg. CNFC 1 per cent Jeddah. The importers were unanimous in their opinion that Indian Teas are very expensive, when compared to Sri Lankan Teas. Ours are not adequately promoted. A few parties expressed interest in Tea Bags under their own brands.
- OP/OPA grades are very popular which one hardly makes. Our high grown whole leaf grade has potential market there. Private Trade is keen on importing good quality Tea—both bulk and packeted. Members of the delegation met the trade both collectively and individually. Substantial quantity of Orthodox OP can be sent from South India to cater this market. Delegates offered wide range of Orthodox broken and Nilgiri OP and good response is awaited. A few blenders and packers showed interest in CTC broken but insisted that standard should be close to that of Assam.
- The Indian Consulate at Jeddah had given wide publicity for the visit of Indian Tea Delegation and also organized meetings with several prominent importers.

- There had been a meeting with some Tea Importers at Jeddah who met delegates at the Red Sea Palace Hotel.
- One or two of those importers mentioned that they had some problems with Sri Lanka but did not elaborate.
- Saudi imported 12 million kgs, on an average of Tea from Sri Lanka and 23 million kgs from England. However, she imports from India only 2 million kgs.

(2) *Egypt*

- Egypt is a very price sensitive Dust/Fanning Market. Average import is around 55 million kgs annually. The Egypt Tea market is currently overstocked with Teas of various origins, mainly Sri Lanka, Kenya and Indonesia. In fact, Kenyan teas eaten substantially into the market share of Sri Lankan teas. Today Kenyan tea has approximately 40 per cent of the Egyptian market – slightly ahead of Sri Lanka with around 35 per cent. These teas are of very good quality. The market is no longer interested in secondary Dust grades that were once popular in Egypt. In fact, there is interest now only for primary Dust grades (PF/PGS) but at heavily discounted prices. Assam Teas command good respect but good South Indian CTC dust priced 20 to 30 U.S. cents below Assam levels very good chance in the market.
- It was indicated that packets were being imported from Sri Lanka at USD 1.90 per 2.00 per kg CNF Port Said/ Alexandria and bulk teas from Kenya at USD 1.45/ 1.50 per kg. Indonesian teas in bulk are available at cheaper rates ranging from $ 1.30 to 1.35 per kg CNF Port Said/Alexandria. Bulk teas from Sri Lanka are also available in the USD 1.30 to USD 1.40 per kg range. Some importers are buying Asian tea at a higher price level of US 1.50/1.60 per kg. CNF. While TTLS standard of secondary dust grades (MS/SRFD/GD) did not attract any interest, the two primary standards of Non RCPF and MSPD/Normal PD in bulk (chests) attract attention at the indicated price levels of US$ 1.20 to

US$ 1.30 per kg CNF Port Said. These parties were unwilling to place immediate orders on the grounds of being over stocked. They can however, be actively followed up for future sale possibilities.

- It is well known that Egypt has been second largest importer of South Indian Tea and that they been importing CTC and Orthodox Teas, well-made Fanning, Grainier Teas and other grades in the lower price brackets.
- Prominent among the private importers that the delegation called upon were Mr. Nasar of Crown Tea Company who market the leading 'Crown' brand of tea in Egypt.
- During the discussions with private importers and with representatives of MISR and SHEMTO another feature emerged was that the market is increasingly moving away from imports of packaged teas to bulk purchases that are then repacked in factories at the Free Trade Zone in Alexandria. The Government is also actively engaged in encouraging full capacity utilization at home and levies an import duty of 50 per cent on packed teas as against only 35 per cent on bulk teas.
- The delegation also met and had extensive discussions with Mr. Nasser El Sharkawy, the then Chairman of the MISR import & Export Co., which is the apex trading body in Egypt. Some members of the delegation sought to the 150 ppm limit on Iron Filings that is stipulated by Egyptian Food Laws reviewed through the good offices of MISR They were told that the chances of success were extremely low. The delegation also requested them to consider gunny bags as alternative packaging to tea chests and they agreed to consider the same when the container handling facilities are mechanized. Rejecting suggestions to buy directly from producers instead of through the auctions, Mr. Sharkawy mentioned that MISR did often purchase upto 100 MT of Packet Tea through the negotiations with private exporters in the origins. They indicated that the 'River Nile standard is available with their representative office at Kolkata who would also be in

a position to know when additional quantities are being considered for purchase. Mr. Sharkawy then wanted to know whether India would be interested in a barter arrangement against their teas. Egypt could ship out Rock Phosphate, Creosole Oil or Cotton Yarn. He was advised that Delegation was not competent to comment on this but would request the Indian Mission at Cairo to follow up the matter with the concerned Ministry in New Delhi.

- The Delegation attended a luncheon meeting hosted by India Egypt Business Council at Cairo at which the then External Affairs Minister, GoI Madhav Singh Solanki and S K Aggarwal, the then Counsel (Commerce) Jeddah participated.
- On enquiry with the Customs Authorities at Cairo regarding alleged discriminatory duty on Indian Tea they said that duty is being levied uniformly at the rate of 30 per cent for loose Tea and 50 per cent for packaged Teas and that there is no discrimination. The duty may be higher on Indian Tea because of its higher price.
- At present Tea imports into Egypt are monitored by two sources namely their Government imports, canalized through A.R.E. Trade Center at Kolkata with Agents who buy through the auction and the private Trade imports by open tender system canalized through their Agent SHEMTO.
- Teas shipped from South Indian to United Arab Emirates consist of mainly orthodox medium description. Tea shipments been only small during the last three years and there is scope for further increase.
- The Delegation had meetings with number personalities concerned with tea import.
- The delegates visited a Private Tea Packing Factory, which was partially mechanized. Teas Packed in gunny bags from Sri Lanka and Kenya reach here in blended form and the quality of these are far below that of ours. They do not even poly lining and look like second hand gunny bags.

(3) Syria

- In Syria (Capital Damascus) the population is about 15 million and the per capita income is about 25,000 Syrian Pounds and the annual trade with India for 1990-91 stood at US $ 10 million and the Indian imports from Syria stood at US $ 0.2 million.
- Tea is one of the most popular beverages in Syria. The annual consumption often has increased from 4 million kgs in 1974 to 2 million kgs at present.
- Syrian bulk tea imports include maximum of well-made and lesser orthodox medium broken such as GBOP and BOPS. Exports of tea, on an average from South India to Syria was nil and in 1990 it was about two lakh kgs.
- Sri Lanka has been the main supplier of Tea to Syria. The delegation was told that Indian Suppliers are under erroneous impression that the Syrian Market consumes tea similar to that supplied to Egypt and Sudan. Accordingly, they were quoting against Syrian Tea Tenders by sending samples of inferior quality. There seems to be good scope for improvement in Indian Export of Tea to Syria by adhering to the quality standards and by sending competitive offers to compete favourably and effectively with Sri Lanka. Intensive publicity campaigns must be further strengthened in order to create awareness among Syrian Public regarding the availability of good Tea from India. The common person in Syria is so imbued with Sri Lankan publicity that he thinks automatically that the best Tea is only Ceylon Tea.
- The delegation understood during the Annual Damascus International Fairs, a Tea kiosk sponsored by the Tea Board is usually set up for sampling of Indian Tea. This drew large crowds. In 1974, a two-week publicity campaign for Indian Tea was organized through the Syrian Advertising Agency in the Press, television, cinema, etc and this proved quite successful. Such publicity campaign has to be kept up at regular

intervals in order to leave an indelible impression in the minds of the people here.

- Extensive publicity campaigns would be more effective and impressive than touch-and-go approach. Therefore, the Tea Board should earmark more funds for future participations in the Fair. This is preferably in a separate kiosk. The Board has to launch large-scale publicity campaigns covering the entire range of the mass media in this country. It recommends that a permanent tea stall similar to Sri Lanka's should be constructed on the Fair grounds. This may be suitably taken up with the Tea Board/Commerce Ministry.
- During the discussions with GEZA Officials in Damascus, the delegation emphasized the need for import of packaged tea from India as Tea in Syria is being sold to the consumer mostly in bulk and one can never know the origin. The report of the Delegation contained a list of all leading private Syrian Tea Importers.
- GEZA, the state owned company imports nearly 30 million kgs per year by floating Global Tenders in which Suppliers form all producing countries participate. Tea is heavily subsidized by GEZA through PDS and hence they buy at lowest possible rates. The decisions were wholly based on price considerations with the severe Foreign Exchange shortage in Syria. The tender awarded to Indonesia was at 1.27 (otx) USD C & F Lakathi. The other packet teas that are available at higher prices are mainly smuggled from borders. Private trade is keen on establishing business with us but on very low prices. Though the market potential at the moment is limited, we can pick up some business once the private trade commences operating on a much larger scale. The delegates emphasized the need for import of packaged Teas from India and offered the samples to Private Trade. GEZA can look at the samples only in response to tender. This country has lower exchange rate for import at incentive rates for domestic business.

- While Sri Lanka sells bulk teas at prices ranging from \$ 1.40 to 1.80 per kg CNF Lattakia, it was widely believed that GEZA has purchased Indonesian bulk Teas recently at considerably lower prices—as low as \$ 1.27 kgs CNF Lattakia.
- The bulk of the teas are sold through the official fair price shops in bulk form and at subsidized rates. However, recently the Government relaxed its import restriction on Tea and permitted private importers to carry on business. Not surprisingly, there was mad scramble to import Teas from all origins and this naturally led to fierce price competition with its inevitable shake out. The Private Trade is relatively quite small and controls less than 25 per cent of the total Tea imports. It is primarily interested in the imports of package Teas in 500 gm polybags with inner liner.

The delegation also called upon the General Director of GEZA, Mr. Hamid Abdul-Rahim, who invited all Indian Importers to participate in the next Syrian tender for Bulk Tea as the current one had recently closed. GEZSA will communicate all relevant details of the next tender individually to each importer in due course.

18

Kenya Tea Growers' Association—The Driving Force Behind Recognition of Kenya Tea

Introduction

Kenya, being one of the African countries, entered into the world of tea at a later date. Tea was first planted in Kenya in 1903, although tea production in Malawi had started on a commercial scale since 1891. International Tea Agreement, lasting between 1930 and early 1950, halted the faster expansion of the Kenyan Tea Industry. The early efforts for expansion also were disappointing. By 1924, only 155 hectares were under tea. However, the Kenyan Tea Growers Association (KTGA), which was set up in 1931, was the driving force behind the recognition of Kenyan teas in the world tea market. After independence, the Kenyan Tea Development Authority was formed in 1964 to promote small tea growers of Kenya. Because of their sustained effort, the small tea holders emerged as the backbone of the Kenyan Tea Industry. At present, the small growers own nearly 80 per cent of the planted tea area and large estate owners 20 per cent. The KTGA alone directly employs nearly 60 thousand people, which accounts for about 50 per cent of total labour force engaged in the tea industry as a whole. The average age of tea bushes under small growers is lower than that of the large estate sector. The average size of small holdings is only 0.38 hectare. Such a situation is comparable with the conditions of small holdings of India and Indonesia.

Kenya Tea Growers' Association

The role played by Kenya Tea Growers Association is the driving force behind the recognition of Kenyan Tea in the world tea market. The formation of Kenyan Tea Development Authority for promotion of small tea growers of Kenya, the share of area under cultivation and crop produced by small tea growers to total area and production are the focal points. In the process efforts have been made to analyze data relating to area, production and yield over a period of 56 years. Quantity of exports, value of exports and unit value of exports are some of the aspects that deserve special attention. Production, export and sale; disposal of tea, origin of Mombassa Auction, market behaviour and promotional efforts are the areas of concern. Further types of manufacture, taxes and duties, tea prices are given attention.

Origin and Development of Kenya Tea Industry

The entire tea industry operates under the aegis of Ministry of Agriculture. It was first brought under Statutory Committee in June 1950 when the Tea Board of Kenya was set up. The Tea Board now exercises licensing control over tea planting and manufacturing facilities and is financing Kenyan Tea Research Foundation. The Tea Board of Kenya now undertakes the task of tea promotion in the world. At present Kenya is the topmost tea producer in Africa and ranks fourth in the field of world tea exporters after India, Sri Lanka and China. Tea is Kenya's second most important foreign exchange earner after coffee. The two crops account for about 52 per cent of the total export earnings while these alone accounts for nearly 25 per cent of the total export earnings of the country. There was a leap in tea production to a level of 86.29 million kgs during 1977 from the previous year's level of 61.98 million kgs in Kenya. Similar commendable achievements were also made in 2001 from the level of 1982. Kenya reached a record level of production during 2000 surpassing all the records of the past. It was 294 million kgs in 2001 compared to 236 million kgs in 2000. Production in 2002 recorded at 287 million kgs. It was estimated that the tea production will rise to the level of 298 million kgs in 2007 compared to 295 million kgs in

2006. Such achievement in production has enabled Kenya to occupy the position in the global tea production after India, China, Sri Lanka and the USSR.

Types of Tea Manufacture in Kenya

At present nearly CTC type tea accounts for 46 per cent of world tea production. India occupies the first position in production of CTC teas accounting for 30 per cent of the global production. Kenya occupies the second position accounting for nearly 19 per cent of the global production. About 99 per cent of the total tea production of Kenya is of CTC type. Kenya produces negligible quantity of Orthodox teas. The per capita domestic consumption of tea in Kenya has been increasing over the years. In recent years, the per capita consumption of tea has risen nearly 800 grams per head from earlier consumption of nearly 600 grams per head. The estimated domestic consumption of tea in Kenya has also reached a level of 25 million kgs during 2006 from the level of nearly 6 million kgs in 1970. Such increases in tea consumption can be explained largely by the increases in population and of real income. In fact, nearly, the Kenyan people consume 20 per cent of the total production of Kenya during 2006.

Marketing of Kenyan Tea at Auctions

The fluctuations at different periods in world tea prices are also influencing the movement of prices of Kenyan teas. Kenyan tea also enjoyed the advantage of the sharp rise in world tea prices during 1977 as also the boom in world tea prices in 1983 and 1984. In fact, a sizeable quantum of Kenyan teas is being sold in the domestic auction of Mombasa as also in London auctions. A small quantity of tea is being sold at Singapore auction. A statement on quantum of Kenyan teas sold and prices realized in different auctions in the world is shown in Table 18.1.

Table 18.1: Quantity Sold and Price Realized of Tea in Kenya per kg during 1970 to 2006

Year	*Quantum of Kenyan Tea Sold at (thousand kgs)*			*Price per kg of Kenyan tea fetched at*		
	Mombasa Auction	*London Auction*	*Singapore Auction*	*Mombasa Auction (Sh)*	*London Auction (in Pernce)*	*Singapore Auction (US cents)*
1970	6,630	15,132	90	6.61	48.6	175.40
1975	14,533	14,771	110	8.55	65.8	195.50
1980	32,264	22,677	140	13.70	111.30	215.45
1985	67,448	16,712	172	25.47	172.60	239.90
1990	97,450	15,856	150	24.24	125.40	210.17
1995	140,341	14,199	140	38.90	109.65	243.06
2000	179,443	850	130	204.01	140.45	368.56
2003	217,062	1020	100	185.45	145.20	239.91
2004	227,094	1345	90	175.45	144.25	191.84
2005	228,540	1450	110	180.25	145.75	200.45
2006	229,022	1570	120	179.45	142.15	215.25

Source : Tea Statistics, Tea Board, India, Kolkata, Various Issues.

Quantum of Kenyan tea sold at Mombassa Auction in 1970 was 6.63 million kgs, which increased by 35.49 times i.e. 229.02 million kgs in 2006. During the last four years, average quantum of tea sold was to the level of 225.25 million kgs. Similarly, between 1995 and 2000, sale of tea at the auction was 159.5 million kgs. The sale was only 130.91 million kgs, on an average, during 1970 to 1980. Kenya tea sold at London auction stood at 9.45 million kgs on an average during 1970 to 1995. Tea sold at Singapore auction averaged 110 thousand kgs during 1970 to 2006.

Growth Variables of Tea in Kenya during 1950 to 2006

More than 85 per cent of the total production of Kenyan teas is available for export, which has been increasing over the years. The exports of Kenyan teas during 1985 achieved a level of 126 million kgs, which enhanced to 278 million kgs in 2006. The UK is the major buyer of Kenyan tea. Pakistan ranked second, Sudan and Egypt ranked 3rd and 4th respectively. Tea of Kenya is being exported to nearly 36 countries of the world. Kenya is also able to export tea at lower unit export price compared to Indian tea. A statement, showing area, production, yield, quantum of export, value of exports etc. of Kenyan tea is shown in Table 18.2.

Table 18.2: Area, Production, Yield, Exports, and Unit Value of Tea in Kenya during 1950 to 2006

Year	*Area (hectare)*	*Production (thousand Kgs)*	*Yield (kgs per ha)*	*Quantity Exported (thousand Kgs)*	*Value of Exports (thousand US dollar*	*Unit Value of Exports (US dollar per kg.)*
1950	7,642	6,776	886	4,704	3,998	0.85
1960	15,936	13,776	864	11,871	11,277	0.95
1970	40,278	41,077	1,020	36,099	37,904	1.05
1975	61,511	56,730	922	52,630	62,558	1.19
1980	76,550	89,893	1,174	74,799	156,339	2.09
1985	831,372	116,172	1,755	126,086	232,972	1.85
1990	97,020	197,008	2,031	169,586	274,910	1.62
1995	110,450	240,450	2,170	220,150	520,245	2.36
2000	122,236	236,480	1,934	216,990	460,713	2.12
2003	135,000	290,140	2,149	270,145	470,245	1.74
2004	136,125	294,150	2,160	272,452	475,215	1.75
2005	137,000	293,240	2,140	275,375	477,415	1.73
2006	138,450	295,450	2,134	278,450	480,450	1.72

Source : Tea Statistics, Various Issues, Tea Board India, Kolkata.

Total area under tea in 1950 was 7642 hectares, which enhanced to 138,450 hectares indicating an increase of 1711.70 per cent over a period of 56 year. Thus, average annual rate of growth was 30.57 per cent. As regards production, it went up from 6.78 million Kgs to 295.45 million kgs accounting for 4260.25 per cent during the same period. In terms of average annual growth rate, it was 76.60 per cent. Yield of tea was improved from 886 kgs per ha to 2138 kgs per ha representing 140.85 per cent increase. The average annual growth rate was recorded at 2.52 per cent. The increase in production was mainly due to expansion of area and partial improvement of yield per kg.

Production, Exports and Sale of Kenya Tea

It is interesting to note the in 1989 Kenya's share of export to total production was 90.02 per cent, which was reduced to

86.02 per cent in 1991. It again increased to 97.18 per cent in 1999. It was hovering around 93 per cent during 2002 to 2006. Out of total production of 181 million kgs, 81 million kgs was sold through Mombassa auction (44.75 per cent) in 1989. Quantity sold in the Auction was 126 million kgs in 1991 (62.06 per cent), 179 million kgs (72.17 per cent) in 1999, 211 million kgs (73.52 per cent) in 2002 and 229 million kgs (77.62 per cent) in 2006. Thus, Kenya's export to total production varied between 86 to 97 per cent during the period from 1999 to 2006. The details are shown below:

Table 18.3: Production, Export and Sale of Tea in Kenya during 1989 to 2006

(in million kgs)

Particulars/ Year	*1989*	*1991*	*1999*	*2002*	*2003*	*2006*
Production	181	203	248	287	290	295
	(7.21)	(7.72)	(8.37)	(9.40)	(9.25)	(9.82)
Exports	163	175	241	267	270	278
	(14.00)	(16.27)	(19.11)	(18.71)	(19.22)	(17.70)
Sold	81	126	179	211	217	229
Export as per cent of Production	90.02	86.02	97.18	93.07	93.10	94.22
Sale as per cent of Production in Mombasa Auction	44.75	62.06	72.17	73.52	74.82	77.62

Source: Tea Statistics, Tea Board, Kolkata, India, various Issues.

Notes—(i) Figures in parentheses indicate share of production and export to global production and export and (ii) Sum total of exports and sale may not add up to total production because of stock left over.

Disposal of Tea at Mombasa Auction by Country and Year

Various countries like Kenya, Uganda, Tanzania, Zaire, Rwanda, Burundi, Malawi and Zimbabwe sell their teas through Mumbasa auction. Total tea sold through this auction in 1998 stood at 89 million kgs, which increased to 126 million kgs in 1991, 148 million kgs in 1994, 166 million kgs in 1997. Quantum of sale further went up to 221 million kgs in 2000 and 222 million kgs in 2003 and 225 million kgs in 2006. Of the total sale, share of Kenya was maximum in all the years. The table below brings out the details:

Table 18.4: Quantity of Tea sold at Mombasa Auction during1988 to 2006

(million kgs)

Country/ Year	*1988*	*1991*	*1994*	*1997*	*2000*	*2003*	*2006*
Kenya	75.0	120.0	130.0	144.88	179.43	217.06	229.02
Uganda	0.67	3.29	8.80	16.17	25.63	32.73	34.85
Tanzania	Neg.	0.53	7.04	3.22	9.66	14.57	16.67
Zaire	0.93	0.86	0.32	0.66	-	0.93	0.95
Rwanda	2.13	0.34	0.11	1.40	1.78	10.65	12.45
Others*	2.06	1.24	2.08	0.29	-	9.90	11.30
Total	88.79	126.26	148.35	166.62	221.60	285.84	305.24
Per cent of Kenya Tea to Total	84.46	95.24	87.84	86.92	80.97	75.93	75.02

* Include Burundi, Malawi and Zimbabwe.

Source : Tea Statistics, Various Issues, Tea Board India, Kolkata.

Share of total tea to Kenya tea sold in Mombasa market in 1988 accounted for 84.46 per cent, which hiked to 95.24 per cent in 1991. The share, however, reduced to 87.84 per cent and 86.92 per cent in 1994 and 1997 respectively. During 2000 to 2006, the share reduced from 80.97 per cent to 75.05 per cent. Quantity of Uganda tea sold though the auction in 1988 was 67 thousand kgs, which enhanced to 3.29 million kgs in 1991, 8.80 million kgs in 1994. The quantum of tea was almost doubled in 1997 (16.17 million kgs) and tripled in 2000 (25.63 million kgs). In 2003 and 2006, the quantum of tea sold was 32.73 million kgs and 34.85 million kgs respectively.

Market Behaviour

It became apparent by the first quarter of 2006 that production from the main tea growing areas of the world was set to be well ahead of 2005 and at the year end both India and Sri Lanka reflected significant increases. India's domestic needs and the offtake by Russia has kept the international supply and demand equation relatively well balanced. Russia became increasingly more selective finally dropping out of the market. The gap left by Russia was to some degree filled by increased demand from Eastern Europe and the Egyptian Private Sector. With all these factors taken into account price levels in real terms could be considered as satisfactory. The weather during the first two months of the year was unsettled and Kericho suffered hail in February with approximately 30 per cent of the crop in some areas destroyed. Widespread seasonal rain fell in March. Total production for the first quarter was 56.22 million kgs, 24.49 per cent above the same period in 2005. The seasonal rains continued into April and May giving way to cold, dry, sunny conditions in June. The half yearly crop figure stood at 108 million kgs, 18.3 million kgs more, a gain of 20.50 per cent over the six months of the previous year. In the third quarter, there was mainly dry weather with intermittent rain, some hail and low temperatures although Nandi, in contrast, reported some heavy rain. The cumulative crop was 184.95 million kgs or up by 14.09 per cent. Hot and generally dry weather was reported during the final three months. Kericho and Nandi received some heavy rain towards the end of October but the expected arrival of the short rains receded and gave way to unsettled, often windy conditions in the west and cold temperatures in the east. The final crop figure in 2007 is expected at 196 million kgs compared to 184.50 million kgs or an 8.5 per cent advance over last year; perhaps lower than had been predicted in some quarters.

Support from Importing Countries

In the Mombasa auction, there was continued widespread support from a number of importing countries. The UK and Pakistan were the most active in varying degrees but Russia became progressively more selective upto May and dropped out of the market in Mid June; Eastern Europe and mainly Poland bought larger quantities. Buying for the Egyptian State was only intermittent but the Private Sector lent useful support. There was good enquiry from Iran while Iraq showed interest. There was selective buying for Ireland, Europe, North America and Canada with a few orders from Australia, the East and Ethopia. Sudan was active on teas for price. Somalia purchased at bottom market levels but was often out priced. The United Arab Emirates was a welcome new entry although for only small quantities.

Exports of Kenya Tea by Destination

Kenya has curtailed London auction shipments considerably

so far. This is a new marketing strategy adopted by Kenya and tends to give the impression that they have now succeeded in penetrating other markets through their own effort. About market promotion, their latest achievement is the successful conquest of the Pakistan and Egyptian markets. The country has virtually knocked the spots of Sri Lanka, enjoying a monopoly until very recently. Shipments to Pakistan from Kenya have improved. More significant is the improvement in the value of Kenyan teas shipped to Pakistan over the years.

Table 18.5: Exports of Kenya Tea by Destination during 1990 to 2006

(in million kgs)

Country / Year	*1990*	*1999*	*2002*	*2006*	*percentage*
United Kingdom	60.28	85.90	94.95	99.37	35.67
Pakistan	49.36	70.36	77.57	81.74	29.21
Egypt	28.93	41.45	46.05	47.73	17.12
Sudan	4.57	6.52	7.28	7.39	2.71
Netherlands	2.73	3.88	4.30	4.40	1.61
Ireland	2.63	3.75	4.20	4.25	1.56
Afghanistan	2.57	3.66	4.09	4.14	1.52
United States of America	2.45	3.49	3.90	3.95	1.45
Yemen	2.22	3.18	3.55	3.60	1.32
Djibouti	2.06	2.94	3.28	3.33	1.22
Somalia	2.06	2.92	3.25	3.30	1.21
Canada	2.03	2.89	3.25	3.27	1.20
Belgium	1.28	1.83	2.04	2.07	0.76
Singapore	1.25	1.78	1.99	2.02	0.74
Germany	0.56	0.81	0.91	0.93	0.34
Australia	0.64	0.77	0.86	0.87	0.32
South Africa	0.41	0.58	0.65	0.67	0.24
India	0.41	0.58	0.65	0.67	0.24
Japan	0.35	0.51	0.56	0.57	0.21
Sri Lanka	0.35	0.51	0.56	0.57	0.21
Botswana	0.30	0.43	0.48	0.49	0.18
Oman	0.30	0.41	0.45	0.46	0.17
France	0.25	0.36	0.40	0.41	0.15
United Arab Emirates	0.25	0.33	0.38	0.38	0.14
Hong Kong	0.13	0.19	0.21	0.22	0.08
Sweden	0.13	0.17	0.18	0.19	0.07
Italy	0.10	0.15	0.16	0.16	0.06
Ethiopia	0.08	0.12	0.13	0.14	0.05
Turkey	0.08	0.12	0.13	0.14	0.05
Tanzania	0.08	0.12	0.13	0.14	0.05
Hungary	0.07	0.09	0.10	0.11	0.04
Israel	0.07	0.04	0.05	0.05	0.02
Iran	0.02	0.04	0.05	0.05	0.02
Saudi Arabia	0.02	0.02	0.03	0.03	0.01

Argentina	0.02	0.02	0.03	0.03	0.01
U S S R (CIS)	0.02	0.02	0.03	0.03	0.01
Switzerland	0.02	0.02	0.03	0.03	0.01
Kuwait	0.02	0.02	0.03	0.03	0.01
Others	0.02	0.02	0.03	0.03	0.01
	169.00	241.00	267.00	278.00	100.00

Source : Customs & Excise Department, Nairobi for Stabex.

It is observed from the above table the Kenya exports to United Kingdom, Pakistan, Egypt, Sudan, Netherlands, etc. During the year 1990, total exports were 169 million kgs, which increased to 241 million kgs in 1999, 267 million kgs in 2002 and 278 million kgs in 2006. The exports showed an increasing trend. Out of the total exports in 2006, United Kingdom constituted 35.67 per cent followed by Pakistan 29.21 per cent, Egypt 17.12 per cent, Sudan 2.71 per cent, Netherlands 1.61 per cent, Ireland 1.56 per cent, etc.

Growth Variables—Comparative Study between Kenya and World

The table below shows the share of Kenya's tea to world tea area, production and exports during 1992 to 2004.

Table 18.6: Area, Production and Export of Tea during 1992 to 2006—Kenya and World

Year	*Area (thousand ha)*			*Production (million kgs)*			*Export (million kgs)*		
	Kenya	*World*	*Percent*	*Kenya*	*World*	*Percent*	*Kenya*	*World*	*Percent*
1992	102	2450	4.16	188	2438	7.71	167	1017	16.37
1993	105	2533	4.15	211	2553	8.27	188	1156	16.30
1994	110	2448	4.50	209	2523	8.30	183	1036	17.67
2001	131	2638	4.97	294	3035	9.71	258	1392	18.55
2002	140	2646	5.29	287	3055	9.40	270	1441	18.88
2003	135	2713	4.97	290	3174	11.24	270	1401	19.27
2004	136	2775	4.90	324	3306	9.82	333	1540	17.66
2005	137	2779	4.92	293	2871	9.70	275	1590	17.29
2006	138	2778	4.95	295	2905	9.85	278	1570	17.70

Source : Tea Statistics, Tea Board, India, Kolkata, Various Issues.

The area under tea in Kenya increased by 35.25 per cent while global tea area enhanced by 13.66 per cent during 1992 to 2006. It shows that the percentage rise in area for Kenya is higher than World, Similarly rate of growth of production of Kenya is higher (59.44 per cent) compared to world (19.36

per cent). As regards exports, it went up by 66.46 per cent for Kenya and 47.83 per cent for world. Kenya accounted for 4.16 per cent of world area in 1992 and 4.95 per cent in 2006. Kenya's share in world production was 7.71 per cent and 9.85 per cent in 1992 and 2006 respectively. Further, Kenya constitutes 16.37 per cent in 1992 and 17.70 per cent in 2006 of world export.

Taxes and Duties

There is no export duty in Kenya. Manufacturing cess @ k shs 46 per100 kgs of made tea has been levied. Value added Tax (VAT) was introduced @ 18 per cent of local rates only with effect from 15 July 2000. Further, the local government @ 1 per cent of Gross Income to the farmer imposed Agricultural Produce cess. The presumptive income tax was reintroduced with effect from 1 January 2002 @ 2 per cent of the Gross income to the farmer. The import duty of green tea (not fermented) in immediate packing of a content not exceeding 3 kgs was levied @ 15 per cent per kg. Import duty of other green tea (not fermented) and partly fermented tea not exceeding 3 kgs whether or not flavoured was imposed @ 15 per cent per kg. As regards 'other black tea (fermented) and other partly fermented, whether or not flavoured', import duty was levied @ 15 per cent per kg. Import duty on instant tea concentrates (hot water soluble in powder form per cold water soluble in powder form per hot water soluble in other forms per cold water soluble in other forms) was imposed at the rate of 15 per cent per kg.

Conclusion

The Kenya has been increasing its promotional efforts in certain selected and established areas through the UK Tea Council. It has received the largest share of 67 per cent of the Kenyan Tea Board's promotional funding. A new strategy may also be deployed to meet the situation confronting global tea. Efforts are intensively made by the Kenyan Tea Board to find new markets apart from the traditional ones. All efforts are made for increased production of tea. It is significant to note that out of the total 290 million kgs of made tea produced from July 2005 to June 2006, the estates sector accounted from 50.7

per cent while the small holders under the management of the Kenya Tea Development Authority accounted fro 49.3 per cent. Apart from this, there is genuine regret that in some tea circles the buyers market was developed on the high side in all these years. There is no common understanding among the major tea producers. They should bring about an atmosphere in which there would be the least room for undercutting prices and remaining at the mercy of buyers. Great hopes were raised to arrive at an understanding initially between India and Sri Lanka to look into the aspects deeply. In such an atmosphere, only the buyers will divide and rule the prices in their own interests.

19

Exports of Green Tea in Japan

Japanese green tea gives a lemon yellow or greenish yellow liquor without anything of brown. The manufacture of green tea, a typical non-fermented tea, developed by Japan has been discussed. Further, a comparison on the method of production of green tea between Japan and China has been made. The hand processing of green tea known as 'Temomi', which covers nine different operations and takes about four hours. Japan has opted 'Aracha' that means crude tea mechanically produced. Besides, processing freshly plucked leaf, manufacture of refined tea, health aspects of green tea, and prospects of liquid tea market, retail ready black tea etc are the areas that make special attention. Prospects of Indian tea in Japan, herbal tea and varieties of tea like green, black, oolong, barley teas have been documented. Area, production, yield, exports, value of exports of tea from Japan during the last one decade has been analyzed. In addition, share of Japan to world production and export of tea; exports of tea from Japan by destination and Import pattern of tea in Japan have been covered.

Japanese Green Tea—Lemon Yellow or Greenish Yellow Liquor

All tealeaves are green. However, when processed, some of these change their colour and those are known as Black Tea. Some they do not, and are known as Green Tea. The tea that Indians usually take is Black tea. Green tea is scarcely produced in India. Percentage wise India produces only about 2.5 per cent of its production as Green Tea. The industry has has developed the taste for it too. America consumes quite some quantity of Green tea. Soviet Russia also has its own method of processing it as well. However, the traditional homes for Green teas are China and Japan. It is according to the taste developed over the centuries that tea is cultured and processed there for manufacture of Green tea.

The Japanese Green Tea, preferred in Japan and USA, gives lemon *yellow or greenish yellow liquor without any tinge of brown.* The liquor of Chinese Green tea however has a tinge of brown, which is liked by consumers in China and North African countries. All teas are same, even the green tea. It is not particularly due to a difference in variety but to in processing. Some teas have come to be called Green Tea. It may, however, be noted that tea leaves containing a good quantum of amino acid and less of tannin are better suited for Green tea production as much as leaves rich in tannin are good for Black tea. The Green tea is actually green in colour because enzymes do not break down the green colouring matter in the leaves, the chlorophyll, and therefore retains its colour.

In tea processing, an important aspect is the way in which the *oxidizing enzyme* contained in the leaves is used. When the enzyme is active, we call it fermentation. When it is inhibited, we call it non-fermentation. If fresh leaves, after plucking are at once treated with high temperature (at 100 degree Celsius in the steam method or 300 to 350 degree Celsius in pan to fired method) in the factory, the enzymes in them become immediately inactivated. This is how Green Tea; a typical non-fermented tea is manufactured. Japan has developed some mechanical device for processing of Green tea, particularly 'Sencha', their most popular variety. There are other varieties called Gyokuro or 'Perarl Dew', Matcha or ceremonial tea, Bancha and Kamairicha. The *method of production of Green tea in China and Japan vary in details.*

A Comparative Method of Production of Green Tea between Japanese and Chinese method is depicted below:

(Japanese method)	(Chinese Method)
Streamline	Primary panning

Cooling	Rolling
Rolling drying	Rotary panning
Rolling	Final panning
Rotary drying	Sorting & Polishing
Twisting	-
Final drying	-

Source: The Assam Review and Tea News, Various issues

Green Tea Processing of Japan

We are here concerned with production of Green tea particularly in Japan. As in other countries, Japan also began with hand processing of tea, known as "temomi". According to this process, all operations, after steaming of raw tealeaves, used to be carried out on a table called 'hoiro' that had a fire furnace under it. Steamed tealeaves were made to a thin long form on the table by skillful handling. Temomi process consisted of 9 different operations and took about 4 hours. Japan has now opted for 'Aracha', which means crude tea mechanically produced and has left behind the hand processing of tea. Today in Japan a large-scale factory produces about 10 tons of crude tea (Aracha) in a day.

In Japan freshly plucked tealeaves have to undergo 6 different processing through many machines. These are *(i) Tea Steaming Machine, (ii) Primary Drying Tea Roller, (iii) Tea roller, (iv) Secondary Drying Tea Roller, (v) Final Drying Tea Roller and (vi) Tea Drier. The tea-steaming machine is made* up of a net drum and stiring shaft, both covered with a long drum. During this process, the steam heat kills the oxidizing enzymes contained in the fresh leaves. When the fermentation stops, the steamed leaves take on a fresh green colour. The leaves contain at this stage about 75 per cent water. The tea then passes through drying tea rollers primary, secondary and final. *The primary drying tea roller* is made up of an air-heating furnace and a main shaft with press arms and stir arms in the drying chamber. The steamed leaves are twisted and dried in this machine until the moisture of the leaves is reduced to about 50 per cent. The next machined called *tea roller* has a jacket in mortar form with a press cap and a weight on the table with a pleated top. The tealeaves are stuffed into the revolving jacket with weight and twisted without heat. The objective is to break the cells of the tea leaves, create flexible and uniform moisture. The *secondary drying tea roller* has a dried fired furnace, a main shaft with press arms in the rotary drum. It presses and dries tea leaves to limit the moisture content to roughly 30 per cent. The *final drying tea roller* is made of a burner, rolling hands and pans with many pleats. Its function is to reduce moisture to about 13 per cent. The characteristic shape and fragrance of tea are the result of the pressing and heating operations. The last process is done by way of the *Tea drier*, which consists of an air heating furnace, a drying chamber, and net conveyers. The aim of this step is to reduce the moisture content in the leaves from about 13 per cent to 6 per cent while maintaining the quality and fragrance.

Refined Tea Manufacture

It is interesting to note that the Japanese farmers have reached mechanical sophistication to attain a level that the above processes producing crude tea are usually carried out by farmers themselves. The tea wholesale dealers called "Chashou" in Japanese carry out the next stage for manufacture of refined tea in the consuming districts. These wholesalers come into the picture because the crude tealeaves, coming out of the farmers' factories, are not uniform in size. Their appearance is comparatively poor and fragrance unsatisfactory. Because of high water content in the leaves, these are not also suitable for storage. There is therefore no way out other than drying out the crude tea completely. The leaves are sifted to produce uniform size with good shape and to improve fragrance and taste. The sifted tea is usually classified according to size and quality. It is then packed into a can or a gas barrier sack. What is interesting to note is that this process is carried out to remove the greenish aroma and to add slightly scorched flavour.

The factory of the wholesale dealer is provided with a tea refining machine, tea firing machine optical tea stalk separator, tea cutter, tea blender and tea packing machine. Particular reference may be made to the Tea refining machine and the optical tea stalk separator. *The tea-refining machine* is composed of various sieves of different sizes. Crude tea is classified according to size by this machine. The *Optical tea stalk separator* is a device that separates the stalk and the branch in crude tea. Perceiving the difference of colour of tea and a stalk by the light sensor, only a stalk and branchy are blown off by compressed air in a few thousand of a second. It processes about 300 kgs. in an hour. Finally, 1kg of black tea is produced from 4.2 kgs to 4.8 kgs of green leaves or about 4.6 kgs to as much as 6.1 kgs depending on the method of manufacture, are required for production of 1 kg of green tea. The story will not be complete without a reference to the method of preparation of the beverage. The golden rules that are applicable to preparation of black tea are also applicable to preparation of green tea, except the milk is scrupulously avoided. The brew of green tea is generally lighter and consumers outside Japan, say; in North African countries have a strong preference for sugar and flavour additives like mint.

Liquid Tea and Retail Ready Black Tea in Japan

In recent years, consumption of liquid tea has remarkably increased in Japan. Available information indicates that the total leaf consumption today is more than 50 per cent of the volume that is used in making liquid tea. In fact, this popularity of black tea as a canned beverage began around the middle of 1980s. At the time canned black tea consisted mainly of tea products that did not contain milk and were not sweet indeed. Liquid tea consumption has sharply increased in the restaurants and fast food centers in Japan with a view to saving labour. This development has also been noticed in other establishments as tearooms and hotels. It is held in the industry circle that the liquid tea will soon see the brightest days in Japan's market. Contextually it may be recalled the black tea consumed in Japan is mostly imported. Its own production is negligible and that is produced only in few areas of the country. Import of Black Tea has increased significantly from 8 million kgs in 1985 to 51 million kgs in 2006.

However, it may be noted that the retail to ready black tea is mostly from European countries such as Great Britain and France, producing well to known brands. Great Britain is the largest exporter to Japan. The other exporter of retail ready packaging was the USA (2.5 million kgs), Sri Lanka (2 million kgs), France (2 million kgs) and India (1 million kgs). The import trends over the past five years indicate a decline from USA and France but simultaneously a rise from Great Britain by 1245 per cent , Sri Lanka by 117 per cent and those from India by 47 per cent respectively.

Health Aspect of Green Tea

Green tea has another aspect. It is not merely a beverage but is a healthy drink too. Not just the Japanese Green tea; any Green tea properly manufactured and properly prepared can, fortify the health system of the imbiber. The tea is rich in several vitamins such as those of Vitamins of 'B' group, Vitamin 'C' and Vitamin 'P'. Fresh tealeaves are rich in Vitamin 'C. Though black tea's loss of the Vitamin is considerable, green tea retains much of it. Again, like black tea it is rich in some group of Vitamin 'B' particularly thiodiamin and riboflavin. Researches have shown that the tannin preparation of green tea is much more active than that of black tea in strengthening the walls of capillaries. Researches in Japan and USSR have reportedly demonstrated the cholesterol-reducing quality of Green Tea. In addition to these, a strong infusion of green tea induces significant anti bacterial activity as was demonstrated in the large-scale use of green tea infusion in combating plague in Japan in 1951. Subsequent clinical trials carried out in Russia demonstrated that a strong infusion of green tea is useful in the treatment of bacillary dysentery also. Even so, the consumption of green tea in Japan accounts for about 20 per cent of tea of all varieties of beverage. It continues to the preferred drink, though recently its consumption has slightly decreased, coffee replacing it. Not green tea alone or in Japan alone, all teas everywhere has suffered the same fate with instant coffee getting popular among young people. Tea has to take the challenge.

Tea in Japan

Japanese market for tea has grown steadily since 1985. It had grown to 59 million kgs in 1999 from 10 million kgs in 1988. It however, reduced to 50 million kgs in 2000 and again went up to 51 million kgs in 2006. In fact, expansion of liquid tea market has significantly contributed to this growth. The market size in value for tea in 2006 stood worth Y 425.5 billion, comprising tea in leaf and tea bag Y 95.4 billion, liquid tea Y 3145.5 billion, and instant tea Y 14.6 billion. Although overall consumption of tea including black tea, green tea and other teas has almost remained unchanged over the past 40 years, a look to the market indicates rapid increase in the demand of leaf tea since 1995 when the demand stood at 10000 kgs and had reached to 40000 kgs in 2006. However, the demand for tea bags grew only slightly, from 15000 kgs in 1998 to 55000 kgs in 2006. Available information further indicates that the share of tea bag to total demand for black tea dropped from 65.5 per cent in 1991 to 50 per cent in 2006. It may be emphasized that the change in market share is attributable to the rapid growth in liquid tea market.

Prospect of Indian Tea in Japan

The Director of Tea Board of India, New York observed that the tea drinking habit in Japan has been changing slowly and steadily. As a traditional tea drinker they specially preferred green tea. Nevertheless, the consumption curve has been showing a downward trend during the last two decades, while the demand for black tea is increasing. Noting the changing habit pattern in Japan, the Director hoped Darjeeling Tea, in near future, will surely further command a very lucrative price from the opulent and quality conscious Japanese market. This may, however, be testified from a recent auction when Darjeeling tea fetched $ 200 per pound. Of course, this does not mean the average Japanese would consume tea priced at $ 200 a pound. However, their leaning towards black tea is evident which may be utilised introducing tea bags at a comfortable price between $4 and $5 per pound. India is the second largest black tea exporter to Japan. In 2006, Japan's import of black tea from India stood 5000 thousand kgs and the figure is 46 per cent higher over than the previous year, the trade division of Indian Embassy in Tokyo reported. However, the need at this moment is a comprehensive market survey to identify the nature of requirement and the buyers' eagerness to pay. It is equally important that India's tea traders should introduce sophisticated packaging to lure the aesthetic minded Japanese buyer.

Tea Varieties in Japan—Green Tea, Black Tea, Ooolong Tea, Barley Tea

Many different types of tea are drunk in Japan. However, popular among them, widely drunk in other words, are Green (Sencha), Black, Oolong, and Barley (Mugicha) tea.

Green Tea: In Japan, this tea is called 'Sencha'. It constitutes the pivotal sector within Japanese tea market. Sencha, the traditional Japanese tea, is sold in loose-leaf form and is grown locally by small producers. The retail market constitutes around 55 per cent of the total Sencha market. Retail sales in 2006 stood around 50 million kgs, up by 5 per cent comparing the previous year.

Black Tea: The popularity of Black Tea, which began 10 years ago, is moving towards the peak. The Japanese today thinks the black tea brings hospitality, the sharing of thoughts and kindness. This brings people closer together and foster communication. The popularity of black tea is also rising among women, many of who are joining classes and seminars. Industry circle thinks, in Japan the black tea will shortly pass through the boom phase of trade cycle. Once this tea was regarded primarily as a luxury drink. Now it is considered as a gift item. However, it has lost much of its appeal since the 1970s, with the fall in retail prices because of lifting the import restrictions. The produce of India and Sri Lanka dominates the market of this tea. It is the smallest sector within Japanese tea market, and is sold in tea bag form. The retail demand is currently standing at around 6 million kgs. Moreover, this demand tends to increase further with the erosion of the popularity of loose-leaf tea in Japan.

Oolong Tea: According to the Japan Central Tea Association, Chinese Oolong tea is widely consumed in Japan. The demand for the drink has increased by 521 per cent between 1995 and 2006 compared with a fall of 7 per cent in the demand for Green Tea.

Barley Tea: In Japan, roasted Barley tea is also known as 'Mugicha', which is widely drunk iced in the summer. It is the second largest sector within the Japanese tea market and the demand, to some extent, is depending on the weather. The retail sales stood at around 20 million kgs in 2006, 40 per cent of the market in other words. Currently, the tea market in Japan stands at some 110 million kgs, up 4 per cent from 2005. As a percent age of total hot drinks' market, tea occupies around 30 per cent in quantity and 53 per cent in value. The estimated market value of the hot drinks is around Y1200 billion at present. And interestingly, tea is the highest value sector.

Area, Production and Yield of Made Tea in Japan

Japan has an area of 56.70 thousand hectares in 1992. It however reduced to 50 thousand hectares in 2004 showing a decline of 11.82 per cent . The decline started from 2001. As regards production, Japan harvested 92.13 million kgs in 1992 and 100.26 million kgs in 2006. The increase in production was due to enhancement of yield. Area, production and yield during 1992 to 2004 are depicted below:

Table 19.1: Area, Production and Yield of Tea in Japan during 1992 to 2004

Particulars/ Year	*Area (in ha.)*	*Absolute increase/ decrease*	*Production (thousand (kgs)*	*Absolute increase/ decrease*	*Yield (Kgs per ha)*	*Absolute increase/ decrease*
1992	56700	–	92103	–	1626	–
1993	55700	(-) 1000	92103	–	1654	(+) 28
1994	54500	(-) 1200	86303	(-) 5800	1584	(-) 70
2001	50100	(-) 4400	90371	(+) 4068	1804	(+) 220
2002	49700	(-) 400	83677	(-) 6694	1684	(-) 120
2003	50000	(-) 300	91930	(+) 8253	1839	(+) 155
2004	50000	–	100262	(+) 8332	2005	(+) 166

Source : Tea Statistics, Tea Board, India, Kolkata, Various Issues.

Exports, Value of Exports and Unit Value of Tea during 1992 to 2004

Japan exported 290 thousand kgs in 1992. It however went up by 3.18 times i.e. 923 thousand kgs in 2004. In value terms, it was US dollars 3883 thousand in 1992 and US dollars 16748 thousand in 2004. Increase in value of exports was attributed to higher unit value. The details are given below:

Table 19.2: Exports, Value of Exports, and Unit Value of Tea in Japan during 1992 to 2004

Particulars/ Year	*Exports (in thousand kgs)*	*Absolute increase/ decrease*	*Export (in thousand US $)*	*Absolute increase/ decrease*	*Unit value (in thousand US $ per kg)*	*Absolute increase/ decrease*
1992	290	–	3883	–	13.39	–
1993	328	(+) 38	4981	(+) 1098	15.19	(+) 1.80
1994	345	(+) 17	5494	(+) 513	15.92	(+) 0.73
2001	760	(+) 55	9961	(+) 4467	13.10	(-) 2.82
2002	806	(+) 46	11766	(+) 1805	14.60	(+) 1.50
2003	845	(+) 39	13765	(+) 1999	16.29	(+) 1.69
2004	923	(+) 78	16748	(+)2983	18.15	(+) 1.86

Source : Tea Statistics, Tea Board, India, Kolkata.

Production and Export of Tea—World and Japan

Japan's share in global production varied from 2.74 per cent to 3.78 per cent during the period from 1992 to 2004. Her share started declining from 1993 (3.61 per cent) to 2002 (2.74 per cent). It however registered an increase from 2003 (2.90 per cent) to 2004 (3.03 per cent). Japan's share in total exports was less then 0.06 per cent.

Table 19.3: Production and Export during 1992 to 2004 World and Japan

Year	*World production (in million kgs)*	*Japan's share (per cent)*	*World exports (in million kgs)*	*Japan' share (per cent)*
1992	2438	3.78	1017	0.03
1993	2553	3.61	1156	0.03
1994	2523	3.42	1036	0.03
2001	3035	2.98	1392	0.05
2002	3055	2.74	1441	0.06
2003	3174	2.90	1401	0.06
2004	3305	3.03	1540	0.06

Source: Tea Statistics, Tea Board, India, Kolkata.

Japan exports tea to ten countries. Her exports stood 8700 thousand kgs in 1951. It was however, reduced to 7719 thousand kgs in 1962 and 923 thousand kgs in 2004. Destination wise exports of tea from Japan is depicted below:

Table 19.4: Exports of Tea from Japan during 1951 to 2004 (in thousand kg)

Destination	*Year*									
	1951	*1961*	*1971*	*1984*	*1989*	*2000*	*2001*	*2002*	*2003*	*2004*
U Kingdom	73	588	3	9	8	19	26	23	30	30
France	0	70	3	–	–	–	–	–	–	–
Germany	2	138	2	65	19	106	61	102	63	60
Netherlands	–	415	0	–	–	–	–	–	–	–
Canada	196	291	96	29	26	92	52	56	49	57
USA	1504	1023	1214	138	514	213	201	265	279	292
Libya	64	411	–	–	–	–	–	–	–	–
Morocco	2240	1415	70	–	–	–	–	–	–	–
Tunisia	50	600	–	–	–	–	–	–	–	–
Australia	–	49	1	–	–	–	–	–	–	–
Other countries	4571	2719	35	104	104	274	285	360	424	484
Total	8700	7719	1424	345	671	704	625	806	845	923

Source : Tea Statistics, Tea Board, India, Kolkata, various issues.

It is evident from the data (Table 17.4) that Morocco was the major buyer of Japanese Tea upto 1961, followed by USA. Exports of tea from Japan to Morocco were 2240 thousand kgs in 1951 and 1415 thousand kgs in 1961. In case of USA, it was 1504 thousand Kgs and 1023 thousand Kgs in two points of time. The countries like UK, Canada, and Germany slowed down purchase of Japanese tea from 1971 on wards. France, Netherlands, Libya, Australia, Tunisia and Morocco did not buy Japanese tea. All these had an effect on fall of exports in 2004.

Import Pattern of Tea in Japan

Japan imports tea from countries like India, Sri Lanka, Indonesia, Kenya, Uganda, Tanzania, China, Taiwan, and UK etc. In 1951, she imported 15.52 million kgs, which enhanced to 56.20 million kgs in 2004, representing an increase of 269.05 per cent (i.e. average annual growth rate of 5.30 per cent). The black tea constituted 41.71 per cent and green tea 58.29 per cent of total tea in 1951. The trend however was reversed in 2004. The share of 'black tea', 'green tea' and 'other teas' were 28.88 per cent, 30.25 pr cent and 40.87 per cent respectively. Import pattern of tea in Japan is depicted below:

Table 19.5: Import Pattern of Tea in Japan during 1951 to 2004 (in thousand kgs)

Imports from	*Year*								
	1951	*1961*	*1971*	*1994*	*2000*	*2001*	*2002*	*2003*	*2004*
India	1011	1494	914	2697	4287	2909	2653	2910	2962
Sri Lanka	3654	3878	2792	5627	8624	7507	7922	8170	9224
Indonesia	–	35	61	879	1256	1182	1181	1334	1337
Kenya	5	38	142	482	604	1470	1245	1175	1150
Uganda	2	0	–	–	–	–	–	–	–
Tanzania	4	2	50	–	–	–	–	–	–
China	27	119	1332	22887	37432	43118	35478	30741	38943
Taiwan	8863	6121	5311	3333	1398	1111	1230	1233	829
U.K	1874	2163	2145	1242	739	640	613	521	507
Other Countries	112	269	1582	3808	3433	2049	1165	1048	1245
Total	15552	14119	14329	40955	57773	60056	51487	47132	56197
	(100)	(100)	(100)	(100)	(100)	(100)	(100)	(100)	(100)
Of which	6489	7511	7431	14187	17950	15181	15029	15500	16299
Black Tea	(41.72)	(53.19)	(51.86)	(34.64)	(31.06)	(25.29)	(29.19)	(32.88)	(28.88)
(per cent)									
Green Tea	9063	6496	5628	4718	14328	17739	11790	10242	16995
(per cent)	(58.28)	(46.02)	(39.28)	(11.51)	(24.80)	(29.53)	(22.90)	(21.73)	(30.25)
Other Teas	-	112	1270	22050	25495	27136	24668	21389	22903
(per cent)	-	(0.79)	(8.86)	(53.85)	(44.14)	(45.18)	(47.91)	(45.39)	(40.87)

Source : Tea Statistics, Tea Board, India, Kolkata.

It is observed from the table that on the one hand both share of black and green trees during 1951 to 2004 reduced. On the other hand the share of other kinds of tea like Oolong, Barley increased. `Other teas' were nil in 1951 and meager in 1961 (0.79 per cent). It's share enhanced from 1971 (8.86 per cent). During 1994 to 2004, the share of "Other kinds of Tea" varied from 40.87 to 53.85 per cent.

Conclusion

Tea consumers in Japan are both quality and health conscious. According to a report published recently in the Nikkei Weekly, consumers in this country are turning to herbal varieties of tea. Their leaning to Tochucha, caffeine–free Chinese tea made from the leaves of the tochu plant, is increasing gradually.

Tochucha is rich in medicinal properties, the report further added. It has twice as much alkali as oolong tea and contains iron. Soft beverages in different forms are very much popular in Japan today. They include carbonated beverages, fruit juice, cola, coffee and tea of different variety. It has been reported that 2.5 million vending machines are quenching the thirst of the nation, serving hot and cold drinks during winter and summer respectively. World Coffee & Tea remarks, popularity of black tea in this country is very high due to overwhelming attention directed to quality of tea swerved by the breweries. They are in keen competetion to develop high quality oolong tea and run heavy advertisements. Still now, canned coffee is the market leader in the canned soft beverage market. Its distinctive merits have placed it favourably in comparison to homemade 'regular coffee' and instant coffee.

20

Export Potentials of Indian Tea in Germany

Backdrop

As many as 15 countries export tea to Germany. Total tea exports to Germany recorded at 3023 million kgs. in 1951. It however, increased to 20.77 million kgs in 2004. In other words, exports enhanced by a multiple 6.43 times showing a growth rate of 543.75 per cent i.e., average annual rate of growth of 23.64 per cent. On an average Sri Lanka exports 439.4 thousand kgs followed by India (4282 thousand kgs), Indonesia 3900 thousand kgs and Argentina 849 thousand kg. India's exports to Germany ranged from 1279 thousand kgs to 5718 thousand kgs during the period 1951 to 2004. Further India's exports to Germany went up by 4.08 times from 1279 thousand kgs in 1951 to 5222 thousand kgs in 2004 representing growth rate of 308.29 per cent (i.e. average annual growth rate of 5.82 per cent). India's share to total exports to Germany in 1951 worked out to 39.63 per cent, which was reduced to 25.14 per cent. This calls for scope of exports of India tea to Germany. The table below shows country-wise and year-wise exports of tea to the Germany.

Further, India may explore the possibility of enhancing of quantum of exports in the UK through aggressive campaign. It is interesting to know Sri Lanka's share to total exports of tea in UK increased over the years. Thus question arises, India must be ready to compete with Sri Lanka and Indonesia.

Table 20.1: Exports of Tea from Various Countries during 1951 to 2004

(qty. in '000 kgs)

Year/ Country	*India*	*Sri Lanka*	*Indo-nesia*	*Bangla-desh*	*Kenya*	*Moza-mbique*	*Malawi*	*Mauri-tius*	*Rwanda*	*Argen-tina*	*Others@*	*Total*
1951	1279	361	173	1113	–	–	–	–	204	2	95	3227
1961	1583	1258	3605	566	–	331	–	–	133	138	349	7963
1971	3341	2948	3409	611	293	601	193	–	23	2	15	11436
1981	5082	4848	1877	1281	127	–	31	–	5	15	40	11436
1990	4082	3596	3438	437	1426	150	1066	–	–	2517	449	13306
1997	5712	5777	1913	76	413	–	480	17	–	129	450	14969
1998	5233	5695	1663	81	604	–	841	20	36	198	570	14371
1999	5265	5735	4555	81	659	–	848	10	–	202	640	17995
2000	4573	4735	6229	72	452	–	524	–	20	1347	450	18402
2001	4178	5129	6426	8	1035	–	344	–	–	1375	645	19140
2002	5002	5452	5837	8	579	–	111	–	–	1672	542	19203
2003	5116	5740	5740	8	609	–	121	–	–	3440	490	21264
2004	5222	5849	5840	8	603	–	279	–	–	2422	560	20774
Av.	4282	4394	3900	436	618	360	440	16	70	849	364	1598

Source: Tea Statistics, Tea Board, Kolkata, various issues and ITC, London.

(-) indicae Nil. @ include Brazil, Japan, Taiwan, China and Turkey.

Import Pattern

Germany imports on an average, 40.51 million kgs. She imports mainly from India, Sri Lanka, Indonesia, East Africa, Mozambique, China, Taiwan etc. In 1951 Germany imported 2.12 million kgs which went up to 6.70 million kgs (by 3.16 times) in 1961. In the next ten years i.e. 1971, it was 9.77 million kgs that hiked to 28.86 million kgs in 1994, 35.02 million kgs in 2000. The quantum of import increased over the years i.e., 2001 to 2004. It was 37.75 million kgs in 2001, 40.59 million kgs in 2002, 45.79 million kgs in 2003 and 43.34 million kgs in 2004. The details of import pattern are given in Table 20.2.

Table 20.2: Import Pattern of Tea in Germany during 1989 to 2005

Imports from	*1951*	*1961*	*1971*	*1994*	*2000*	*2001*	*2002*	*2003*	*2004*
India	1156	2743	4360	7290	7207	7544	6079	6672	5471
Sri Lanka	339	1546	3100	5805	5139	6576	6143	4345	5695
Indonesia	558	1826	1070	4013	5939	6404	6484	7348	7804
East Africa	13	9	262	2141	–	–	–	–	–
Mozambique	–	120	52	–	–	–	–	–	–
China	3	84	140	5172	6767	6078	6397	7137	7700
Taiwan	7	135	36	73	79	85	90	51	78
Other countries	48	237	749	4362	9895	11071	15398	24538	16662
Total	2124	6700	9769	28856	35021	37758	40586	45792	43412

It is clear from the data referred to above table that quantum of imports into Germany increased sharply over the years. During 1951 to 2004, India's share to total imports was highest followed by Sri Lanka and Indonesia. Imports from China gained prominence from 1994 onwards. It shot up from 5.17 million kgs in 1994 to 7.70 million kgs in 2004. Thus India's objective is to ensure Germany must procure more quantity of tea from India. Accordingly comprehensive study is to be undertaken to suggest strategies on long term basis for enhancing India's exports to Germany.

The German Tea Council introduced a new corporate concept resulted in a restructuring process and a tighter and more efficient organization. All available financial means are channeled into concrete promotional measures and transparently documented with a minimum of overhead expense. In order to have a sound operating basis before pressing ahead with the new campaign the supervisory board carried out a tea potential survey in many times. The investigation, carried out by Messrs Marplan, concluded that today, with values such as healthy living, proper nutrition and physical well being taking top priority in consumer consciousness, tea is a drink with unbeatable credentials—benign, delicious, refreshing, versatile and calorie-free. The enormous variety and the reasonable price are further arguments in its favour, matched by no other beverage. The survey pointed out a little realized fact: Tea offers a singularly unique combination of virtues, which can be summed up briefly as "enjoyment without side effects". In addition, it confirmed that there is great potential for tea in the field of catering.

Consumption of So Called Healthy Drinks: The consumption of so called "healthy" drinks such as mineral water and fruit juice again increased considerably, with Germans now drinking more of these beverages than any other nation. Market figures suggested that the consumer was inclined towards a higher intake of herbal infusions and fruit-based *tisanes*. Household statistics indicated that home consumption decreased slightly, in spite of virtually unchanged prices. However, since the borders separating east and west Germany opened, the consumption situation was influenced by the influx of sizeable amounts of tea into east Germany. Stocking up by east German citizens living close to the borders had easy access to shopping facilities in west Germany. Consequently, the statistics painted a somewhat unprecise picture. The tea tax figures (the most reliable indicator of actual consumption) confirmed this, having shot up by 20 per cent during the first 6 months of 2006.

Salient Features of Market Survey: The salient features of the market survey has been outlined below. The market survey pointed clearly to the target group for an advertising campaign. This target group belong to young people who tend to drink tea only occasionally, and who are not yet committed to a particular beverage. Gesellschaft for Teewerbung entrusted the task to Hamburg agency Windi Winderlich Design-Kommunikation with the creation of a young, dynamic campaign inviting direct participation from its readers. A total of 172 black-and-white quarter-page and one-third page advertisements appeared in selection of appropriately selected magazines. The advertisements in cartoon-style had witty headlines and invited readers to submit an even wittier one, with a change of winning a prize. Some five thousand individual entries were received during the first six months the campaign ran. The campaign provided as a spin-off useful and interesting material for the continuation of the same. A new brochure presenting tea from the classic tea producing countries—India, Kenya and Sri Lanka—as a thoroughly up to the minute drink was developed and produced to complement the campaign. Closer attention was devoted to the catering trade, having seen that there are considerable resources in this field. A separate advertising directed at this target group appeared in a selection of the most important trade magazines. The full-page advertisements explained the objectives of the consumer campaign and invited participation.

Public Relations: At the beginning of 1990, Gesselschaft fur Teewerbung entrusted the public relations agency BMC Concept PR with the task of developing and implementing a PR campaign. The objectives were to: *(i)* project an image of tea that does this beverage justice, *(ii)* to spread knowledge of the Tea Council as a center of information, and *(iii)* to make documentation. The PR agency and the advertising company operate hand in hand and drew on a joint fund of knowledge and experience in order to ensure that all measures were ideally coordinated. The agency compiled and evaluated market data and passed the prepared information to the press as well as trade members for their own use. It monitored the positioning of tea in the media through permanent observation, with the object of recommending suitable lines of action.

News Streamlined: The press bulletins, "Tea News" has been streamlined to match the Council's new corporate identity. It is a vehicle for conveying facts and figures on tea and the Tea Council itself to the media. Our long standing excellent relations with individual representatives of the press were boosted by personal meetings, chats and tea tasting sessions. As a direct result, there were numerous full spread features in the highest circulation magazines as well as in trade journals, besides television and radio broadcasts. To complement and enhance the effect of the advertising campaign in trade journals, the PR agency together with Windi Winderlich Design-Kommunikation produced an information and eye-catching brochure of specialized information of particular interest to caterers and the trade in general.

Existing promotion Aids and Informative Material Revisited: In addition to the production of a new consumer brochure to complement the advertising campaign directed at young consumers not yet committed to a single beverage, the existing promotion aids and informative material were revised and brought up to date. The shooting at German locations for the documentary tea film, a project approved at the annual general meeting of the council. Production continued in the tea producing countries. The film was constructed in such a manner as to allow its application for a number of purposes and target groups. Video versions was also produced.

Sales Promotion

An analysis of the effectiveness of tea serving activities at trade fairs came to the conclusion that it would be more prudent to invest the funds available for generic promotion in advertising and PR campaigns. For this reason, there were no trade fair activities in the year under report. Lectures on tea at caterers' training colleges were continued. The Tea Council's lecturer, nutrition expert Traute Hartmann, also lectured for the benefit of municipal works and housewives' associations. The lecturing activities were extended to cover other areas.

Internal and External Information Service

The German Tea Council keeps in touch with numerous national and international organizations involved with tea. Thus, has constant sources of news relating to tea at its disposal. This news and information is sifted and sorted to isolate all matters of interest to the members. This information is then translated where necessary and distributed together with monthly news letters. This keeps the members upto date not only on the current activities of the Tea Council but also on international tea news. The Tea Boards of India, Kenya and

Sri Lanka, as well as their representatives offices in Brussels, Bonn and London, receive regular quarterly reports on the Tea Council's activities, and the situation on the German Tea market. The German Tea Council itself has built up a public reputation as a "Tea Consulate". Every enquirer, whether consumer, tutor or journalist, is provided with a "made to measure" package of information. The 5th edition of the German Tea Council's manual on tea, "Tea for the Thirsty-Minded", was printed. This book is a best seller amongst the many books on tea available today.

Tea in Germany

The German consumers of tea are both quality conscious and health and environment conscious. They are also sensitive to reports of residual pesticides and the social situation of pluckers in tea producing. In recent years, Germany's import of tea for consumption revolves around 45 million kgs - 50 per cent of all tea are imported from India and Sri Lanka, the bulk of being Orthodox. The number of tea consumers have increased by about 17 million with the reunification of Germany. In Germany 80 per cent of all tea is hereunto sold in loose packed form and only 20 per cent in tea bags. On the other hand, tea bags are popular in Germany. In the country, however, there are about 2000 speciality tea shops selling garden teas and loose tea straight from the chest. Current consumption pattern indicates that canned ice tea, flavoured ice tea and instant tea are becoming popular.

New Market For Germany's Tea Importers

With the possibility of carrying free trade with Russia, Poland and other European countries where tea has always been a popular beverage, tea importers in Germany expect that the country's export business will prosper. It is further felt that the expansion of the EC to include Scandinavian countries. Austria and Switzerland will open up new vistas for the expansion of tea trade.

Tea-break in Deutschland

Consumer Patterns in the beverage sector are shaping up very well in favour of the good old Eastern drink, tea, in the newly unified State of Germany, says the fifty fourth annual report (2006-07) of the Tea Council of Germany. So called "healthy" and low calorie drinks, having minimum side effects, such as mineral water, fruit juices, and soft drinks have registered soaring graphs in the previous year, and there has been a 20 per cent increase in the tea yield during the first half of 2007. A 4.5 per cent increase in tea consumption, totaling 25 million kgs has also been recorded, It is remarkable that tea could hold its market alongside other competing drinks, tisanes and herbal infusions.

Top Efforts: The German Tea Council based at Hamburg, deserves accolades for stepping up its marketing and promotional programmes in a renewed way. Advertising and public relations, aimed at roping in new consumers and retaining the old ones, have yielded dividends. It invoked greater appreciation for tea as a natural, flavorous and time consistent beverage. The managing director paid an early visit to the principal cities in India and Sri Lanka to acquaint himself firsthand with the indigenous tea industries in these primary producing countries. The visit has evinced great interest in the Tea Board offices there for markets in east Europe. The ratio of payments between German trade and the producer nations may improve as a result of the efforts of the board of directors to attract more contributions from the former.

Setting up Trade Contribution: The council convened three board meetings, two annual general meetings and some meetings of the communication sub-committee and the film committee during the past year. Trade contributions was set up by 30 per cent from the new business year beginning on the first day of October 1991. A few changes were occurred in the constitution of the board of directors: Vice Chairman India. Mr. N.M.N. Rahman, though in touch, left the board following the closure of the Office National Indian du The in Brussels. He was followed successively by Mr. T. Chakraborty from the London office of the Tea Board, and thereafter by Mr. A.K. Sengupta, when the Brussels office reopened. Mr. E Kolthoff of Messrs. J. Bunting Techandelshans Gmb & Co. was elected a new member of the board. The council gained new shareholders and sponsors.

The Arm of Publicity: Some innovative advertisement programmes were launched in the year under review. These included cartoons and illustrations and a slogan competition that invited as many as 7000 entries. The agency Windi Winderlichy Design Kommunikation published more than 150 ads in high-reach city journals like *Stern, Freudin, Prinz,* etc. A parallel campaign targeted at caterers, hoteliers and wholesalers was carried out in the major trade journals, and it spelt out the council's objectives and activities. The consumer and trade publicity was followed up simultaneously by the publication of a special information brochure, and a revised reprint of the basic tea manual.

A whole gamut of public relation (PR) service was offered by the German Tea Council to highlight tea as a modern, healthy, instant and versatile beverage. The PR measures were jointly managed by the council and BMC concept PR, its agency. The East German media were provided with background material, as information and special "tea situation" photographs, for full spread articles and features. Contacts, aggregating 249 million, were achieved. Radio and television broadcasts, the latter incorporating excerpts from the council's own video production, Abenteuer Tea, portrayed the exotic drink. A special drive, "High Tea" (after the British tradition), consisting of information and pictures on various recipes and their serving, was undertaken. The package, presented as folders to the trade, press and around 400 top-notch hotels, evoked a modest response. Journalists received copies of the house new letter. Tea News and the press echoed the same copiously. Market surveys recycled the material needed for brand oriented launches.

Being Tea Conscious: The award, "Golden Tea leaves", has been instituted for meritorious achievement in the field of tea by individuals from tea-producing countries, foodstuff trade, tea business, catering, journalism, etc. *In Quest of Tea,* an instructive and entertaining documentary film which spotlighted tea as it is cultivated in the several districts in India, Sri Lanka and Kenya, was produced by the tea council to generate curiosity and promote consumption in the German Nation. This lively production was made available to national film distributors, educational authorities, consumer boards, etc., and would include an English version, too, for international viewing.

Brooding on the Brew: For the professional interests of learning caterers and dieticians, lectures on tea as an ideal beverage are delivered frequently by Mrs. Traute Hartmann, a nutrition expert. There also exists an information service, both internal and external, offered by the council to its own members as well as to the respective Tea Boards of India, Sri Lanka and Kenya. Members are kept constantly informed on the latest developments concerning tea from the free flow of tea news between numerous national and international tea organizations. The proximity of the German Tea Association, which has five common board members, has also enabled the Tea Council of Germany to remain the de facto genius loci of tea in Deutschland.

Conclusion

The German Tea Council provides facts and figures about the black tea TnSFKeTin Germany. A gain of 2107 th. Kgs in the import during the last five years, on an average, ended 2006 from both general and special trades, with a stable demand inland, was recorded. It attributed to the growing demand in the five new federal states. The break-up of the 24.73 million kgs imported during the last five years showed the major exporters like India, Sri Lanka, China, Africa (including Malawi, Kenya, etc), the Netherlands, Great Britain and South America (Brazil and Argentina)—in that order. This total average valued at DM 138.366 m was 9.3 per cent more in quantity and 7.3 per cent in value than the previous year's.

Figures also revealed that Germany's at-home and out-of-home tea consumption shot up by 11.9 per cent and 7.3 per cent respectively. The highest consumption-per-household statistics have been reported from the North and East Frisia in the former FRG, and the north-eastern and south-eastern regions in the former GDR. The drinking rate is 2.6 per cent less in the East than that in the West. Moreover, while tea bags are twice as popular in the East than in the West, no marked changes in the shares of 'loose' and 'bag' tea, both in value or volume were reported. The major sales points in the

West are hypermarkets, Aldi, conventional Food stores, and speciality tea-shops. Those in the East are conventional food stores, hypermarkets, discounters, and Aldi. This implies that the East is more price conscious than quality conscious.

The consumer preference pattern has not changed very much. Of the 100 different varieties of flavoured black tea, only nine flavours (especially Earl Grey, Vanilla, Wild Cherry, etc.) seem to hold sway. The expenditure for brand advertising and generic promotion of black tea during the last five years ending 2006 amounted to DM 26 million— much the same as in the last five years ending 2001.

21

Teas in Mauritius, Taiwan and Indonesia

This chapter deals with tea economy of like Mauritius, Taiwan, and Indonesia. Moreover, efforts been made to know the extent of area under tea, production and in respect of these countries during the period 1989 to to 2005.

Tea in Mauritius

Small planters occupy maximum tea areas in Mauritius. They enjoy a guaranteed green leaf price. In early season, they normally get free grant of complex fertilizer also. The the Governor of Mauritius, Sir Robert Farquhar, encouraged commercial cultivation of tea in nineteenth century although Father Galloys introduced tea there in 1760. First small export took place in 1948. There is not much of pest and disease. Two months winter dormancy is there. About seventy-five to eighty per cent of tea is exported. Cost of production was so high and profitability so doubtful that the tea industry was at the verge of closure during late eighties. India government is now assisting and Mauritius tea industry is undergoing a three-year plan since the later half of 2001. A tea experimental station was opened at Curepipe town in 1949. Before the Tea Board came into existence in 1975, Tea Control Board under Agriculture Ministry was regulating the tea industry from 1960. The Tea Development Authority has played a constructive role in development of tea. R and D in tea are in the hands of Tea Board since 1992 in Mauritius.

Table 21.1: Area, Production and Yield of Tea in Mauritius during 1989 to 2005

Area in thousand ha, production in million kgs and yield kg/ha.

Year	*Area*	*Absolute incr./decr.*	*Production*	*Absolute incr./decr.*	*Yield*	*Absolute incr./decr.*
1989	3.07	–	5.50	–	1791	–
1990	2.90	–0.17	5.57	+0.07	1980	+189
1991	2.87	–0.03	5.98	+0.41	2063	+83
1999	0.06	–2.81	1.47	–4.31	2195	+132
2000	0.07	–0.01	1.31	–0.16	1960	–135
2001	0.07	0	1.57	+0.26	2302	+342
2002	0.07	0	1.38	–0.19	2097	–305
2003	0.08	–0.01	1.40	+0.02	2130	+33
2004	0.09	+0.01	1.45	+0.05	2160	+30
2005	0.10	+0.01	1.46	+0.01	2165	+5

Source: Tea Statistics, Various Issues, Tea Board, Kolkata.

Area under plantation and production of tea in case of Mauritius declined. There were set backs of area from 3.07 to 0.10 thousand hectares and production from 5.50 to 1.46 million kgs. Despite the fall in area and production, yield has shown an upward trend. It was 1791 kgs per hectare in 1989 and 2165 kgs per hectare in 2005.

Tea in Taiwan

Immigrants from Fukien, a Chinese province, introduced tea in Taiwan nearly 200 years ago and today an area over 20,000 hectares is under tea. Most of which is situated in Central and North Taiwan. The farmers cultivate tea in smallholdings like China. Tea started to be commercially propagated in 1868. Labour shortage is there. Demand of black tea bags is on increase since last fifteen years and they are marketed in shops and markets. R and D are looked after by TTES (Taiwan Tea Experiment Station). It has achieved reputation in tea and now a very interesting range of products like canned tea, instant tea, fruit tea, flavoured tea, tea candy, tea jelly, tea biscuit, caky tea, tea powder, tea dishes, tea wine and tea cocktail are there. Annual production, on an average, in Taiwan is over 20,000 kgs and main variety produced is Chinsin Oolong. Details of area, production yield and exports of Taiwan are brought out in the table below.

Table 21.2: Area, Production, Yield, Exports of Tea in Taiwan during 1989 to 2005

Year	*Area (Thousand ha)*	*Production (Million kgs)*	*Yield (Kgs per ha)*	*Export (Million kgs)*
1989	24.30	22.25	927	7.45
1990	24.40	22.45	917	6.75
1991	24.22	21.50	896	5.05
1999	24.63	22.56	1100	3.45
2000	21.52	20.43	1033	3.40
2001	20.45	20.56	1047	2.75
2002	19.30	20.54	1055	3.50
2003	19.40	21.56	1060	3.45
2004	19.40	21.58	1060	3.25
2005	20.00	21.00	1065	3.55

Source: Tea Statistics, various issues, Tea Board, Kolkata, India.

It is evident from the data presented in the table that area and production remained static during 1989 to 1999. However, yield rate also underwent major change. It varied from 927 kgs per hectare to 1100 kgs per hectare . It is noteworthy that the eexport in absolute amount declined from 7.45 million kgs in 1989 to 3.45 million kgs in 1999 and thereafter it was same at around 3 million kgs from 1999 to 2005. Taiwan did not figure any percentage in terms of world production and world exports. From 2000 onwards are declined and around 20000 hectares. Similar is the position of production. It was about 20.5 thousand kgs duing the last six years.

Tea in Indonesia

Around six per cent of world tea is produced in Indonesia. It is reported that there is scope of further extension of areas, which are available and suitable for tea. Although in Sulawesi island some plantations came up very recently, the main Indonesian tea is grown in two Islands—*Java and Sumatra*. Tea in Indonesia suffered heavily during the period of Second World War. Big tea areas were uprooted. Tea was neglected when post war political unrest was there. The Dutch companies were taken over by Government in 1959.

Tea Business: About seventy five per cent of tea area has crossed the age of 75 years. A five years development programme provided to replant about 25000 hectares in West Java, which represents 80 per cent of total tea area. In Indonesia, the per capita consumption of tea is 280 grams. China first introduced tea in 1826. Subsequently Assam type was introduced in 1878. Out of twenty recommended clones, only three of them were widely used. All new areas since 1968 have clones. Apparent consumption of tea per head in Indonesia during the last four years from 1995-1997 to 2004-2007 is shown in the Table below:

Table 21.3: Apparent Consumption of Tea in Indonesia during 1995-96 to 2004-05

Year	*Total (million kgs)*	*Absolute increase/ decrease (million kgs)*	*Per head (kgs)*	*Absolute increase/decrease (kgs)*
1995-96	61.67	-	0.31	-
1996-97	66.00	(+) 1.67	0.32	0.01
1997-98	64.33	(-) 1.67	0.31	(-) 0.01
1998-99	58.77	(-) 5.56	0.28	(-) 0.03
1999-00	59.10	(+) 0.33	0.29	(+) 0.01
2000-01	60.15	(+) 1.05	0.30	(+) 0.01
2001-02	61.05	(+) 0.90	0.32	(+) 0.02
2002-03	61.00	(+) 0.05	0.31	(-) 0.01
2003-04	61.45	(+) 0.45	0.34	(+) 0.04
2004-05	61.85	(+) 0.40	0.35	(-) 0.01

Source: Tea Statistics, various issues, Tea Board, Kolkata, India.

It is evident from the data incorporated in the above table the total consumption of tea slightly improved from 61.67 million kgs to 61.85 million kgs i.e. by 0.18 million kgs. during the period from 1995-96 to 2004-05. This was due to fall in consumption per head. It was 310 gram per head in 1995-96 and 350 gm per head in 2004-05.

Variety of Tea Leaf: Assam jats are there. For new plantings clones are used which are from local selections. Some clones were brought from Sri Lanka also. From China and Japan tea was introduced in Java in 1684. However, Java tea got its recognition on improvement of quality after Assam tea seed was introduced there in 1878. Assam type thrives on Pengalengan Plateau and produces good liquor. Basis of Indonesian tea soils are volcanic rocks. Java soils are easily eroded. Red soil is highly suitable for tea. High altitudes of Java do not produce flavour like Darjeeling. Indonesia, outside monsoon current's range, is tropical. Rainfall and temperature are expected to be even during the year in Java normally.

Plucking Period of Tea: Indonesian tea does not face a really dry period. Plucking continues round the year. Normally afternoons are cloudy and mornings are sunny in Indonesian tea areas. Indonesia does not winter dormancy. In Java, maximum crop is harvested during the period September–January. May is also a good cropping month. Nine to ten days mean leaf period has been found there. From selected stands of Java tea reached Sumatra. In Indonesia, tea estates owned by the government recorded increase in productivity during last fifteen years coming to over 1970 kgs per hectare, which crossed 3000 kgs in the year 2000.

Type of Manufacture: Indonesia produces Orthodox tea, although CTC production started there in 1986. *Green tea* and *scented tea* are also produced there. While processing orthodox tea, continuous rollers and rotorvane are used. Domestic demand is met by green tea added with *Jasmine* reprocessed and made aromatic. Jasmine tea is supplied both in pack and in bottles and cartons as soft drink. Maximum black tea is exported. Export of black tea is done after obtaining quality certificate from government laboratories who are authourized to issue such certificates.

Grades of Tea: Indonesian green tea looks, to some extent, like the Taiwan. The important grades "*Peko*" has tender leaves while "*Jikeng*" consists of coarse leaves. Green tea and fresh Jasmine flower aroma constitute Jasmine tea. This is popular for its briskness, strength, and pleasing aroma. It is black due to heating and carbonizing. Particles are curled and large. Drying of tea with Jasmine flowers is done in continuous drying machine to make Jasmine tea. In Jakarta Joint Marketing Office holds weekly auctions.

Tea Experiment: Tea Experimental Station was started in 1902 at Buitenzorg, which later came under government control. New Tea Research Institute at Gamburg near Bandung is working since 1974. RITC (Research Institute for Tea and Cinchona) was established in 1973. High yielding clones GMB 1, 2, 3, 4, and 5 were released in 1988. Liquified fertilizer application (NPK, Mg) once in two months boosted the production of leaves by fifty per cent in comparison to thearea receiving solid fertilizer. Indonesian Research Scientists identified rice field weed named Azolla, which is found in fish ponds also, as an alternative nitrogen supplement. This was used as organic fertilizer. In India, at Titabar in Assam and elsewhere Azolla has been found increasing the yield of paddy. It was subsequently used in tea commercially. In Java, Wellensiek became successful in rooting tea cuttings in 1933. TRI 2025 is the most popular clone in Indonesia. However, new clones having better potential of yield in comparison to TRI 2025 since come up. Indonesia has the distinction of undertaking the first work for identifying the deficiency symptom of mineral on the plant at its Tea Research Institute. Dolomite application is popular in Indonesia. Area, production, yield, and exports of tea in Indonesia is depicted in the table below:

Table 21.4: Area, Production, Yield and Exports of Tea in Indonesia during 1989 to 2005

Year	*Area (Thousand ha)*	*Production (Million kgs)*	*Share of World Production (Percentage)*	*Yield (Kgs per ha)*	*Export (Million kgs)*
1989	129	147	5.86	1135	115
1990	134	160	6.21	1189	111
1991	137	152	5.79	1116	110
1999	159	161	5.42	1027	98
2000	158	157	5.26	999	105
2001	160	161	5.21	1001	100
2002	162	166	5.36	1025	100
2003	164	170	5.40	1055	101
2004	166	172	5.43	1060	102
2005	169	173	5.45	1062	103

Source: Tea Statistics, various issues, Tea Board, Kolkata, India.

Indonesia covered an area of 169 thousand of tea under cultivation with an annual production of 173 million kgs in 2005 as against 129 thousand hectares of tea and 147 million-kgs of tea in 1989. Yield rate improved to 1062 kgs per hectares in 2005 from 1135 kgs per hectare in 1989. The country accounted for 5.45 per cent of world production and 7.45 per cent of world exports. Exports were maximum at 115 million kgs in 1989 and minimum at 98 million kgs in 1999. The per capita tea consumption reduced from 320 gm to 280 gm during the period.

22

Tea in South Africa and Some Other Countries

In South African tea areas wind is strong, day temperature is high and night temperature low. The areas of Zululand, Natal and Transkei saw extension of tea in 1967 after the beginning of tea plantation on commercial basis in 1964 in Northern Transvaal. In Zimbabwe tea area is more in Chipinga than Inyanga. Assam types are suitable considering the pattern of temperature there. Rainfall is not sufficient for healthy tea bushes. Commercial tea plantation in Zimbabwe was started in 1925.

Tea in Mozambique, Tanzania, Uganda, Rwanda etc.

Mozambique is fortunately placed with very good scope for tea extension. Maximum tea estates are situated in Gurue and Socone districts, although initial planting was done in Milange. Tea is there now in Tacuane also. In all these districts the distribution of rain is better than Milange. Some soils of Mozambique have sulphur deficiency. Seasonal change in temperature is there. Plucking is done throughout the year in Tanzania where hybrid seed was used in early planting. Subsequent use of large leaf types has been there. Sulphur deficiency is there in some soils of Tanzania. In Southern Tanzania, there is seasonal change in temperature. Although tea is there in other areas also, main tea districts are Mengo and Toto in Uganda. Betjan jat faired quite well. Soils are deep and highly weatherd. They are rich in organic matter. Every month some rain is there in Uganda. June, July, August, December, January and February are the months they face solid water deficit. Plucking is done during the whole year. Of course, in every month the volume of crop is not same. Dormant season as such is not there. Climate and the pattern of harvest in Rwanda are like Uganda. Rwanda tea is located in Southeast from Lake Kivu. The planters know Ethopiean tea. Area under tea cultivation in the country was 2000 hectares in 1989. However, it increased to 3500 hectares in 2005. Crop harvested was to the level of 1800 thousand kgs. In 1989, it was almost doubled at 3400 thousand Kgs in 2005. Yield worked out to 950 Kgs per hectare. The country in 1989 exported 1000 Kgs of tea, which was reduced to 750 thousand kgs. in 2005. The share of production and exports of tea was 0.04 per cent and 0.05 of world production and exports respectively.

Tea in Nyasaland, New Guinea

Nyasaland tea industry is the oldest in Africa. Kivu, the mountainous district, has the maximum tea areas in Zaire. Harvest comes all around the year. Climatic conditions are almost like Uganda. The place St. Helena in Cameroons has tea. In 1980, Cameroon had over 1000 hectares of tea. An area of about 2000 hectares of tea was there in Burundi by mid seventies. It increased to 6840 hectare in 1989 and 9000 hectares in 2005. As regards production, it was 3862 thousand Kgs in 1989 and 7000 thousand Kgs in 2005. Yield worked out to 750 kgs per hectare. Quantum of tea exports in 1989 was 3696 thousand kgs and 600 thousand kgs in 2005. Area under cultivation and production in New Guinea were more or less constant at 4000 hectare and 6200 thousand kgs during 1989 to 2005. Yield rate was 1610 kgs per hectare. Exports hovered around 5800 thousand kgs during the period. Tea reached New Guinea from selected stands of Java. Planting on large scale was taken up in 1954 and the main tea area is in Wahgi Valley. New Guinea does not come under monsoon currents' range and is tropical. Winter dormancy is not there.

Tea in Rhodesia, Georgia etc.

Tea area is there in Rhodesia. Marked seasonal change is found in temperature there. In the history of tea irrigation, Rhodesian achievement in early years is acknowledged. Tea is planted in Belgium, Congo. From 1920s tea spreaded in Georgia, though it is there since the middle of last century. China tea occupies the most of the plantations there. Tea remains dormant in autumn and winter there. Easy erosion of soil is there . But measures been adopted to conserve the soil. Tea Institute is there at Anaseouli in Georgia. Field machinery researches are taken care of by State Designing Bureau situated in Tibiliai. In erstwhile USSR tea plantations were first started in Georgian republic. Subsequently, it got expanded in Azerbaijan and Krasundar. Rainfall in Azerbaijan is less than half of what is received in Georgian Western parts.

Tea in Turkey

With USSR seeds tea in Turkey was taken up in 1930 in Rize and then Trabzon and Giresun in phases. Tea was extended to Ordo also at the end of fifties. China bushes are grown there. There is government restriction on the size of the holdings of tea and they are small. Frost and snow are there in winter and temperature is very low. Normally theseason of plucking starts in May and ends in October. Stations for tea research are situated at Rize and Giresuin. In 1989, area under tea cultivation in Turkey stood at 90 thousand hectares, which increased to 91 thousand hectares in 1990. It again reduced to 89thousand hectares in 1991 and 77 thousand hectares in 1999. It remained constant upto 2005. In 1989 production was 142 million kgs, which declined to 127 million kgs and 137 million kgs in 1990 and 1991 respectively. Production increased to 171 million kgs in 1999. It again declined to 145 million kgs in 2002 and 150 million kgs in 2005. Yield rate went up from 1581 kgs per hectare in 1989 and 1900 kgs per hectare in 2005. Export declined sharply from 25 million kgs to 5 million kgs during the period. Share of production to world production was about 5 percent while it was 1 percent of world exports.

Tea in Malawi, Cameroon

Malawi tea industry is the oldest in Africa. Beginning of the tea industry of Africa took place in Malawi with small plantation at Lauderdale in the second half of 1880s. China hybrids were early species followed by Assam types. Polyclonal stocks and clones propagated vegetatively are there in use in Malawi for new plantations. The period December to April has been found to be maximum cropping period at Cholo. Soil water deficit occurs during the months of August, September, October and November when dry and hot weather prevails and humidity is low. Seasonal change in temperature is observed. Yield is quite less in dry and cold months. Complete winter dormancy is not there . However, the harvest weight is very small in a winter monthousand. Alluvial deposits are found in Malawi. Sulphur deficiency is there in Malawi tea soils. Due to "Yellow" disease tea bushes suffer which may be attributed to Sulphur's non-availability. While manufacturing copper compounds were sprayed in Malawi for fermentation, as available copper was immobilized due to high organic matter in some soils there. Selected stands of Java became the source of Malaya tea. Cameroon highlands maximum tea. Coastal region at lower elevations has also some tea. Tea area of about 2500 hectares was there in 1980. The distribution of rain is good. The months of April, May, September and October higher intensity of rainfall. Malaya falls outside the monsoon currents' range and climate is tropical. Normally, during the whole year rainfall and temperature are expected to be even. Malawi has an area of 19 thousand hectares under tea cultivation having annual production of 42 million kgs with an average yield of 2100 kgs per hectare in 2005. The country exports substantial quantity to the level of 40 million kgs. Area and production increased @ 1 percent and 4 percent per annum during the period from 1989 to 2005.

Tea in Australia, New Zealand and Queensland

Australia's own requirement of black tea to thelevel of approximately five per cen of total tea consumed is supplied by an area of about 300 hectares in North Queensland where growing of tea started in mid sixties. Selected stands of Java were the sources from where the tea came to Queensland. In Australia, irrigation is necessary when season is dry. Most of the rain is there in the first half of the year. Near Innisfall, tea

Table 22.1: Area, Production, Yield and Exports of Tea in South Africa, Mozambique, and Kenya during 1989 to 2005

Year	(a) Area in thousand hectare			(b) Production in million kgs.			Yield in Kgs per ha			Exports in million kgs		
	South Africa	Mozambique	Kenya	South Africa	Mozambique	Kenya	South Africa	Mozambique	Kenya	South Africa	Mozambique	Kenya
1989	7	2	87	12.7	1.8	181	1895	900	2065	-	1	163
1990	6	2	97	12.2	2.0	196	1934	1000	2031	-	0.75	170
1991	7	2	101	12.1	2.0	204	1808	1000	2023	-	1.34	176
1999	7	2	120	10.6	1.8	249	1519	900	2066	4.95	0.60	241
2000	7	3	122	10.6	2.5	237	1516	893	1933	6.0	0.65	217
2001	7	3	132	10.7	3.0	295	1463	938	2239	6.63	0.70	258
2002	8	3	133	10.9	3.0	287	1453	909	2175	6.40	0.75	267
2003	8	3	134	11.0	3.1	288	1460	910	2190	6.45	0.79	273
2004	8	3	135	11.1	3.2	289	1465	915	2195	6.50	0.80	284
2005	8	3	136	11.2	3.2	290	1470	920	2200	6.55	0.82	295

Source: Tea Statistics, various issues, Tea Board, Kolkata, India.

plantation was taken up commercially in 1960. Australia occupies only 800 hectares of land under tea plantation in 2005 with an annual production of 14 lakh kgs. The yield rate worked out to 1750 kgs per hectare. There is gradual expansion of black tea industry in Australia. With imported plants, the Australian tea industry is developing green tea in the Southern state. Black tea is not produced in New Zealand where it is produced in Motueka. The New Zealand Tea Cooperative does the planting there and they got about sixty hectares plantation. The cost of production is high in Australia and New Zealand.

Tea in Vietnam

Vietnamese tea came from selected stands of Java. Tea became an industry in Vietnam in 1918. Devastation of tea bases occurred during war affecting the industry and tea production got boost only after the independence war ending in 1975. Real strength to tea production came in past 1888 period on the formation of UTE (The Union of Vietnam Tea Farming Industry Enterprises) which now has 80 thousand hectares under cultivation producing 34 million kgs of tea annually comprising *black tea, green tea, flavour tea, scented tea, red tea and yellow teas.* Out of which one third comes directly from UTE. They assist local tea companies also. Vietnamese Tea Association is there of which both UTE and local tea companies are the members. Growing conditions in South Vietnam suit all tea types. Vietnam can be taken as a monsoon land where dry and wet seasons are found. Vietnam Tea Research Institute came into being in 1918 and is located in Vinh Phu near Hanoi. Vietnam has 85 thousand hectares of tea in 2005 with a production of 85 million kgs constituting 4 percent of world production. Quantity of exports recorded at 76 million kgs in 2005 accounting for 5 per cent of world export. Yield rate was about 1800 kgs per hectare. Details of area, production, yield and exports of tea in respect of Turkey, Iran, Malawi, Australia, and Vietnam are given in the Table 22.2.

Tea in Peru, Brazil, Argentina, Equator, Balvin, Columbia, etc.

Peru had 4000 hectares of tea in 1980. Tingo Maria area is

Table 22.2: Area, Production, Yield and Exports of Tea in Turkey, Iran, Malawi, Australia and Vietnam during 1989 to 2005

Year/	Area in thousand hectare					Production in million kgs.				
Country	Turkey	Iran	Malawi	Australia	Vietnam	Turkey	Iran	Malawi	Australia	Vietnam
1989	89.5	32.0	18.5	0.66	65.0	141.6	46.5	39.5	0.71	30.2
1990	90.6	32.0	18.2	0.77	60.0	126.7	44.4	39.0	0.77	32.2
1991	88.6	32.0	18.3	0.77	65.0	136.8	45.5	40.5	0.72	33.6
1999	76.7	32.0	18.8	0.80	77.0	170.5	60.4	38.5	0.13	65.6
2000	76.7	34.7	18.7	0.80	80.0	130.6	53.2	42.1	0.13	70.6
2001	76.6	34.7	18.8	0.80	82.0	142.9	46.7	36.7	0.13	80.0
2002	76.6	34.6	18.8	0.80	84.0	145.0	48.4	39.8	0.13	84.6
2003	76.8	34.6	18.9	0.81	84.5	146.0	49.4	40.7	0.14	84.9
2004	76.9	34.7	18.9	1.82	84.6	148.0	50.2	41.8	0.15	85.0
2005	77.0	34.7	19.0	0.83	84.7	150.0	51.1	42.0	0.15	85.3

Year/			*Yield in kgs per hectare*				*Exports in million kgs*			
Country	*Turkey*	*Iran*	*Malawi*	*Australia*	*Vietnam*	*Turkey*	*Iran*	*Malawi*	*Ausiralia**	*Vietnam*
1989	1581	1438	2133	1084	1534	24.9	1.6	39.9		15.0
1990	1400	1375	2146	997	1537	27.6	1.5	41.0		13.6
1991	1544	1406	2215	929	1527	2.34	1.5	37.1		10.0
1999	2222	1731	2045	1625	1746	4.5	4.0	42.7	10.0	36.4
2000	1703	1529	2245	1625	1772	6.4	3.5	38.4	11.0	55.7
2001	1864	1327	1960	1625	1793	4.8	4.0	38.2	11.5	68.1
2002	1890	1385	2087	1750	1793	5.1	3.0	39.4	12.0	74.8
2003	1895	1395	2090	1705	1795	5.2	3.2	39.5	12.4	74.9
2004	1898	1400	2095	1780	1798	5.4	3.4	39.7	12.5	75.4
2005	1900	1401	2100	1785	1800	5.4	3.5	40.0	12.6	75.7

* Figures from Georgia is available.

Source: Tea Statistics, various issues ,Tea Board, Kolkata, India,

more favourable. In 1981, tea was there in Brazil with an area of about 5000 hectares. On the border of Brazil, Argentina's commercial tea cultivation was started in Misiones around 1947. Some tea is there in the South of Misiones also. World's most Southerly tea areas of Misiones and Corrientes in Argentina are well known. 1958 was the year when Argentina tea came to London market for the first time. Major portion of Argentina tea is Cambod (Indo China) type. Assam hybrids and China type of bushes are also there. Rainfall is unregularly distributed. Growing conditions are not very good. Tea in Misiones, however, grows better than other areas. Winter dormancy is therefor three-four months. Drop in night temperature is big. Temperature has marked seasonal change. Small growers play an important role in the cultivation of tea. The labour is costly and scarce and mechanical harvesting is done. The period of tea harvest there is normally from September/October to April/May. The 1982 Falkland war snatched the market of UK from Argentina. Argentinian teas are mostly exported to Chile, USA and Pakistan. A Research Station is situated at Carvo in Argentina. Equador also produces tea. Tea is grown in Bolivia, Colombia, Corsica, Mexico and Paraguay also. Although in a very small experimental way, it has also started in USA. Taking into account of three countries, total area owned stood at 45 thousand hectares, production 75 million kgs with a yield rate of 1666 kgs per hectare. They also exported 62 million kgs in 2005. Area, production, yield and exports of tea for Peru, Brazil and Argentina are brought out in the table ahead.

It is observed from the table that the yields of tea is lowest in Peru compared to Brazil and Argentina. It was 992 kgs per hectare in Peru against 1448 kgs per hectare in Brazil and 1732 kgs per hectare in Argentina in 2005. Quantum of tea exported from Argentina was 54.6 million kgs in 2005 whereas it was 0.2 million kgs for Peru and 4.2 million kgsfor Argentina. There was fall in exports for Peru and Brazil during 1989 to 2005. The exports increased in the case of Argentina from 43.4 million kgs to 54.6 million kgs.

Area under Tea in Major Producing Countries of the World

Tea is cultivated in 33 countries, out of which China has the

Table 22.3: Area, Production, Yield and Exports of Tea in Peru, Brazil, Argentina during 1989 to 2005

Year/ Country	*Area in thousand hectare*			*Production in million kgs.*			*Yield in kgs per ha*			*Exports in million kgs*		
	Peru	*Brazil*	*Argentina*	*Peru*	*Brazil*	*Argentina*	*Peru*	*Brazil*	*Argentina*	*Peru*	*Brazil*	*Argentina*
1989	4.0	5.0	41.3	3.0	11.0	40.0	750	2200	969	0.2	9.0	43.4
1990	3.0	5.5	41.3	3.5	9.5	43.0	1167	1727	1042	0.2	7.5	46.0
1991	3.0	5.5	41.4	3.5	9.5	43.7	1167	1727	1055	0.2	7.3	36.0
1999	2.5	5.5	39.0	2.4	7.5	55.0	960	1364	1410	0.1	2.9	52.0
2000	2.6	5.5	39.0	2.5	7.0	63.0	962	1273	1615	0.1	3.7	50.0
2001	2.7	5.0	39.0	2.6	7.0	59.0	963	1400	1639	0.1	4.1	56.6
2002	2.8	5.0	36.0	2.7	7.0	62.0	982	1440	1722	0.1	4.0	54.0
2003	2.9	5.2	36.0	2.8	7.2	62.3	985	1445	1725	0.2	4.1	54.2
2004	3.0	5.4	36.3	2.9	7.3	62.4	990	1446	1729	0.2	4.2	54.5
2005	3.1	5.5	36.4	3.0	7.4	62.5	992	1448	1732	0.2	4.2	54.6

Source: Tea Statistics, various issues, Tea Board, Kolkata, India.

maximum area under tea cultivation (1084 thousand hectares), followed by India (420 thousand hectares), Sri Lanka (222 thousand hectares), Indonesia (138 thousand hectares), Kenya (102 thousand hectares), Turkey (89 thousand hectares), Vietnam (68 thousand hectares), Japan (57 thousand hectares) etc. Table below shows the details of area under tea in different producing countries.

Table 22.4: Area under Tea in Different Producing Countries in World during 1992 to 2004

(Area in hectare)

Name of the countries	*1992*	*1993*	*1994*	*2001*	*2002*	*2003*	*2004*
India	420289	418363	425966	509806	515832	519598	521403
Sri Lanka	221836	221836	187310	188971	187971	188199	188720
Indonesia	138736	129231	128503	150938	150723	143620	142782
Bangladesh	47781	47888	47847	49313	49500	50000	50400
China	1084200	1170800	1134600	11407000	1134200	1207300	1262310
Taiwan	22177	23087	21218	18938	18329	18500	18600
Japan	56700	55700	54500	50100	49700	50000	50000
Vietnam	68000	70000	72000	82000	85000	87000	90000
Papua and New Guinea	4000	4000	4000	3800	3700	3700	3700
USSR/CIS	1600	1600	1600	40600	40500	41300	41800
Iran	31874	34650	34650	34664	34500	34500	34000
Turkey	89345	89330	76971	76653	76600	76639	77000
Kenya	101845	104864	110222	131581	139976	131419	131418
Uganda	20500	20500	20500	20870	21170	21570	21720
Tanzania	19415	19415	19881	21371	21316	21984	22287
Malawi	18587	18705	18801	18761	18800	18694	18663
Mozambique	2000	2000	2000	3200	3200	3200	3250
Zaire	9000	9000	9000	6000	6200	6200	6250
Mauritius	3133	3151	3028	659	680	681	674
Rwanda	12566	12566	–	12825	12862	12862	12849
Burundi	8363	8750	9065	8709	8625	8800	8900
Cameroon	1512	1531	1547	1500	1500	1550	1600

at 3 per cent. Countrywise India produces 892 million kgs , followed by China (835 million kgs), Kenya (324 million kgs), Sri Lanka (308 million kgs), Turkey (165 million kgs), Indonesia (165 million kgs),etc. Myanmar produces less than 80 thousand kgs. Most interestingly, Nepal started tea cultivation from 1997on words. She produces 8 million kgs annually.

Further, percentage share of major countries in world production displayed the fact the India's share in global output has declined over the years. The table below depicts the fact.

Table 22.6: Share of Major Tea Producing Countries in Global Production during 1992 to 2004

(in percentage)

Name of the countries/Year	*1992*	*1993*	*1994*	*2001*	*2002*	*2003*	*2004**
India	30.04	29.80	29.84	28.13	27.41	27.67	27.01
Sri Lanka	7.34	9.14	9.65	9.76	10.17	9.55	9.32
Indonesia	5.94	5.35	5.08	5.50	5.31	5.35	4.99
Bangladesh	2.01	1.98	2.05	1.87	1.76	1.84	1.68
China	22.96	23.50	23.32	23.21	24.40	24.20	25.26
Taiwan	0.85	0.80	0.87	0.65	0.67	0.66	0.64
Japan	3.87	3.61	3.42	2.98	2.74	2.90	3.03
Vietnam	1.48	1.48	1.59	2.64	2.88	2.98	2.87
Papua & New Guinea	0.24	0.23	0.26	0.20	0.20	0.20	0.20
USSR/CIS	2.26	1.17	0.71	0.49	0.47	0.46	0.47
Iran	1.97	1.96	2.29	1.94	1.62	1.83	1.66
Turkey	6.41	5.00	5.32	4.71	4.65	4.88	4.99
Kenya	7.71	8.27	8.30	9.71	9.40	9.25	9.82
Uganda	0.37	0.48	0.53	1.10	1.11	1.15	1.08
Tanzania	0.75	0.91	0.94	0.82	0.90	0.93	0.93
Malawi	1.15	1.55	1.39	1.21	1.28	1.31	4.52
Mozambique	0.06	0.08	0.08	0.08	0.10	0.10	0.09
Zaire	0.12	0.12	0.12	0.09	0.09	0.09	0.09
Mauritius	0.24	0.23	0.20	0.02	0.05	0.05	0.04
Rwanda	0.56	0.37	0.16	0.59	0.49	0.49	0.43
Burundi	0.24	0.22	0.27	0.30	0.22	0.23	0.23
Cameroon	0.14	0.15	0.14	0.14	0.14	0.14	0.14
Argentina	1.80	1.80	1.66	1.94	1.90	1.89	1.91
Brazil	0.37	0.39	0.32	0.15	0.15	0.15	0.15
Peru	0.12	0.12	0.11	0.09	0.09	0..09	0.09
Ecuador	0.06	0.06	0.07	0.05	0.06	0.06	0.06
Zimbabwe	0.32	0.55	0.53	0.74	0.74	069	057

Myanmar	0.00	0.00	0.00	0.00	0.00	0.00	0.00
Malaysia	0.27	0.23	0.24	0.18	0.17	0.13	0.14
South Africa	0.40	0.42	0.46	0.35	0.38	0.34	0.17
Australia	0.02	0.03	0.05	0.04	0.05	0.05	0.05
Ethiopia	-	-	-	0.15	0.15	0.15	0.15
Nepal	-	-	-	0.25	0.26	0.25	0.25
Grand Total	100.00	100.00	100.00	100.00	100.00	100.00	100.00

*Provisional, *Source:* Tea Statistics, various issues, Tea Board, Kolkata, India.

Data presented in the above table showed the share of India, Japan, USSR per CIS, Iran, Turkey, Brazil etc to total production has declined over the years. On the contrary, share of Sri Lanka, China, Vietnam, Kenya, Uganda, Malawi, Mozambique, Cameroon etc to global output has gone up. The share of world production remains the same for Nepal (o.25 per cent), Ethiopia (0.15) and Australia (0.04 per cent).

Yield of Tea by Different Producing Countries

It is interesting to note the output per hectare has been sharply improving in all the tea producing countries on account of various developments the took place over the years. These are economic, social and fiscal, environmental, political measures. Table below brings out yield of tea per hectare of different countries.

Table 22.7: Yield of Tea in Major Producing Countries in World during 1992 to 2004

Name of the countries	*1992*	*1993*	*1994*	*2001*	*2002*	*2003*	*2004**
India	1742	1819	1768	1675	1625	1690	1713
Sri Lanka	806	1052	1300	1568	1652	1611	1633
Indonesia	1044	1057	998	1106	1076	1182	1154
Bangladesh	1024	1055	1080	1152	1083	1166	1104
China	516	512	519	615	657	636	662
Taiwan	933	884	1031	1047	1110	1135	1129
Japan	1624	1654	1584	1804	1684	1839	2005
Vietnam	532	539	556	976	1035	1069	1056
Papua & New Guinea	1488	1500	1625	1605	1675	1730	1757
USSR/CIS	34375	18750	11250	369	353	351	374
Iran	1506	1443	1667	1702	1435	1683	1618

Turkey	1749	1430	1745	1864	1854	2022	2143
Kenya	1847	2014	1900	2239	2051	2235	2470
Uganda	445	599	657	1593	1598	1691	1644
Tanzania	946	1197	1195	1158	1291	1341	1377
Malawi	1514	2112	1869	1960	2084	2230	2684
Mozambique	750	1000	1000	938	938	1000	954
Zaire	333	333	3000	433	435	452	480
Mauritius	1865	1882	1681	929	2032	2109	2199
Rwanda	1086	756	to	1389	1162	1204	1104
Burundi	708	631	757	1035	766	839	843
Cameroon	2260	2549	2306	2800	2800	2774	2813
Argentina	1063	1111	1050	1639	1611	1667	1736
Brazil	1500	1667	1333	885	912	961	942
Peru	1500	1500	1350	963	1000	964	982
Ecuador	1769	1601	1922	1684	1789	1895	1927
Zimbabwe	1214	2183	2085	3291	3291	3208	2755
Myanmar	845	915	852	867	875	882	889
Malaysia	2139	1959	1971	1746	1632	1224	1286
South Africa	1580	1753	1909	1463	1766	1699	890
Australia	0670	1118	2114	1625	1750	1765	1824
Euthopia	-	-	-	1957	1958	2000	1958
Nepal	-	-	-	7000	7182	6957	7009
Grand Total	995	1008	1031	1151	1154	1170	1190

*Provisional, *Source:* Tea Statistics, various issues, Tea Board, Kolkata, India.

Cameroon attained maximum yield at 2813 kgs per hectare, followed by Zimbabwe (2755 kgs per hectare), Malawi (2684 kgs per hectare), Turkey (2143 kgs per hectare), Kenya (2470 kgs per hectare), Mauritius (2199 kgs per hectare), , Japan (2005 kgs per hectare), The yield rate was minimum for china (643 kgs per hectare), followed by Zaire (445 kgs per hectare). Although Nepal entered into tea cultivation in 2001, her yield exceeded all the countries. The yield was 2.49 times more than Cameroon. Low yield countries must ensure to improve their productivity.

Exports from Different Producing Countries

The producing countries export tea to many countries. The table below shows the details.

Table 22.8: Quantum of Tea Exports from Major Producing Countries in World during 1992 to 2004

(In thousand Kgs)

Name of the countries	*1992*	*1993*	*1994*	*2001*	*2002*	*2003*	*2004**
India	174962	175318	150690	182588	201002	173684	197668
Sri Lanka	177801	209942	224235	287503	285985	290567	290604
Indonesia	121243	123926	84916	99721	100185	88175	98572
Bangladesh	27160	31914	23640	12925	13653	12173	13435
China	175526	201435	179679	249678	252273	259980	280193
Taiwan	5296	5142	4373	2451	2592	2713	2388
Japan	290	328	345	760	806	845	923
Malaysia	286	272	378	400	440	450	500
Vietnam	12967	18000	20000	68217	74812	59900	70000
Nepal	22	25	30	70	2090	2800	3100
Iran	1000	1700	1038	4000	8457	7014	8000
Turkey	5048	3961	5199	4809	5160	7042	5904
Kenya	166518	188390	183147	258118	272459	269268	333802
Uganda	7817	10251	10971	30427	31073	34069	29686
Tanzania	17853	19387	18570	22060	22563	20416	24170
Malawi	35363	35270	38652	38261	39386	42015	46599
Mozambique	800	300	500	700	750	800	900
Zaire/Congo	1500	2353	1501	2000	2100	2200	2200
Ethiopia	–	–	–	1000	1100	1200	1200
Mauritius	5461	4392	4036	41	39	41	42
Rwanda	13045	7200	4500	11000	11200	11500	13000
Burundi	5651	5760	6009	8709	6510	6926	7000
Zimbabwe	6089	8065	9688	17154	17634	17056	14912
South Africa	–	-	–	6632	7400	7168	3500
Georgia/CIS	–	–	–	8000	7000	7000	7300
Argentina	36529	43594	43230	56645	57107	58191	66374
Brazil	8211	8335	8377	4082	3979	4209	3593
Peru	248to	388	205	100	100	100	100
Ecuador	1458	1512	1470	1300	1185	1094	1036
Cameroon	2479	5780	3176	4200	4300	4400	4500
Papu & New Guinea	5648	6441	6300	6100	5500	5600	6500
Others Countries	800	1000	1500	2000	2000	2200	2300
Grand Total	1017042	1155992	1036376	1391651	1440840	1400796	1540001

* Provisional, *Source:* Tea Statistics, Tea Board, Kolkata, India, various issues.

Data revealed the Kenya exported 334 million kgsfollowed by Sri Lanka (291 million kgs), China (281 million kgs), and India (181 million kgs). Exports declined over the years from countries like Indonesia, Bangladesh, Taiwan, Mauritius, South

Africa, Brazil, Peru, Ecuador. The reasons for fall in exports are attributed to increase in domestic consumption, lack of aggressive marketing of product in othercountries, competition from soft drinks, preference to organic tea etc..

Share of Major Countries to Global Exports

The table below show cases percentage share of major countries in global exports:

Table 22.9: Share of Major Producing Countries in Global Exports of Tea during 1992–2004

(In percentage)

Name of the countries	*1992*	*1993*	*1994*	*2001*	*2002*	*2003*	*2004**
India	17.20	15.17	14.54	13.12	13.95	12.40	12.87
Sri Lanka	17.48	18.16	21.64	20.66	19.85	20.74	18.87
Indonesia	11.92	10.72	8.19	7.17	6.95	6.29	6.40
Bangladesh	2.67	2.76	2.28	0.93	0.95	0.87	0.87
China	17.26	17.43	17.34	17.94	17.51	18.56	18.19
Taiwan	0.52	0.44	0.42	0.18	0.18	0.19	0.16
Japan	0.03	0.03	0.03	0.05	0.06	0.06	0.06
Malaysia	0.03	0.02	0.04	0.03	0.03	0.03	0.03
Vietnam	1.27	1.56	1.93	4.90	5.19	4.28	4.55
Nepal	–	–	–	–	0.15	0.20	0.20
Iran	0.10	0.15	0.10	0.29	0.59	0.50	0.52
Turkey	0.50	3.43	0.50	0.35	0.36	0.50	0.38
Kenya	16.37	16.30	17.67	18.55	18.91	19.22	21.68
Uganda	0.77	0.89	1.06	2.19	2.16	2.43	1.93
Tanzania	1.75	1.68	1.79	1.59	1.57	1.46	1.57
Malawi	3.48	3.05	3.73	2.75	2.73	3.00	3.03
Mozambique	0.08	0.03	0.05	0.05	0.05	0.06	0.06
Zaire/Congo	0.15	0.20	0.14	0.14	0.15	0.16	0.14
Ethiopia	–	–	–	0.07	0.08	0.09	0.08
Mauritius	0.54	0.38	0.39	0.00	0.00	0.00	0.00
Rwanda	1.28	0.62	0.43	0.79	0.78	0.82	0.84
Burundi	0.56	0.50	0.58	0.63	0.45	0.49	0.45
Zimbabwe	0.60	0.70	0.93	1.23	1.22	1.22	0.97
South Africa	–	–	–	0.48	0.51	0.51	0.23
Georgia/CIS	–	–	–	0.57	0.49	0.50	0.47
Argentina	3.59	3.77	4.17	4.07	3.96	4.15	4.31

Brazil	0.81	0.72	0.81	0.29	0.28	0.30	0.23
Peru	0.02	0.03	0.02	0.01	0.01	0.01	0.01
Ecuador	0.14	0.13	0.14	0.09	0.08	0.08	0.07
Cameroon	0.24	0.50	0.31	0.30	0.30	0.31	0.29
Papu & New Guinea	0.56	0.56	0.61	0.44	0.38	0.40	0.42
Other Countries	0.08	0.09	0.14	0.14	0.14	0.16	0.15
Grand Total	100.00	100.00	100.00	100.00	100.00	100.00	100.00

*Provisional, *Source:* Tea Statistics, various issues, Tea Board, Kolkata, India.

Kenya accounted for 21.68 per cent of world exports, while it was 18.87 per cent for Sri Lanka and 18.19 per cent for China, Indonesia, Vietnam, Argentina constituted less thousand 8 per cent each of global exports. Taiwan's share to global exports varies from 0.16 to 0.52 per cent. Japan and Malaysia registered negligible share about 0.06 per cent and 0.04 per cent respectively. Similarly Peru's share to world exports is very negligible i.e. less thousand 0.03 per cent. India, the leading tea producing country represented less thousand 15 per cent during 1994 to 2004. It's share to world production declined from 17.20 per cent to 12.84 per cent during 1994 to 2004.

It is needless to mention here that the Producing Countries are earning considerable amount through exports. The Table below exhibits the value of tea exports in respect of tea producing countries for a period of 12 years from 1992 to 2004.

Table 22.10: Value of Tea Exports from Producing Countries

(Value in Thousand US Dollars)

Name of Countries	*1992*	*1993*	*1994*	*2001*	*2002*	*2003*	*2004**
India	384031	380830	315276	356485	360787	341394	406290
Bangladesh	32434	42627	29000	16037	16237	15736	
Sri Lanka	328307	390964	408035	654674	639636	653368	700564
Indonesia	140823	155696	96181	99854	103426	95818	116018
China (Mainland)	–	–	–	342389	304979	357633	436845
Japan	3883	4981	5494	9961	11766	13765	16748
Taiwan	17011	–	–	15277	16043	17921	16758
Turkey	6200	45807	5529	4078	4400	5389	6854

Vietnam	–	–	–	78406	82523	66000	78000
Burundi	10646	–	–	40940	8864	10105	
Kenya	294818	321903	325889	450705	431712	451167	548750
Malawi	33766	35589	29907	35476	34697	37635	47212
Mauritius	6118	5821	4623	216	223	231	348
Rwanda	23913	–	–	–	–	–	–
South Africa	–	–	–	15857	16766	12498	–
Tanzania	21432	24392	19807	27967	27493	24663	30059
Uganda	7762	10565	11765	33165	34802	34069	46200
Zimbabwe	7355	9999	11322	6571	–	–	–
Argentina	38515	38225	–	40462	39471	33205	39181
Brazil	–	–	–	6455	5553	5693	5470
Papua New Guinea	6728	7341	–	7000	7200	7000	7000

Source: ITC London, *Provisional.

Value of Exports of tea in case of Sri Lanka stood at US Dollars 700,564 thousand in 2004 followed by Kenya US Dollars 548,750 thousand and China Mainland US dollars 436,845 thousand. India ranks fourth position (US dollars 406,290 thousand) followed by Indonesia (fifth position – US Dollars 116,018 thousand). Mauritius earns negligible amount of US dollars 348 thousand. Vietnam, earns less thousand US dollars 80 thousand where as Malawi and Uganda less thousand US dollars 50.

Bibliography

PUBLICATIONS by Dr G.D. Banerjee

A. Six Books and one Ph.D. Thesis

1. Banerjee, G.D., Structural Changes in Tea Industry since 1956, unpublished thesis submitted to Jadhavpur University, Kolkata.,1982
2. Banerjee, G.D. (1996), *Tea Plantation Industry in India between 1815 and 1992,* Lawyers Book Stall, Guwahati, Assam.
3. Banerjee, G.D. Hundekar and Das Edited, (1997), *Challenges before Small Scale Industries,* Horizontal Publishers, Allahbad, Uttar Pradesh, India.
4. Karmakar, K.G. and Banerjee, G.D., (September 2005) *The Tea Industry in India – A Survey,* Department of Economic Analysis and Research, NABARD, Mumbai.
5. Banerjee G.D. and Banerji, Srijeet, *Darjeeling Tea— The Golden Brew,* (2007), International Book Distributing Company, Lucknow, Uttar Pradesh, India.
6. Banerjee G.D. and Banerjee, Sarda (2008), *Sustainable Tea Plantation Management,* International Book Distributing Company, Lucknow, Uttar Pradesh, India.
7. Banerjee, G.D. and Banerjee, Sarda, (2008), *Agriculture and Rural Development Policy Agendas in the New Millennium,* International Book Distributing Company, Lucknow, Uttar Pradesh, India

B. Eleven Reports

1. Socio-Economic Implications of High Yielding Varieties of Food Grains in the Eastern Region of India, UNDP Global Project, Agro-economic Research Centre, Santiniketan.
2. Efficiency of Small Farms Under Different Tenurial Conditions with Special Reference to North Bengal, ICAR, New Delhi - 1.
3. Techno-Economic Survey of Darjeeling Tea Industry, Tea Board, India, Kolkata, West Bengal.
4. Techno-Economic Survey of Tripura Tea Industry, Tea Board, India, Kolkata, West Bengal.
5. Techno-Economic Survey of Small Tea Gardens in Kottayam and Idukki (Kerala), Tea Board, India, Kolkata.
6. Techno-Economic Survey of Small Tea Gardens in Kangra (H.P.), Tea Board, India, Kolkata.
7. Techno-Economic Survey of Nilgiri Tea Industry, Tea Board, India, Kolkata, West Bengal.
8. Techno-Economic Survey of Cachar Tea Industry, Tea Board, India, Kolkata, West Bengal.
9. Evaluation Study Report on Inland Fisheries in Nadia District NABARD, West Bengal Regional Office, Kolkata.
10. Evaluation Study Report on Inland Fisheries in West Tripura, Tripura, NABARD, Assam Regional Offic, Guwahati.
11. Evaluation Study Report on Poultry Farming (Broiler) in Medinipur District, NABARD, West Bengal Regional Office, West Bengal, Kolkata.

C. About 160 Papers published by Dr. G.D. BANERJEE

a. *Indian Journal of Agricultural Economics,* Indian Society of Agricultural Economics, Krishi Vikas Sadan, First Floor (Near Dr Antinio De silva Technical High School), Veer Savkar Marg, Caddle Road, Dadar (west) Mumbai 400028, Tel—022 24374789, Fax—022

24374790 E. mail- isae@bom7. vsnl.net. in; website www.isacindia.org

1. Changes Overtimes In the Levels of Income of the Weaker Sections of Rural Community (WB), Annual Conference Issue June- July 1972.
2. Impact of Agro Processing on Incomes of Primary Producers, Annual Conferences, Dec. 2003.

b. *TAI News Letter* published by Tea Association of India, Indian Exchange Palace, Kolkata 1, (West Bengal).

3. Problems and Prospects of Tarai Tea Industry, Feb. 1983, Vol.16, No. 2.
4. Problems and Prospects of Indian Tea Exports, March 1983, Vol. 16, No. 3.
5. The Role of FAO, UNCTAD and ITPA for Development of World Tea, May 1983, Vol. 16, No. 5.
6. Export Prospects of Indian Tea in Tunisia, July 1983, Vol. 16, and No.7.
7. Tea Plantation of India (North), September-October 1983, Vol.16, Nos. 9 and 10.
8. Structural Development in Tea Industry, November 1983, Vol. 16, No. 11.
9. Evolution of Tea Industry in India (Part I), December 1983, Vol. 16, No. 12.
10. Evolution of Tea Industry in India (part II), February 1984, Vol. 17, No. 2.
11. Ownership of Tea Estates, March 1984, Vol. 17, No. 3.
12. Japan As A Base of Indian Tea, August 1984, Vol. 17, No. 3.
13. Changes in Pattern of Management, September 1984, Vol. 18, No. 9.
14. Area, Production and Yield of Tea in Different Excise Zones, December 1984, Vol. 17, No. 12.
15. Changes in the Pattern of Ownership, February 1985, Vol. 18, No. 2.
16. Market Research, March 1985. Vol. 18, No. 3.
17. The Role of Tea in Indian Economy, April 1985, Vol. 18, No. 4.

18. Export Prospects of Indian Tea in Nigeria, June 1985, Vol. 18, No. 6.
19. Export Prospects of Indian Tea in Singapore, November 1985, Vol. 18, and No. 11.
20. Tea Plantation in South India, October 1986, Vol. 19, No. 10.
21. Impact of Area, Production of Tea in New Planting, Yield Rates, Exports and Quantity Retained for Domestic Consumption, November 1986, Vol. 19, No. 11.
22. Efficiency of Tea Estates, January 1987, Vol. 20, No. 1.
23. Role of Tea Plantation in North India, May 1987, Vol. 203, No. 5.
24. Export Prospects of Indian tea in Iran, January 1988, Vol. 21, No.1.
25. Structural Changes in Tea Exports in India, February 1988, Vol.21, No. 2.
26. Export Possibility of Indian Tea in Arab Republic of Egypt, May 1988, Vol. 214, No. 5.
27. Export Prospects of Indian Tea in Canada, July 1988, Vol. 21, No. 7.
28. Export Prospects of Indian Tea in Poland, September 1988, Vol.21, No.9.
29. Export Prospects of Indian Tea in Syria, January 1989, Vol. 22, No.1.
30. International Tea Promotion, March 1989, Vol. 22, No. 3.
31. Export Prospects of Indian Tea in Libya and Jordan, May 1989, Vol. 22,No. 5.
32. Tea in South India, July 1989, Vol. 22, No. 7.
33. Production and Exports of Value Added Teas in India, October 1989, Vol. 22, No. 10.
34. Problems and Prospects of Coimbatore Tea Industry, July 1990, Vol. 23, No. 7.
35. Problems and Prospects of Wynaad Tea Industry, October 1990, Vol. 23 No. 10.
36. Tea Statistics, Tea Boards of India, various issues.

37. Tea Directory, Tea Boards of India, various issues.
38. FAO 1995, 1999: Impact of Uruguay Round Agreement on the World Economists position, 2005 and Current Situation and Short Term Outlook, paper presented to Inter Government Group on Tea Ottawa September, 2005.

c. *The Assam Review* and *Tea News* Published by Assam Review Publishing Company, 27A, Waterloo Street, Kolkata –69, Phone to 033-2 2248251

39. World Markets of Tea and Its International Arrangements, January 1985, Vol. 73, No. 11.
40. Tea Economy in South India, February 1985, Vol. 73, No. 2.
41. Export Prospects of Tea in Singapore, July 1985, Vol. 73, No. 7.
42. Structure of Tea Industry, August 1985, Vol. 73, No. 8.

The Entire Thesis, namely, "Structural Changes in Tea Plantation Industry since 1956", was published by the above publisher in 17 instalments.

43. October 1985, Vol. 74, No. 10.
44. November 1985, Vol. 74, No. 11.
45. December 1985, Vol. 74, No. 12.
46. January 1986, Vol. 75, No. 1.
47. February 1986, Vol. 75, No. 2.
48. March 1986, Vol. 75, No.3.
49. April 1986, Vol. 75, No 4.
50. May 1986, Vol. 75, No.5.
51. June 1986, Vol. 75, No.6.
52. July 1986, Vol. 75, No. 7.
53. August 1986, Vol. 75, No. 8.
54. September 1986, Vol. 75, No. 9.
55. October 1986, Vol. 75, No. 10.
56. November 1986, Vol. 75, No. 11.
57. December 1986, Vol. 75, No. 12.
58. January 1987, Vol. 76, No. 1.

59. February 1987, Vol. 76, No. 2.

60. Export Possibility of Indian Tea in Iraq, I, January 1988, Vol. 77, No. 1.

61. Export Possibility of Indian Tea in Iraq, II, February 1988, Vol. 77, No. 2.

62. International Tea Promotior., May 1989, Vol. 78, No. 5.

63. Tea in South American Countries, July 1989, Vol. 78, No. 7.

64. Production and Export of Value Added Tea in India, August 1989, Vol. 78, No. 8.

65. Export pospects of Indian Tea in Jordan, October 1989, Vol. 78, No. 10.

66. Export Prospects of Indian Tea in Iran, February 1990, Vol 79 , No. 2.

67. Export Prospects of Indian Tea in Libya, June 1990, Vol. 79, No. 6.

68. Export Prospects of Indian Tea in Japan, August 1990, Vol 79, 8.

69. Export Prospects of Indian Tea in Argentina, March 1991, Vol. 80, No. 3.

70. Export Pospects of Indian Tea in South America, May 1991, Vol. 80, No. 5.

71. Export Prospects of Indian Tea in Poland, September 1991, Vol. 80, No. 9.

72. Export Prospects of Indian Tea in Australia, June 1993, Vol. 82, No. 6.

73. Export Prospects of Indian Tea in Egypt, October 1993, Vol. 82, No. 10.

74. Export Prospects of Indian Tea in Germany, November 1993, Vol. 82, No. 11.

75. Export Prospects of Indian Tea in Netherland, December 1993, Vol. 82, No. 12.

76. Export Prospects of Indian Tea in Srilanka, January 1994, Vol. 83, No 1.

77. Export Prospects of Indian Tea in Indonesia, February 1994, Vol. 83, No. 2.

78. Export Prospects of Indian Tea in China, March 1994, Vol. 83, No. 3.
79. Export Prospects of Indian Tea in Peru, April 1994, Vol. 83, No. 4.
80. Export Prospects of Indian Tea in Pakistan, May 1994,Vol. 83, No. 5.
81. Export Prospects of Indian Tea in Canada, June 1994,Vol. 83, No. 6.
82. Export Prospects of Indian Tea in Ethopia, September 1994,Vol. 83, No. 9.
83. Export Prospects of Indian Tea in Kenya, October 1994,Vol. 83, No. 10.
84. Export Prospects of Indian Tea in Tanzania, November 1994, Vol. 83, No. 11.
85. Export Prospects of Indian Tea in Uganda, December 1994, Vol. 83, No. 12.
86. Export Prospects of Indian Tea in Vietnam, January 1995, Vol. 84, No. 1.
87. Export Prospects of Indian Tea in South Africa, February 1995, Vol. 84, No. 2.
88. Export Prospects of Indian Tea in Zimbabwe, March 1995, Vol. 84, No. 3.
89. Export Prospects of Indian Tea in Mozambique, April 1995, Vol. 84, No. 4.
90. History of Darjeeling Tea, December, 1999, Vol. 88, No. 12.
91. Development Issues of Tea Industry, February, 2000, Vol 89, No 2
92. Development Issues of Tea Industry, March 2000, Vol. 89, No 3.
93. Development Issues of Tea Industry, April 2000, Vol. 89, No. 4.
94. Structural Issues in Tea industry, May, 2000, Vol. 89, No. 5.

d. *Chai ki Bat* published by Bharatiya Chai Parishad, 25 Ballyganj, Circular Road, Kolkata 700 019.

95. Export Prospects of Tea in Canada, January 1988, Vol. 33, No. 1.

96. Export Prospects of Tea in Saudi Arabia, February 1988, Vol. 33, No. 2.

97. Export Prospects of Indian Tea in Iran, April 1988, Vol. 33, No. 4.

98. Export Prospects of Indian Tea in Poland, May 1988, Vol. 33, No. 5.

99. Structural Changes in the Tea Exports of India, August 1988, Vol. 33, No. 8.

100. Export Possibility of Indian Tea in Arab Republic of Egypt, January 1989, Vol. 34, No. 1.

101. Availability of Tea in Internal Market or Maximisation of Export Earnings, March 1989, Vol. 34, No. 3.

102. Export Prospect of Tea in Iraq, May 1989, Vol. 34, No. 5.

103. Market Research on Tea Consumption, August 1989, Vol. 34, No. 8.

104. Market Research on Tea Consumption, October 1989, Vol.34, No. 10.

105. Green Tea (Part I), March 1992, Vol. 36, No. 3.

106. Green Tea (Part II), April 1992, Vol. 36, No. 4.

e. *The Northeast Times*, G.L. Publications, MG Road, Guwahati.

107. Industrialisation Sets Back to Farm income, 21 January 1992.

108. Economics of Green Tea, 28 May 1992.

109. Indian Tea in Syria, 16 June 1992.

110. Indian Tea in Jordan, June 21, 1992.

111. Indian Tea in Libya, July 07, 1992.

112. National Bank's Role for Tea Development, July 12, 1992.

113. The Role of National Bank for Development of Tea Industry, July 15, 1992.

114. Dry Land and Rain fed Farming, November 18, 1992.

115. Potentials of Horticulture Crops, November 28, 1992.

116. Market Potential of Indian Tea in Syria, December 10, 1992.

117. Cashew Nut Plantation, December 19, 1992.

f. *Financial Express,* Mumbai

118. Green Tea Peep Into the Past, 07 November, 1992.

119. Rain Fed and Dry Land Farming: A Balanced Agricultural Strategy Vital, 02 January, 1993.

g. *Eastern Miror,* Dimapur, Nagaland

120. Economics of Organic Farming – A case for Banana Plantation, Dec, 27, 2005.

121. Dairy Industry in 21st Century, January 4, 2005.

122. Problems of Agricultural Marketing in Nagaland, February 26, 2005.

123. The Role of SHGs in Poverty Allivation, October 20, 2005.

124. The Development of Handicrafts and Handloom in Nagaland, November 16, 2005.

125. Economics of Tea cultivation in Kangra, December, 18, 2005.

126. Himachal Pradesh Tea Industry –A Revival Package, 15 January 2006.

127. Agricultural Economy of Nagaland—Opportunities and Challenges, 20, February 2006.

128. Village Development Board as Financial Institution—Published in three instalments on 15, 16 and 17 April 2007.

h. *National Bank News Review,* NABARD, Department of Economic Analysis, and Research, Plot No. 24, Block—G, Bandra Kurla Complex, Bandra (East), Mumbai-400051

129. A Fresh Insight Into the Problems of Rural Development in the North East Region, February 1992.

130. Brackish Water Fish Culture A Case Study, January-March Issue, 1995.

131. Agro Processing Sector—Some Issues, July-September, 2004.

i *Financing Agriculture,* Agriculture Finance Corporation, Dhanaraj Mahal, Ist Floor, Chatrapati Shivaji Marg, Mumbai 400001, Tel No 2028924,Fax 022 *2028966, E mail (i) afcl@bom vsnl.net.in,*

132. Horticulture Strives Well in Food and Nutritional Security, April-June 2000, Vol 32, No. 1.

133 Agricultural Extension Assessment of various Models, October-December 2000, Vol. 32, No. 2.

134. Bio-technology for Indian Farmers, July-September 2001, Vol. 33, No. 3.

135. Water Resources Management–A Long Term Planning and Judicious Use of Water and Food Security, October-December 2001, Vol. 33, No. 4.

136. Evaluation Studies of Self Help Groups, April–June 2002, Vol. 34, No. 2.

137. Economics of Medicinal Plants, July–September 2003, Vol. 34, No. 3.

138. Boosting of Agricultural Exports—Opportunities and Challenges, Janurary- March 2005, Vol. 36, No. 1.

139. Dairy Development in the Context of Globalization, January – March 2006.

j. *Man and Development,* Center for Research in Rural and Industrial Development, Sector 19 A, Madhya Marg, Chandigarh-160019, E mail: cridchd@sancharnet.in

140. Agricultural Extension: A Critical Analysis of Various Models, September 2001, Vol. XXXIII, No. 3.

k. *Indian Journal of Agricultural Marketing,* Indian Society of Agricultural Marketing, Nagpur, 57/IV, Seminary Hills, Nagpur 440006, Email – kumar 81@indianet.

141. Primary Marketing of India Tea, Annual Conference Issue, December 2000.

142. Marketing of Indian Tea: A Review, Sept 2001, Vol 33, No 3

l. *Afro-Asian Journal of Rural Development,* No 2, State Guest Houses Complex, Chanakyapuri, New Delhito 110021, Phone (011) 24100475, 26877783, 61115936, Fax No (011) 24672045, 26115937, E mail aardohq@nde.vsnl.net.in

143. Marketing of Mango processing under Institutional Finance—A Case Study in Andhra Pradesh, July-December 2001, Vol. 34, No. 2.

m. *Indian Association of Social Science Institutions (IASSI) Quarterly Journal,* Care of Institute of Applied Man Power Research, Indraprastha Estate, New Delhi, Gram: SAMAJ VIDYA, New Delhi, Tel: 23315284, 23356834, E mail stiassi@ bol. net. In, website—www. Iassi. nic.in

144. Indian Tea No Longer A Fashionable Slogan, April-June 2002,Vol. 22, No. 4.

145. Agro Processing – A Link between Agriculture and Industry, Jan-March, 2004 (jointly with Dr K.G. Karmakar), Vol. 23, No. 1.

146. Sustainable Tea Plantation Management, Jan-March 2004 (jointly with Sarda Banerjee) Vol. 23, No. 1.

147. China's Pu'er Tea-Tea with Miraculous Function, October- December 2005, Vol. 24, No. 2.

148. Product Diversification and Value Addition of Tea, October-December, 2006, Vol. 25, No. 2.

n. *Times Agriculture Journal,* The Economic Times and NABARD, The Times of India Building, Dr. D.N. Road, Mumbai- 400001, Eto mailprittik@marwar.com (ii) b2bedit @ timegroup.com

149. All Hands on Deck, September-October Issue, 2002.

150. Horticulture An Over View Poised for Golden Revolution – November-December Issue, 2002.

151. Financing Horticulture January-February, 2003.

152. A Difficult Terian, July-August 2003.

o. *Waste Lands News Society for Promotion of Waste Lands Development,* 14 A, Vishnu Digamber Marg, New Delhi-110002, e mail: spwd@vsnl.com, Editor Sujata Kausik.

153. Water Vision, jointly with Dr. K.G. Karmakar and Sarda Banerjee, November, 2004 January, 2005.

p. *Kurukshetra,* A Journal of Rural Development, Room Noto 655 /661, Nirman Bhavan, A wing, (Gate No.5) Ministry of Rural Development, New Delhi to 110011, E mail- kurupage@ yahoo. co. in. Editor Anjani Bhushan, Assistant Editor Kalama.

154. Corporate Partnership for Agricultural Development, April 2005, Vol –53, No. 4,

155. Eco Labeling in Agriculture, January 2006, Vol. 54, No . 1

q. *Yojana,* Yojana Bhavan, Samsad Marg, New Delhi – 100001, Ph—(011) 23096738, 23717970, E mail-editoryojana@hotmail .com / ceyojana48@yahoo.com , Chief Editor—Anurag Mishra, Editor—Dr. Sapna N. Singh, Webpublicationsdivision.nic.in

156. Tea Industry At the Cross Roads, Independence Special Issue, 15 August, 2005S

r. *Agriculture Today – The National Agriculture Magazine,* Editor– M.J. Khan, C 17, III Floor, Lajpat Nagar I, New Delhi – 110024, E mail : agricult@del3.vsnl.net.in and editor@agriculturetoday.org

157. Economics of Organic Farming, October 2005, Vol. VIII, No. 10.

158. Ecolabeling in Agricultural Products—Business Opportunities in 21 st Centuries v December issue, 2005.

s. *NAB LAW,* Law Department, NABARD, Plot No. 24, Block-G, Bandra Kurla Complex, Bandra East, Mumbai-400051, Chief Editor—U.N.Srivastava, Chief General Manager, E Mail—nablaw@vsnl.com, nablaw@gmail.com

159. Agricultural Marketing Infrastructure in NAGALAND—Challenges and Opportunities, Vol. 23, No.1 April-June, 2007.

t. *Technical Digest,* Technical Service Department, NABARD, Plot No. 24, Block-G, Bandra Kurla Complex, Bandra East, Mumbai-400051, Ph-022-26530038, E. Mail—nabtsd@bom5vsnl.net.in.

160. Opportunities and Challenges of Indian Dairy, Issue 9, 2006, web—www.nabard.org.

D. Books by Other Authors

161. Sarkar Gautam K. (1972), *The World Tea Economy,* New Delhi, Oxford University Press.

162. V.N. Asopa, (2004) *Competitiveness of Global Tea Trade*, Oxford and IBH Publishing Company Pvt Ltd. New Delhi

163. Banerjee, Barundev (1993): *Tea Production and Processing*, New Delhi: Oxford and IBH Publishing Company.

164. Arunachalam, K. (1995), *A Handbook of India Tea*, Coonoor, The Tamil Nadu Tea Plantation Corporation Ltd.

165. Dr. K.G. Karmakar (1995), *Agricultural Project & Management for Banks*, Popular Prakashan, Mumbai.

166. Dr.K.G. Karmakar (1999), *Rural Credit, Micro-Finance and SHGs*, Saga Publications, New Delhi.

167. Dr K.G. Karmakar (2002), *The Silent Drums: A Review of Tribal Economics Development*, Northeren Book Center, New Delhi.

168. Dr. K G. Karmakar, about 28 papers are published in the various fields viz. Agriculture, Rural Development, Management, Plantation & Horticulture etc. in the leading Journals of National and Internation repute.

169. Vijay Dudeja, *Spot Light of Tea*.

170. Culpin, Claude (1986) : *Tractors – Use of Farming and Farm Machinery*.

171. Kamble, H.G. and Panwar, J.S., (1985) Pattern of Use and Maintenance of Tractors on A Mechanised, Farm– A Case Study, *Journal of Institution of Engineers*, Agricultural Engineering 67 : 111–113

172. Maheshwari, S.K. and Singh, B. (1987), Analysis of Repair Cost of Various Systems of Indigenous Agricultural tractors, Paper presented at Annual Convention of Indian Society of Agricultural engineers held at JNKVV, Jabalpur, 9-11 March.

173. Singh, B. and Singh, K.N., (1991) Utilization of Different Models of Tractors on Large Mechanized Farms. Proceedings of Annual Convention of Indian Society of Agricultural Engineers held at IARI, New Delhi, India, 9-11 October.

174. Shyam, M., (1992) Farm Tractor Utilization in Selected Districts of Madhya Pradesh, *Indian Journal of Agricultural Engineering* 2(1) : 12-16 March.

175. Barua, D.N. (1989), *Science and Practice in Tea Culture*, Tea Research Association, Jorhat, Assam, India.

176. Shri D. Ganguly, CTC Segment Roller and its Reshaping at the Tea Factory, Director Vikram, Agro Tech Services Pvt. Ltd.

177. Shri C.E. Sooria Moorthi, Advanced and Microwave Technology, Dept. of Solar Energy Service, Madurai Kamraj University

178. J.K. Bhavannani and S. Sareen (1990), Standardisation in the field of Processed Foods. *Ind. Food Packer.* Mar–Apl.

179. B. Roy 1991. Safety of Tea Packaging in Plastic Films and Laminates. Seminar Flexible Packaging in Tea, IIP.

180. R.N. Chatterjee, Commercial Model of MC Tear Rotorvane Technical Manager, Andrew Yale Co. Ltd.

181. Rupai Tea Estate, James Waren Group, Annual Resports 1991, 1994, 1995, 1996, 1997

182. Tea Research Association, Jorhat, Assam, "Two Leaf and a Bud".

183. C. A. Harler, Tea Manufacture.

184. Surjeet Ghosh, CTC Roller Driver System, Group Engineer Warant Tea Company Ltd. and Member of Technical Committee of TRA, TOCKLAI, Jorhat.

185. Anonymous, (1999) , Banks to assist West Bengal Small Tea Growers, *The Assam Review & Tea News*, 88(9) p.38-39.

186 I. Sharma, Khemraj, (1999), *Tea industry in India: An Introduction*, N L Publishers, Dibrugarh, Assam.

187. Eden, T., *Tea*, Third Edition, Londan

188. Eden. T., *World Crops.*

189. Forests Denys, *Tea for the British.*

190. Suchanti, R. (Ed.) (2000), *Tea Market.*

191. *The Statesman*, Where the Land under Tea is disputed? 14.10.1994:7 (Pabitra Dey)

192. *Uttarbanga Sambad*, Naya Cha Bagan : Jatilata Door Hachhe, 03.02.2000:5

193. *Uttarbanga Sambad,* Chhoto Cha Bagan Niye Ashabadi Tripurar Mantry, and 22.02.2000:4.

E. Report, Buletins, etc

1. Annual Administrative Reports of (i) Tea Association of India; (ii) Indian Tea Association; (iii) Chakibat; (iv) Kolkata Tea Traders Association; (v) UPASI; (vi) Tea Research Association, TOCKLAI; (vii) Indian Institute of Plantation Management – 11 PM, Bangalore; (viii) National Tea Research Foundation etc.
2. Barooah Committee Report on Tea, New Delhi, Government of India.
3. Domestic Marketing of Tea, National Council of Applied Econmic Research, Indraprastha Marg, New Delhi.
4. Report on Adhoc Committee on Tea, Govt of India.
5. Reports on Financial and Cost Survey of Tea Industry, Tea Board, India, Kolkata.
6. Report on Plantation Inquiry Commission, Part I & II, Govt of India, 1956.
7. Report of the Committee on Tea Marketing, Tea Board, India, 1978.
8. Techno Economic Survey Reports on (i) Tripura Tea Industry, 1978; (ii) Small Tea Garden's in Kottayam and Idukki, 1979; (iii) Nilgiris Tea Industry, 1980; (iv) Coimbatrore Tea Industry, 1984; (v) Assam Tea Industry,,(vi) Darjeeling Tea Industry published by Tea Board, India, Kolkata.
9. *Tea Statistics and Tea Directory,* Various issues, Tea Board, India.
10. *Tea Statistics and Tea Digest,* J. Thomas and Company Pvt. Ltd, Kolkata.
11. Economic Survey, Various issues, Govt of India.
12. Reserve Bank of India, Bulletin, Various Issues.
13. *Statistical Abstract,* Govt. of India, Central Statistical Organization, Various issues.
14. Perspective of Tea Management in 2000 AD, Kolkata Management Association.

15. Proceedings of Various National and International Tea Conventions and Tea Meets held upto December 2007.
16. Annual Report, Darjeeling Tea Research Centre, Kurseong, Various issues.
17. FAO Tea Trends and Prospects, Commodity Bulletin Series, Rome
18. FAO Agricultural Commodity Projections for 1975, 1985, 1995 and 2005.
19. Tea Research Association – *Two Leaf and a Bud,* Various issues
21. James Warren Group, Annual Report, Rupai Tea Estates, 1991 & 1994-1999.

F. Periodicals, Year Books, Journals & News Papers

1. *The Assam Review* and *Tea News,* Various Issues
2. *Chakibat,* Bharatiya Cha Parishad, Kolkata, *Business World.*
3. *Capital,* Kolkata; *Monorama Year Book. Hindustan Year Book*
4. *Kishan World, Tea Chronicals, Business World, Economic Times*
5. *India Today, Financial Express, Hindustan Times, Times of India.*
6. *Statesman Year Book, Telegraph, DNA, Assam Tribune*
7. *North-East Times,* Guwahati
8. *Sentinel,* Guwahati
9. *The Economic Times*
10. *Financial Express*
11. *Business Standard*
12. *Business Line.*

■■■